MORTAL MINDS

MORTAL
THE BIOLOGY OF NEAR-DEATH EXPERIENCES
MINDS

DR. G. M. WOERLEE

Prometheus Books
59 John Glenn Drive
Amherst, New York 14228-2197

First published in the United States in 2005 by Prometheus Books

Published in English in 2003 by de Tijdstroom, Utrecht, The Netherlands

Inquiries should be addressed to
Prometheus Books
59 John Glenn Drive
Amherst, New York 14228–2197
VOICE: 716–691–0133, ext. 207
FAX: 716–564–2711
WWW.PROMETHEUSBOOKS.COM

09 08 07 06 05   5 4 3 2 1

Library of Congress Cataloging-in-Publication Data

Woerlee, G. M.
    Mortal minds : the biology of near-death experiences / G.M. Woerlee.
        p. cm.
    Includes bibliographical references.
    ISBN 1–59102–283–5 (alk. paper)
    1. Near-death experiences. 2. Parapsychology and science. I. Title.
BF1045.N4W64 2005
133.9'01'3—dc22

2004060270

Printed in the United States of America on acid-free paper

Contents

Preface		page 7
Chapter 1	Questions	page 11
Chapter 2	Death of the Body	page 19
Chapter 3	Separate Body, Mind & Soul	page 35
Chapter 4	Properties of the Soul	page 43
Chapter 5	Animation by the Soul	page 51
Chapter 6	Control by the Soul	page 59
Chapter 7	Paranormal Senses	page 73
Chapter 8	Dreams & Visions	page 89
Chapter 9	The Aura	page 107
Chapter 10	Disembodiment Defined	page 119
Chapter 11	Sensation, Body & Mind	page 127
Chapter 12	Disembodied Feelings	page 135
Chapter 13	Diabolical Dreams	page 155
Chapter 14	Body, Mind & Soul	page 171
Chapter 15	Dying	page 177
Chapter 16	Oxygen Starvation	page 191
Chapter 17	Dying Eyes	page 207
Chapter 18	The Experience of Dying	page 217
Chapter 19	A Vision of Eternity	page 227
Appendices		page 239
References		page 249

Preface

Years ago I asked myself whether near-death experiences were proof of a life after death. So I searched for explanations for these experiences, as well as proofs of the apparent reality revealed by these experiences. But none of the books or scientific articles I read, none of the radio or television programs I heard or saw, and no-one with whom I spoke could give me adequate explanations for these experiences, or proofs of the reality revealed by these experiences. This dearth of adequate explanations and proof stimulated me to embark upon my own study of near-death experiences.

An initial survey revealed a vast literature about near-death experiences, and much good scientific research in matters relating to these experiences. The sheer quantity of this literature, as well as the quantity and quality of experimental studies relating to all aspects of near-death experiences, meant that any personal research and experimentation would be no more than a hasty repetition of existing studies. So I decided to limit my investigation of near-death experiences to an extensive literature study.

During the years I studied near-death experiences, I learned how changes in the functioning of the body generate these experiences. Simultaneously with other researchers, I learned how these changes in the functioning of the body revealed a physiological basis underlying many religious beliefs, as well as revealing the nature of death. Gradually this book evolved into a personal investigation into the personal experience and meaning of death. The final result is a curious mixture of religion, the paranormal, and hard facts about the functioning of the body. The sequence of chapters explaining all these things may seem strange, but is actually carefully worked out to provide a logical flow of argument answering my questions about the nature of death.

1   Chapter 1 ('Questions') asks three questions about the nature of death. What is death? What will I experience as I die? Is there a life after death? It also explains my reasons for wanting to know answers to these questions.
2   Chapter 2 ('Death of the Body') carefully defines death of the body. This is necessary, because ideas about the definition of death of the body differ considerably between people and societies.
3   Chapter 3 ('Separate Body, Mind & Soul') describes how our ancestors possibly came upon the idea of a difference between the mind and the body, the concept of the soul, as well as the belief in a life after death.
4   Chapter 4 ('The Soul') uses the texts of major world religions to define the three fundamental properties of the soul manifested by the body. These are: the soul interacts with the body, the soul interacts with the body to animate the body, and the soul interacts with the body to control the body.

5 Chapter 5 ('Animation by the Soul'),and Chapter 6 ('Control by the Soul'), discuss the proofs that a soul with these properties really exists.

6 Chapter 7 ('Paranormal Senses'), Chapter 8 ('Dreams & Visions'), and Chapter 9 ('The Aura'), discuss whether apparently immaterial senses and aspects of the body are indirect evidence for the reality of a soul.

7 Out-of-body experiences provide the most direct evidence for the reality of an invisible and immaterial human soul. Chapter 10 ('Disembodiment Defined') defines the properties of apparently disembodied souls.

8 The properties of the out-of-body experiences defined in Chapter 10 necessitated a rigorous discussion of the way the mind perceives sensations. So Chapter 11 ('Sensation, Body, & Mind') discusses how the mind perceives sensations.

9 The discussions in chapters 10 and 11 enabled an accurate discussion of out-of-body experiences in Chapter 12 ('Disembodied Feelings'), and nocturnal demonic attack in Chapter 13 ('Diabolical Dreams').

10 Chapter 14 ('Body, Mind & Soul') summarises all the evidence for an invisible and immaterial aspect of the body that survives the death of the body, such as the mind, or the soul. The conclusion is that there is no soul, that the mind is a product of the functioning of the mechanisms of the body, and that the mind dies with the body.

11 The discussions in the preceding chapters answered my questions about the nature of death, and the possibility of a life after death. However the question of how I will feel while dying remained unanswered. In order to learn about the experience of dying, it is first necessary to define the nature of dying, and why people die. Chapter 15 ('Dying') discusses and defines these aspects of dying. The discussion in this chapter reveals that more than nine in ten people lose consciousness, and die of disorders causing loss of consciousness and death due to oxygen starvation, while less than one in ten people lose consciousness and die of other causes.

12 Oxygen starvation determines the final dying experiences of more than nine in ten people, so Chapter 16 ('Oxygen Starvation') is a discussion of the experiences generated by different degrees of oxygen starvation.

13 Chapter 17 ('Dying Eyes') discusses the causes of the visual experiences reported by dying people.

14 All this knowledge about the experience of dying is combined in Chapter 18 ('The Experience of Dying') to provide a description of the process of dying, and the experiences that people may undergo while dying. This answered my question about the experiences undergone by the dying.

15 Chapter 19 ('A Vision of Eternity') is a personal reflection upon the philosophical problems raised by the knowledge revealed within this book.

Many references are made to scientific journals reporting the results of experiments whose data are used to support arguments in the text. I give these references so interested people with access to this information can determine the accuracy of my reasoning for themselves. This is standard practice in all scientific literature. After all, some people may claim that what I say cannot be true. Very well, these people can check these experimental reports for themselves to see if they arrive at other conclusions.

Some people may say some of the experiments reported in this book are immoral and unethical. I can only say to these people that these experiments were all performed with consenting adult volunteers according to ethical standards current at the time, as well as conforming to ethical standards set by the reputable international scientific journals publishing these experimental results at that time.

Some people may say that some of what I have written in this book is not new. They are correct. But this book explains and uses this knowledge in new ways. Some people may even say some things in this book are self-evident. Indeed, some things are self-evident. Some things are even so self-evident, that some people say they need no explanation at all. Yet, even though some things are obvious and self-evident when explained, for some reason they were neither obvious nor self-evident before I devised these explanations. Furthermore, I can only say that I have never seen or heard many of these things explained this way before, either by other people, or on the television, or on the radio. I am widely read, yet I have never come across many of these explanations before.

A large part of this book is devoted to an investigation of the reality of a human soul. But this book is not about the human soul as such. An extensive discussion of the human soul was necessitated by the fact that all current thinking about the possibility of a life after death involves some sort of belief in a soul. In fact, at the time of writing, most people still believe that each person has a soul, and all current societies are heirs to millennia of intense communal belief in the reality of the human soul. So any discussion of the mortality of the human mind had to discuss the many apparent evidences for the reality of a soul.

Another important point was made evident to me by people who read early versions of this book. Different people had different ideas about the meanings of fundamental terms such as 'life', 'soul', 'mind', 'dying', and 'death'. So I have taken great pains to carefully define these terms, and these definitions are used consistently throughout this book.

G.M. Woerlee,
Leiden, October 2003

Chapter 1

Questions

'I know there is a time for coming,
And a time for going,
And that which lies between,
Yes, that is my life.'[1]

This verse started me thinking about my own mortality. I never thought about death when I was young. Indeed, in the arrogance of my youth I regarded death as something that only happened to other people. So I disregarded all thoughts of personal mortality. I was even impatient with those who told me of these things, because I never associated them with myself. But I was no longer young when I first heard this verse. I saw this in my reflection. I recognised this in the decline of my body functions. I recognised this in the ways my thought processes had changed with the passage of time. And I began to notice the days, the weeks, and the years flying past at an ever-increasing pace. All about me I saw those among whom I live and work ageing along with me, and some even passed away. These evidences of my own frailty and my own mortality became increasingly more evident to me. Finally, I realised deep within myself that I too will eventually die.

Realisation of my personal mortality profoundly disturbed me. It was an idea I found difficult to fully comprehend, even though my work as a physician made me familiar with the dying and the deaths of others. I specialised in anaesthesiology shortly after finishing my medical studies, and have worked as an anaesthesiologist for many years. Anaesthesiology is not just knocking people out and keeping them unconscious during operations. Anaesthesiology is also a specialisation teaching a way of thinking and managing basic body functions, so as to be able to sustain the lives of people undergoing large operations, as well as to be able to sustain the lives of desperately sick or injured people. So I knew a lot about the functioning of the human body, about the processes of life, and how to sustain life. Yet when I first heard the verse above, I knew very little about the personal consequences of dying and death, even though these things are as much a part of my life as my conception, birth, and existence.

Furthermore, my work confronted me with what I called the wonders I saw when I administered general anaesthesia to people undergoing operations. I still call these things wonders, because I have always regarded general anaesthesia as a strange and wondrous condition. A person arrives in the operating theatre as a living, vital, conscious, speaking individual. I administer anaesthetic drugs, and suddenly the condition of this person is reduced to that of a biological mechanism. No longer a vital personality, this person has become an unconscious vacant shell, a machine made of flesh and blood undergoing repair by a surgeon. I maintain the vital functions with machines and drugs, keeping the unconscious body of this person in a functional condition, insensible to pain and to the outside world. I maintain this condition until the end of the operation. Then I cease administering some drugs, administer other drugs, and within a few short minutes consciousness and personality return. The vacant shell, the body of that person, becomes a living, vital, conscious, speaking individual again.

This process still evokes a sense of wonder in my mind, despite the passage of more than twenty years during which I have administered general anaesthesia to many thousands of people. It is very similar to what I perceive when a person dies. The consciousness and breathing of the dying person finally cease, and I perceive a strange sense of absence. The body of the deceased person is present, but I, and other observers sense an absence of something in the body of the dead person. This sensation used to puzzle me. I would ask myself why I sensed an absence, and what it was that made each person a vital individual. This same sense of absence also prompted me to ask several questions such as: 'Is the conscious mind somehow different from the body? Does the conscious mind of an individual somehow continue to function, even though that person is in a state where they are no more than a vacant shell, such as during general anaesthesia, or even after death? What is the nature of this very insubstantial something called mind?'

Of all the questions I asked myself about the nature of the mind and the nature of death, the question that most occupied my thoughts was whether some part of me will survive my death. I was not alone in asking this question. Many people feel deep within themselves that there is some form of survival of the individual mind, or self, after death. Indeed, this belief in some form of life after death is so ancient, so intense, and so deep-rooted, that many people do not even question the truth of this belief. Some of those who believe in a life after death even find support for their belief in the messages a few people claim to receive from the dead. One man published the messages he claimed to have received from the dead. And one of these messages told of the nature of life after death in these words:

'We are told that those who have passed from our earth life[2] inhabit the nearer spheres, amid surroundings not wholly dissimilar to those they have known in this world; that at death we shall enter the sphere for which our spiritual developments fits us. We shall not be plunged into forgetfulness. A human being is not transformed into another being.

In the first sphere of light we find trees and flowers like those that grow in earthly gardens; but more beautiful, immune from decay and death, and endowed with qualities that make them more completely a part of our lives. Around us are birds and animals, still the friends of man, but nearer, more intelligent, and freed from the fears and cruelties they suffer here.

We find houses and gardens, but of substance, colour and atmosphere more responsive to our presence; water whose playing is music; wide-ranging harmonies of colour. We find everything more radiant, more joyous, more exquisitely complex, and while our activities are multiplied, our life is more restful. Differences in age disappear. There are no "old" in the Spheres of Light[3], there are only the graceful and strong.'[4]

Who would not want to live for all eternity in such a paradise? Our ancestors believed wholeheartedly in the reality of a life after death in such a paradise. Even now, many people believe they will live for eternity in such a paradise after they die. But what aspect, or what part of the body of each individual survives death to live in such a paradise? Is there really a life after death? This question of the reality of a life after death occupied my mind, just as it has occupied the minds of all people throughout all ages of man. I know this is true, because my own thought patterns, as well as the thought patterns of the society in which I live, are products of philosophies developed to answer this question.

Nonetheless, even though most people have always believed in a life after death, and even though many people still believe in a life after death, this is no proof of the truth of this belief. So I searched for signs and evidences indicating the reality of a life after death. But I am not the only person who has searched for signs and evidences of the reality of a life after death. Many others have also searched for these same signs and evidences. And throughout countless millennia, people have asked those they believed to have special knowledge about the nature of death, whether there really is a life after death.

Malunkyaputta was one of these questioners. He lived thousands of years ago in the north of India, and was greatly attracted to the teachings of the great religious teacher called Siddhartha Gautama, who later became known as 'the Buddha'.[5] Malunkyaputta told the Buddha that he would lead a life according to the teachings of the Buddha, if the Buddha could tell him whether the body and the soul were identical, whether the soul

continues to live after death, and whether the world is eternal. The Buddha
answered these questions of Malunkyaputta with a parable:

> 'Consider the situation of a man who is brought to a surgeon after being
> shot by a poisoned arrow. This man refuses to let the surgeon treat him, say-
> ing: "I refuse to allow my wounds to be treated until I know the name of
> the man who shot me, his age, whether he is tall or short or of average
> length, what sort of family he came from, the names of his family members
> and his friends, what the bow looks like with which he shot me, the mate-
> rials used to make the bow, the type of arrow and the details of its construc-
> tion". This man will die before he learns the answers to all his questions.'[6]

The answer to the problem faced by the man shot with the poisoned arrow
was simple; the arrow had to be removed before his body absorbed a lethal
quantity of poison from the arrow. This man did not have enough time to
learn the answers to all his questions. Furthermore, knowledge of the answers to his questions was quite irrelevant to his treatment. Speedy removal of the arrow was all that was needed. The Buddha told Malunkyaputta with this parable, that answers to his questions were quite irrelevant
to decide how to conduct his life. In addition, the Buddha told Malunkyaputta with this parable, that no-one could learn the answers to his questions during a short individual human life span.
This parable disappointed me. It is evasive. It did not answer my question
whether there is some sort of life after death. Even so, no-one has ever found
a better answer, despite the efforts of many scientists, philosophers, and
theologians during the millennia since Malunkyaputta asked the Buddha this
question. So I searched for other indications of a life after death.
Many people believe in God, an all-powerful, all-knowing, and all-pervading
creator of all that exists within the universe. They also believe that God
chose certain people as prophets and messengers, and that these people
were inspired by God to write books containing the word of God. There
are many religions, each with its own holy books, and all contain the word
of God according to the believers in these religions. And the holy books of
many religions told me that life after death is not a matter of belief, but a
fact. Yet these holy books, as well as the believers in these religions could
offer me neither proofs of the reality of God, nor any proofs of the reality
of a life after death, only their faith in the reality of God, and their faith in
the reality of a life after death. I am a practical man. I was dissatisfied
with the thought I had to blindly believe what these books told me. I was
dissatisfied with mere blind belief in God and a life after death, when
there was no proof for any of these things. I refused to simply believe in a
life after death, only because of what God supposedly told people through

the writings of the prophets. And even though people have always believed in the reality of a God, and a life after death, this did not necessarily mean any of these things are true.

There were also people who told me they did not believe in any form of life after death. These people considered themselves to be logical and realistic people who based their lives only upon the evidence of what they could sense and measure. But these people could also offer me no proofs of their belief that there is no life after death. Often, they could not even explain why they believed there is no life after death. Many had only a deeply rooted belief in the absence of a life after death. And those who were able to formulate reasons for their belief in the absence of a life after death, could only offer analogies, and the absence of evidence for a life after death, but no proofs. In fact, their belief was based upon no more than the fact that centuries of observation, and scientific research, had failed to reveal the reality of God, or any evidence for a life after death. But such a lack of evidence for any of these things is not proof that these things do not exist.

All this questioning confirmed a sad truth. Despite many millennia of intense questioning and intellectual effort, there was still no real proof of a life after death. All my uncertainties remained. Such uncertainty about the reality of a life after death stimulated my curiosity. I wanted proof of a life after death. So I searched for signs indicating the possibility of a life after death, and I found several signs and evidences indicating the possibility of a life after death.

For example, there are indications that there is more to this world than can be experienced or perceived with the senses, or even detected with exquisitely sensitive measuring apparatus. These are indications provided by apparently inexplicable events, phenomena, and wonders such as out-of-body experiences, the ability to see an aura of light surrounding each human body, and paranormal senses. The stories and experiences of some people also seem to indicate that a life after death is possible. For example, some people say they can see and communicate with the dead, while others say they have visited the universe inhabited by the dead. These people really do perceive these things, and really have undergone such experiences. Many people even believe these perceptions, and these experiences, are windows giving the living a vision of the eternity awaiting each person after death. All these things are apparent proofs of the reality of wondrous immaterial aspects to the universe. And throughout many ages, many people believed these things were not only proof of immaterial aspects to the universe, but also proof of the reality of a life after death. Indeed, many believers in a life after death desperately hold these apparently inexplicable events, phenomena, and wonders before them. They listen to stories about these things, tell and retell them, and they are glad. They cherish their belief in these things, because their belief in these things liberates them from the oppressive transience of this mortal life, offering them the comforting prospect of eternal life after bodily death. So they do not critically analyse these events, phenomena, and wonders, to discover whether they truly are signs indicating the reality of a life after death.

I did not dismiss all these things as fantasies and hallucinations. People reporting these experiences are seldom insane or hysterical. They really do undergo these things, and they really do perceive these things. They are reasons why many people believe in a life after death. But these things are also not necessarily proof of a life after death. I was too critical to blindly believe that strange and unexplained experiences, perceptions, phenomena, communications, and wonders were proof of the reality of a life after death. Such things could only be considered proof of a life after death, if they could not be explained by anything else except a life after death. I wanted to be able to explain, and to understand these things, so as to learn whether there really is a possibility of a life after death.

Every living person will eventually die. But death is not an instantaneous transition from being alive to being dead. Nor is death an instantaneous transition from this life to a life in some unseen, and uncertain life after death. People must first die before they are dead. During my work as a physician I see the injured, the sick, and the dying. I hear of the deaths of people known to those with whom I speak. I hear of the deaths of people whom I know. And sometimes I see people die. Some people die peacefully, while others die horribly; but everyone eventually dies. I wanted to know why people die. What is dying? How do the minds of dying people function? How do dying people sense the world around them? What do dying people experience? How does the process of dying modify these experiences? I wanted to know all these things.

To learn these things was not just an abstract intellectual exercise on my part. My thinking, and reading about these things filled me with an ever-increasing sense of the evanescence of my own life. I felt oppressed by the imminence of my own mortality. So I wanted to learn these things, because I realised that I too will eventually die. I wanted to learn about the experience of dying so as to better understand my own sensations when I die. I wanted to learn how the process of dying could affect the way I will see and experience the world about me when I die. I wanted to learn how the process of dying could affect my thinking and my emotions as I die. I wanted to learn whether there was some sort of life after death. I wanted to learn these things so that I could better understand what my family members are undergoing should they die before I die. I wanted to learn these things so I could better understand the experiences of other dying people. Finally, I realised that all my questioning and searching could be expressed in three questions:

1. What is the true nature of death?
2. What will I experience as I die?
3. Will some part of me survive my death?

So I began a systematic study of the true nature of dying and death to find answers to these questions. I believed, and I believe even more firmly now, that knowing answers to these aspects of human life allows me to conduct my life according to a philosophy based upon facts, and not upon blind faith. I believe such knowledge gives me a better understanding of my fellows and myself. I believe such knowledge gives me a better understanding of my relationship to the universe. I believe such knowledge is well worth knowing. And I believe other people also want to know these things.

Chapter 2

Death of the Body

What is the true nature of death? What defines death? Countless millennia of human experience with death, as well as centuries of study of into the definition and nature of death have yielded answers to these questions. Even so, popular conceptions of the definition and nature of death differ considerably between individuals. The most important difference I found when first examining these questions, was that many people believe death of the body and death of the mind to be quite different. Two stories illustrated to me how such an idea could have arisen. The first story is a report of an actual event written by a woman who apparently died and was restored to life. She wrote:

> 'I was in the hospital, but they didn't know what was wrong with me. So Dr. James, my doctor, sent me downstairs to the radiologist for a liver scan so they could find out. First, they tested this drug they were going to use on my arm, since I had a lot of drug allergies. But there was no reaction, so they went ahead. When they used it this time, I arrested on them.[1] I heard the radiologist who was working on me go over to the telephone, and I heard very clearly as he dialled it. I heard him say, "Dr. James, I've killed your patient, Mrs. Martin". And I knew I wasn't dead. I tried to move or let them know, but I couldn't. When they were trying to resuscitate me, I could hear them telling how many c.c.'s of something to give me, but I couldn't feel the needles going in. I felt nothing at all when they touched me.'[2]

The radiologist thought this woman was dead, because she was apparently unconscious, he could no longer detect her heartbeat or breathing, and she appeared dead. But the woman did not believe him at that time, even though she realised she could neither move nor speak, felt no touch or pain, and was being resuscitated from death. This report raises two questions. Was she really dead, and did her mind continue to live after her body was dead? Or was the process of dying not yet sufficiently advanced to cause her to lose consciousness, but still sufficiently advanced so she was paralysed and insensible to pain?

The second story is an account of a live burial. In the past, as in the present, a few persons who gave every sign of being dead, suddenly aroused from death to find themselves in a coffin, in a mortuary, or the subject of funeral rites. Reports of such occurrences are still the subject of much discussion, rumour, and consternation. Such reports are the source of a deep-rooted, almost hysterical fear possessed by many people of being buried alive. The short story writer Edgar Allen Poe[3] once wrote a story called 'The Premature Burial', whose main character was a man who regularly suffered from episodes of loss of consciousness during which he appeared dead. After one such episode, he awoke to find himself inside a coffin:

> '*I knew that I had now fully recovered the use of my visual faculties - and it was dark - all dark - the intense and utter darkness of the Night that endureth for evermore. I endeavoured to shriek; and my lips and my parched tongue moved convulsively together in the attempt - but no voice issued from the cavernous lungs, which, oppressed as if by the weight of some incumbent mountain, gasped and palpitated, with the heart, at every elaborate and struggling inspiration. The movement of the jaws, in this effort to cry aloud, showed me that they were bound up, as is usual with the dead. I felt, too, that I lay upon some hard substance; and by something similar my sides were, also, closely compressed. So far, I had not ventured to stir any of my limbs - but now I violently threw up my arms, which had been lying at length, with the wrists crossed. They struck a solid wooden substance, which extended above my person at an elevation of not more than six inches from my face. I could no longer doubt that I reposed within a coffin at last.*'[4]

This is an exceptionally powerful evocation of the horror aroused by the thought of live burial. It is also another illustration of inaccurate ideas about the nature and definition of death. Those who made the diagnosis of death failed to detect a heartbeat, breathing, consciousness, or any other indication of life in this man. Accordingly, they pronounced him dead, and he was buried. Yet this man awoke in his coffin. But he could not have been dead when he was buried, because dead people never awaken. Millennia of human experience with death teach that the dead are dead, and they remain dead. Even so, is this ages-old knowledge always true? There may be exceptions to this rule. So did this man die and somehow return to life?

These two stories illustrated to me the problem of defining when death is present, as well as the problem of differentiating death of the mind from death of the body. Furthermore, these two stories also illustrated to me why some people believe that the mind does not die together with the body, and why some people believe death of the mind is something quite different from death of the body. The fundamentally different nature of these two beliefs necessitated an accurate definition of death of the mind, as well as an accurate definition of death of the body.

What defines death of the mind, and what defines death of the body? It is impossible to accurately define death of the mind, because it is impossible to observe, or to measure the presence of conscious mental activity in someone who is unconscious, apparently dead, or dead. However, it is possible to measure, and to define, a moment at which death of the body is certainly present. This is measurable, because the body is material, and the functions, as well as the chemical composition of the body are measurable. Therefore I decided to first provide an accurate definition of death of the body. So what is death of the body?

Myriad chemical reactions occurring inside and outside the cells forming the body, build the structures of the body, as well as generate energy for the functioning of the body. The vital functions of the body as manifested by breathing, heartbeat, and nutrition, sustain these vital chemical reactions, which in turn sustain these vital bodily functions; a veritable circle of life, where function sustains function. Death occurs when this circle of life is broken, causing these complex self-sustaining processes to cease. Cessation of these vital self-sustaining processes heralds the beginning of bodily decay and dissolution. Decay and dissolution signify true death of the body, because decay and dissolution signify failure of the circle of life. Millennia of human experience with death confirm this observation; no deceased person whose body had begun to decay ever returned to life. Bodily decay is a certain manifestation of death of the body, and is an accurate definition of the presence of death of the body. But the manifestation of bodily decay is a process that only begins several hours after death, a fact making the presence of bodily decay an unusable definition of death for many judicial, medical, or social reasons. The reasons for this are very practical. For example, in many societies the dead are buried or cremated within hours of death, a period often far too short for any bodily decay to manifest. Organs destined for transplantation must be removed from the bodies of the dead within minutes after death, a period far too short for any bodily decay to begin. The necessity to rapidly, and accurately determine the presence and time of death in these, and other situations, means that the presence of bodily decay is an unusable definition of death, even though the presence of bodily decay is an accurate definition of death of the body. These examples illustrate some of the reasons why it is necessary to have another accurate definition of the moment when death of the body is present.

Usually a person is defined as being dead when breathing has stopped and the heart no longer beats. Indeed, nearly every dead person manifests these signs. This is why cessation of heartbeat and breathing are nearly always used to define the moment of death. Nevertheless, this is a purely practical definition, because cessation of heartbeat and breathing describe only two manifestations of death, but say nothing about the nature of death. Consider the example of the woman whose heart stopped beating. The radiologist said she was dead, because she had no heartbeat, and she had stopped breathing. But this woman was conscious, even though she did not breathe, and her heart did not beat. So did she remain conscious for a while after her breathing and heartbeat stopped, or did her mind continue to live even though her body was dead? This example illustrates that cessation of heartbeat and breathing are sometimes quite inadequate to define the presence of death of the body.

So what is an accurate definition of death of the body? Are there organs or tissues whose removal or destruction always cause death of the body? One way to answer this question is to study what happens to people who lose body parts, organs, and tissues due to diseases, injuries, or operations. Such a study reveals that the human body can survive an amazing degree of damage, injury, mutilation, and removal of many body parts and organs, without dying, losing consciousness, or developing any personality changes. People may suffer horrid mutilation, but still remain alive and conscious, as well as retaining their own unique personalities. An analysis of the effects, and the survivability of loss of different organs and tissues, makes it possible to determine which parts of the body are essential for life. Such an analysis gives an accurate idea of the true nature of death of the body. Accordingly, I performed just such a step-by-step analysis of the effects of organ and tissue removal, injury, and disease.

I began my systematic study with an examination of blood. Our ancestors knew very little about the functioning of the human body. They regarded blood as a wondrous life-giving fluid, concealed, and contained within the blood vessels of the body. The reason for this belief was their certain knowledge that the life and vitality of even the most intelligent and powerful people, as well as animals, faded away as blood drained out of their bodies. So it is not surprising that ancient peoples, such as the Israelites, came to believe that blood was a vital, life-giving fluid. Ancient Israelites even believed blood contained a divine, life-giving something causing the bodies of humans and animals to live. Their God even inspired one of their prophets to write:

> 'For the life of the flesh is in the blood: and I[5] have given it to you upon the altar to make an atonement for your souls for it is the blood that maketh an atonement for the soul.'[6]

This is an understandable way of looking at the function of blood in primitive times. The reasoning behind this way of thinking is clear. Draining the blood out of the bodies of humans and animals causes death, which means that blood contains a divine, life giving something enabling humans and animals to live. This is why the God of the ancient Israelites forbade them to drink, or to eat blood, because to drink or to eat blood was to ingest a divine life-giving substance. Only God, the all-powerful, all-knowing, and all-pervading creator of all living beings, was permitted to receive the divine life-giving something contained within blood in the form of ritual blood sacrifices. But this same reasoning can be applied to all other body tissues. Cut off the head, remove the heart, excise the liver, extirpate the lungs, or destroy the bone marrow, and a person will die as a result of any one of these things. Yet strangely enough, no-one ever claimed these tissues contained some sort of divine, life-giving something causing the body to live.

Blood contains no divine life-giving something, but it is a complex fluid with many functions. Blood is mainly composed of water in which many inorganic salts are dissolved. Blood also contains many different proteins with as many functions. There are enzymes performing chemical transformations, proteins transporting hormones, proteins transporting drugs, and proteins essential for blood clotting. Furthermore, blood contains many different types of cells. There are white blood cells called platelets which are needed for blood clotting, red blood cells which give blood its red colour and are needed to transport oxygen, as well as several different other types of white blood cells which are needed for immune responses. Blood flowing through blood vessels transports oxygen, hormones, salts, and nutrients to all tissues of the body, while simultaneously removing waste products, hormones, and other substances produced by the tissues through which it flows. All this means that blood is an essential transport fluid in the body, transporting substances essential for life to the tissues of the body, as well as transporting wastes away from the tissues of the body to organs where they are excreted. Oxygen is one of the vital substances transported by blood, because oxygen is an essential ingredient in vital chemical reactions occurring within all cells of the body. These vital chemical reactions produce energy-rich substances driving all other chemical reactions within the cells of the body. True, oxygen is only one of many substances vital to the functioning of the body, but unlike all other vital substances, there is no reserve store of oxygen within any tissue of the body. This is why all body tissues require a continual flow of blood. This is why people lose consciousness within five to twenty seconds after the flow of blood to the brain suddenly stops.[7] And this is why the life and vitality of people and animals appears to fade away as they bleed to death.

The volume of blood contained within the average adult human body is about five litres. People who survive operations during which they lose more than ten litres of blood are living proof of the essential transport

functions of blood. A blood loss of more than ten litres during an operation, means that more than twice the volume of blood contained within
the body must be replaced during such an operation. People survive such
massive blood loss during these operations because blood is transfused
into their bodies as fast as it is lost. Blood for blood transfusions comes
from a blood bank, and a blood bank either buys blood from individuals,
or receives blood from people who freely donate their blood. A person who
sells or donates their blood, never sells or donates more than a half litre of
blood at any one time, because to rapidly lose more than a half litre of
blood within a short time causes people to become weak and unwell.
Furthermore, modern blood banks never provide physicians administering
blood transfusions with unprocessed blood: instead, a modern blood bank
only provides blood components. So a person who survives an operation
during which more than ten litres of blood are lost will have received: red
blood cells derived from more than twenty different persons, platelets derived from at least six different persons, blood proteins needed for blood
clotting derived from at least eight different persons, and at least five litres
of water containing inorganic salts from a chemical factory. These people
are bright and alert after awakening from anaesthesia for operations during which they receive such massive blood transfusions, and they manifest
no changes in mental function or personality. This is proof that blood contains no substances determining consciousness, mental function, or personality, as well as further proof that blood is a vital transport fluid within
the body.
Blood is a vital transport fluid. Accordingly, blood must flow into, and out
of tissues, because tissues in which blood stagnates, or tissues in which
there is no flow of blood, die due to lack of oxygen and other essential substances. This is why blood is useless without the heart. So what is the relationship of the heart to death? Ancient Greeks thought the heart was the
seat of the mind, because the heart beats more rapidly or slowly according
to emotions and thoughts. They were wrong. The heart is no more than a
pump, only it is a pump made of meat instead of metal. The function of
the heart is to pump blood around the body. No more, and no less. Each
person is alive because their heart pumps a continual flow of blood containing essential chemicals through all their body tissues. Even so, the human heart is a remarkable pump because it can function for more than
one hundred years without stopping. Few machines are able to function
for so long without stopping, but the heart is able to function so long, because unlike a machine, the heart can heal and repair itself.
The body of an average adult contains about five litres of blood, and the
heart pumps about five litres of blood into the body every minute. So every
minute, the average adult heart pumps a volume of blood approximately

equal to the total volume of blood contained within the body. Blue-coloured, oxygen depleted, carbon dioxide enriched blood, flows through large thin-walled blood vessels called 'veins' to enter the right heart. The right heart pumps this oxygen-depleted, carbon dioxide enriched blood into blood vessels within the tissues of the lungs. Oxygen in the air contained within myriad small cavities in lung tissue called 'alveoli', diffuses into the blood vessels embedded within the walls of these alveoli. This oxygen chemically combines with the blood flowing through these blood vessels, changing the colour of the blood from blue to red as the haemoglobin within the blood combines with oxygen. At the same time, carbon dioxide diffuses out of the blood in the blood vessels embedded within the walls of the alveoli into the cavities of the alveoli. The end result of this process is that oxygen-enriched, carbon dioxide depleted blood flows out of the lung blood vessels into the left heart, which then pumps it into thick-walled blood vessels called 'arteries'. Red-coloured, oxygen-enriched, carbon dioxide depleted blood flows through arteries to all parts of the body. Once inside the various organs and tissues of the body, arteries divide into microscopically thin blood vessels called 'capillaries'. Oxygen diffuses out of blood flowing through capillaries into the surrounding tissues. At the same time, waste carbon dioxide diffuses out of tissues surrounding the capillaries to combine with blood flowing through these capillaries. Blood flowing through the capillaries changes colour from red to blue as oxygen contained within the blood diffuses into the surrounding tissues. Blue-coloured, oxygen-depleted, carbon dioxide enriched blood flows out of the capillaries to enter veins through which it returns to the right heart, where the cycle is endlessly repeated. This endless pumping of blood around the body is called 'the circulation'.

The pumping of the heart circulates blood around the body, and heartbeat is a sign of the pumping action of the heart. Yet sometimes the heart stops beating. There are many reasons why the heart may stop beating, but the effect of cessation of heartbeat is always the same; no blood is pumped through the organs and tissues of the body. Cessation of heartbeat means that no vital substances are pumped to the organs and tissues of the body, and so the body dies. This is why cessation of heartbeat was once considered to be a certain sign of death. Even so, cessation of heartbeat is not always a certain sign of death, because heart massage, and mechanical hearts prove that people can be alive, as well as conscious without any heartbeat, or even without a heart at all. There are several medical treatments demonstrating this.

For example, heart massage can be applied to a person whose heart has stopped beating. The person applying heart massage rhythmically compresses and releases the chest between 60 to 120 times each minute. This rapid rhythmical cycle of increased and decreased pressure in the chest, together with the functioning of the four one-way valves in the heart, mean that heart massage generates a flow of blood around the body, even though the heart no longer beats. The flow of blood generated by heart massage is usually less than what the heart pumps when it beats normally, but is often sufficient to sustain life. About one in five persons applying heart massage performs their work so efficiently, that they generate a flow of blood around the body sufficient to sustain consciousness as well as life.[8] People undergoing such efficient heart massage are not only alive, but are also conscious, even though their hearts do not beat at all.

Some persons have a heart so diseased, that it is incapable of pumping sufficient blood around their bodies to keep them alive. Heart transplantation is the only treatment possible for these people. But suitable transplant hearts are seldom immediately available, and these people often die while waiting for suitable transplant hearts. This is why mechanical hearts are sometimes temporarily implanted in these people. The diseased and failing heart is removed, and a mechanical heart is implanted to take over the function of the failing heart. This procedure sounds simple, but it is actually an expensive, and complicated procedure fraught with many possible medical complications, as well as technical problems, which is why mechanical heart implantation is only performed in a few medical centres in wealthy countries, such as the United States of America.

Such implanted mechanical hearts are capable of sustaining life and consciousness for many months. An example of this was the implantation of a mechanical heart into a 56 year-old businessman called Alvin M. in the year 1995 CE. His diseased heart was removed and replaced with a mechanical heart. This mechanical heart kept him alive for 133 days, (a record number of days at that time), after which a suitable human donor heart became available, and was implanted. Alvin M. remained in hospital all these 133 days, during which time he exercised each day, spent time with his family and friends, as well as conducting his business from his hospital room. He told reporters:

> "'I feel wonderful. I feel better than I have in years," M. says. "However, it was not a record that I was eager to break. As much as I've come to love the people here at LDS Hospital, I'm ready for a donor heart and am ready to go home."'[9]

All this means that the body can live and be conscious without any heart at all, because a mechanical heart can pump and circulate enough blood around the body to sustain life, consciousness, and physical activity. So heart massage, and mechanical hearts, demonstrate that as long as sufficient blood is pumped around the body, a person can live and be conscious without any heartbeat, or even a heart. These things prove the heart is only a pump, pumping blood containing oxygen, carbon dioxide, and many other substances around the body. But oxygen and carbon dioxide must somehow enter into, and leave the body. This raises the question of the relation of breathing to death.

People must breathe to live, because people always die when they stop breathing. Somehow the mechanical process of inhaling and exhaling air is necessary to sustain life. This is why ancient peoples believed air contained some vital life-sustaining principle. And this belief inspired Hindu holy men to write in the Bhagavad Gita that:

> *'I am the fire of digestion in the bodies of all living entities, and I join with the air of life, outgoing and incoming, to digest the four kinds of food-stuff.'*[10]

Indeed, breathing does sustain life, but there is nothing magical about the process. The act of breathing-in sucks normal atmospheric air containing nearly 21% oxygen and 0.03% carbon dioxide into the lungs. A short moment after a person stops inhaling air into the lungs, the muscles used to suck air into the lungs relax, and the lungs empty like rubber balloons. Exhaled air contains about 15% oxygen and 4.3% carbon dioxide, quite a different composition from normal atmospheric air. The different compositions of inhaled and exhaled air reveals the basic function of breathing. Inhaling sucks fresh air into alveoli within the lungs. Oxygen contained in the fresh air within these alveoli chemically combines with oxygen-depleted blood flowing through blood vessels embedded within the walls of these alveoli. In addition, waste carbon dioxide diffuses out of blood flowing through blood vessels embedded within the walls of alveoli to enter the alveoli. Exhaling removes oxygen depleted air and waste carbon dioxide from the alveoli within the lungs. This is a process of gas exchange, and this process of gas exchange is the function of the lungs. But this basic process of getting oxygen into the body, and removing waste carbon dioxide from the body does not have to be performed by breathing. There are a number of situations where people do not breathe at all, but are still alive and conscious.

Sometimes a person cannot breathe because of the effects of drugs, poisons, venom's, or disease. Such a person can be connected to a machine called a 'ventilator' that inflates, as well as deflates their lungs, taking over the function of breathing until the effects of these drugs, poisons, venom's, or diseases have passed, and the person is able to breathe normally again. Mechanical ventilation is used routinely during anaesthesia, as well as in intensive care units all over the world. A person undergoing mechanical ventilation does not breathe, but is alive, and is also conscious, if neither sedated nor under anaesthesia.

Mechanical ventilators use the lungs to get oxygen into the blood, and to remove waste carbon dioxide from the blood. But lungs are not needed to get oxygen into blood, nor are lungs needed to remove waste carbon dioxide from blood. Machines called 'oxygenators' can perform this task without the mechanical process of breathing, or any lungs being required at all. A continuous flow of blood is pumped out of a large vein into the oxygenator. Here, oxygen is transferred directly into the blood, and waste carbon dioxide is removed. The oxygen-enriched, carbon dioxide depleted blood is then pumped back into another large vein, through which it flows into the heart which pumps it around the body. So the basic functions of breathing: the addition of oxygen to blood, and the removal of excess carbon dioxide from blood, can occur without any breathing, or any lungs being required at all. A person connected to an oxygenator does not breathe, yet such a person is alive, and is also conscious, if neither sedated nor under anaesthesia.

The functions of both the heart and the lungs can also be replaced without causing death. A device called a 'heart-lung machine' can take over the functions of the heart, as well as the lungs, by adding oxygen to blood, removing carbon dioxide from blood, and pumping blood around the body. Heart-lung machines are used routinely during heart operations, as well as in intensive care units. A person attached to a heart-lung machine does not breathe, does not use their lungs, and has no heartbeat. Even so, such a person is alive, and is also conscious if neither sedated nor under anaesthesia. These things mean people can live and be conscious without any heartbeat or breathing at all. And these things mean that even though absence of heartbeat and breathing usually are manifestations of death, their absence does not always mean a person is dead.

The human body is made of more than just the blood, the heart, and the lungs. So I continued my systematic evaluation of the effects of injury, surgery, and disease of body parts, organs, and tissues upon mental function and viability.

For example, people can lose both arms and both legs without dying. Horridly crippled but alive, they still retain their normal mental function, and their own unique individual personalities.

Extensive cancer of the pelvic bones and bladder, extensive bedsores in the lower halves of the bodies of paraplegics, and extensive disease of arteries supplying the legs with blood, are all difficult conditions to treat. Drastic operations are sometimes performed to treat such conditions. One of the most drastic of all operations is removal of the whole of the lower half of the body, that is, removal of the legs, the pelvis, and the abdomen below the navel. This operation was first performed in 1960 CE, and by the year 1998 CE about forty-four people were known to have undergone such an operation.[11] The few persons who underwent this operation were literally cut in half! Heroic surgery indeed. The longest recorded survivor of such an operation lived for twenty-eight years after being operated upon.[12] Despite being cut in half, these people are still alive, they are conscious, and they retain their own unique individual personalities.

Kidneys remove waste products from the body by excreting them as substances dissolved in the urine. People can live a fairly normal life after disease or injury destroys both kidneys, or after surgical removal of both diseased kidneys, although they are dependent upon kidney dialysis to remove waste products from their bodies.

The liver is the metabolic powerhouse of the body, regulating the hormonal, metabolic, and chemical housekeeping of the body by performing multiple vital chemical transformations. But a person can live and be conscious for several days after removal of the liver, or total destruction of the liver by diseases or poisons, provided the function of their absent liver is replaced by an artificial liver connected to their blood circulation.

The pancreas produces insulin, a hormone that regulates the glucose concentration in the blood. The pancreas also produces many of the enzymes needed to digest food in the intestines. Total destruction of the pancreas by disease, or surgical removal of a diseased pancreas does not cause death, loss of consciousness, or personality changes. People can live a reasonably normal life without a pancreas. But they must eat pancreas enzymes with their food to replace the digestive enzymes no longer produced by their absent pancreas, as well as inject insulin to treat the diabetes mellitus resulting from absence of insulin production.

Intestines digest food with enzymes produced by the stomach, liver, intestines, and pancreas. Digestion splits food into nutrients, vitamins, and minerals that are absorbed into blood flowing through microscopic blood vessels in the walls of the intestines. Blood transports these substances to all the tissues of the body. Even though the intestines perform a vital function, disease or destruction of the entire intestinal system from mouth to anus need not cause death. People can continue to live even after disease destroys their entire intestinal system, because water, nutrients, vitamins, and minerals can be pumped directly into the bloodstream using a technique called 'total parenteral nutrition'. Total parenteral nutrition is a standard medical technique used to feed people whose intestines no longer function because of disease, surgery, or injury. People receiving total parenteral nutrition are alive and conscious, and the functioning of their minds is unaffected.

The spinal cord conducts nerve signals from the brain to all parts of the body below the head, as well as conducting sensory nerve information from all parts of the body below the head into the brain. Some people suffer spinal cord injuries high in the neck. Such high spinal cord injuries damage the nerves controlling breathing[13], as well as causing loss of control of all parts of the body below the head. The effects of such an injury are devastating: breathing stops, and all parts of the body below the head are paralysed. People suffering from such high spinal injuries require mechanical ventilation to perform their breathing for them. Yet even though these people cannot breathe, and all parts of their bodies below their heads are paralysed, they are still alive and conscious, and the functioning of their minds is unaffected.

All these things mean that all organs and body parts below the head can be removed or destroyed without causing death. I admit that this division of the body into parts below, and above the head is arbitrary, but I made this division for practical purposes. I wanted to demonstrate that provided their functions are replaced, injury or disease can destroy all the organs and tissues below the head without causing death, or changing mental function. So what are the effects of injury and disease of the organs of the head? Injury or disease can also destroy many of the organs and tissues of the head without causing death. For example, injury or disease can destroy large parts of the skull, the jaw, the eyes, the nose, or the ears. All this can occur without causing death, changing the level of consciousness, mental function, or personality. So what does define death? Only the brain is left. Indeed, it is brain destruction that defines the presence of death.

Brain destruction always causes death. This sounds very precise, but is actually quite misleading. After all, does death only occur after destruction of the whole brain? Or does death occur after destruction of part of the brain? And if death occurs after destruction of part of the brain, then which part of the brain determines whether a person is alive or dead? There is only one way to answer these questions, and that is to study what happens when different parts of the brain are absent, are diseased, malfunction, or are destroyed by injury, surgery, or disease.

I will first describe some basic brain anatomy before beginning this discussion. The spinal cord ascends to the neck. Just inside the skull, the spinal cord broadens and forms the brainstem. The brainstem has three parts: the medulla forms the lower part, the middle part is formed by the pons, and the midbrain forms the upper part. The brainstem connects the spinal cord with the two halves of the cerebellum, and the two halves of the brain called cerebral hemispheres. It is called the brainstem because it looks like the stem of a tree. Below the brainstem, the spinal cord forms a long taproot, while above the brainstem, the cerebellum and the two cerebral hemi-

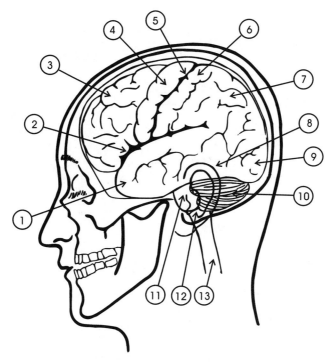

Figure 1   Relationship of the surface of the head to skull and brain structures.

1 Temporal lobe. 2 Fissure of Sylvius, or lateral sulcus. 3 Frontal lobe. 4 Precentral gyrus. 5 Fissure of Roland, or central sulcus. 6 Postcentral gyrus. 7 Parietal lobe. 8 Outline of the ear. 9 Occipital lobe. 10 Cerebellum. 11 Pons. 12 Medulla oblongata. 13 Spinal cord.

spheres form the crown of the tree (see figures 1 and 2).

What happens when different parts of the brain are absent, abnormal, malfunction, damaged, or destroyed?

Sometimes it is necessary to remove one half of a diseased brain. This is done with an operation called 'cerebral hemispherectomy', an operation to remove a diseased cerebral hemisphere. The brainstem and other parts of the brain called the 'thalamus' and 'hypothalamus' are not removed during this operation. People who undergo this operation always develop paralysis of the sides of their bodies opposite to the sides of their operations. They also develop personality changes, but their intelligence is unchanged.

Some of the people who undergo this operation are even able to live reasonably normal lives after undergoing removal of a diseased brain half.[14]

The effects of this operation show that large amounts of brain tissue can be removed or destroyed without causing death, affecting consciousness, or

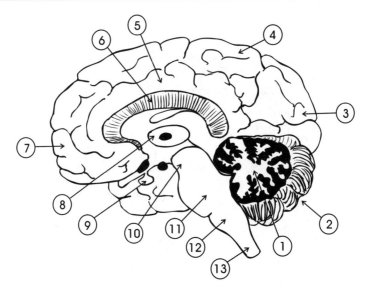

Figure 2   **Cross-section through the middle of the brain**

1 Cross-section through the cerebellum. 2 Cerebellum. 3 Occipital lobe. 4 Parietal lobe. 5 Cingu-late gyrus. 6 Corpus callosum. 7 Frontal lobe. 8 Thalamus. 9 Pituitary gland. 10 Midbrain. 11 Pons. 12 Medulla. 13 Spinal cord.

reasonably normal mental function.

Studies of left and right brain function have been made by injecting small doses of a powerful anaesthetic drug directly into the arteries through which blood flows into the brain. Most of the blood flowing through the left side of the brain, (the left cerebral hemisphere), comes from the left carotid artery, and most of the blood flowing through the right side of the brain, (the right cerebral hemisphere), comes from the right carotid artery. The brainstem receives most of its blood from another two arteries called the vertebral arteries. Accordingly, injection of a small dose of an anaesthetic drug into a carotid artery causes anaesthesia of the brain half supplied by that carotid artery, but does not affect the brainstem. So people who receive such an injection of small dose of an anaesthetic drug into a carotid artery remain conscious and continue breathing, even though they do develop personality changes, as well as paralysis of the opposite sides of their bodies during the period of anaesthesia of one half of their brains.[15] All these studies show the same thing. Large amounts of brain tissue can malfunction, or cease functioning altogether, without affecting consciousness, or reasonably normal mental function.

Two to seven babies in every ten thousand live births are born with a birth defect called 'anencephaly'.[16] These babies are born without a brain or brainstem. Usually such babies never become conscious, and die shortly after birth. But sometimes an anencephalic baby is born with a brainstem, even though the rest of the brain is absent. Such babies can live for a time, and even become conscious. An example of this was the case of an anencephalic boy published in 1949 CE. Two physicians described the mental and bodily functioning of this anencephalic boy who lived for eighty-five days after birth.[17] After he died, a study of his body revealed he had no brain tissue except for a spinal cord, a brainstem, a cerebellum and a hypothalamus. The two physicians described the mental function and physical activity of the baby:

> 'Most interesting to the writers was the presence of instincts and emotions. If we handled the patient[18] roughly he cried weakly but otherwise like any other infant, and when we coddled him he showed contentment and settled down in our arms. When a finger was placed into his mouth he sucked vigorously. He would sleep after feeding and awaken when hungry, expressing his hunger by crying.'

This is a description of reasonably normal mental, and bodily function for a baby. So this anencephalic baby boy slept, awoke, drank, and reacted to his surroundings just like a normal baby. This case history indicates that all that is required for a human body to live, to feed, and be conscious, are a brainstem, a thalamus, and a hypothalamus. Yet even this minimum is not the absolute minimum amount of brain tissue required for life. Careful examination of the effects of birth abnormalities, as well as studies of brain injuries and diseases in adults, reveals that brainstem function is what determines whether the body is alive or dead. All these studies show that destruction, or irreversible failure of brainstem functions invariably causes death of the body.[19]

The brainstem is a small but vital part of the body with an importance out of proportion to its size. Nerve fibres originating within brainstem nerve centres radiate out into all parts of the brain to generate consciousness[20], making it possible for the brain to experience, and to manifest conscious mental function through the mechanisms of the brain. In addition to generating consciousness, nerve fibres originating within other brainstem nerve centres radiate to other parts of the brain and the body to control other vital body functions, such as breathing[21], circulation[22], vomiting, and swallowing.[23] This is why normal brainstem function is essential for life, and the functions of the brainstem explain the effects of brainstem malfunction and failure.

- The brainstem regulates the level of consciousness. Abnormal brainstem function caused by drugs, diseases, or injuries changes the level of consciousness, causing affected people to become drowsy, unconscious, or comatose, depending upon the degree of malfunction.
- The brainstem regulates breathing. Abnormal brainstem function caused by drugs, diseases, or injuries, causes abnormal breathing, or cessation of breathing.
- Failure of all brainstem functions caused by drugs, diseases, injuries, or total brainstem destruction, always causes loss of consciousness, and always causes breathing to stop.

These basic facts of body structure and function explain why brainstem destruction, or irreversible failure of brainstem functions, always causes death. Consciousness, the ability to breathe, to drink, to eat, and to procreate. These are properties defining the living human body. The human body is viable and alive as long as the brainstem functions normally: because normal brainstem function drives unconscious actions such as breathing, swallowing, and circulation, as well as conscious actions such as eating, drinking, and procreation. This is bodily life. Brainstem function determines whether the body is alive or dead, because failure of brainstem functions causes loss of consciousness, after which all conscious mental activity ceases. Failure of brainstem functions also causes breathing to stop, after which the body dies of oxygen starvation. Irreversible failure of brainstem functions means death of the brainstem, resulting in death of the brain, and death of the body. So true death of the body is defined by he presence of brainstem death. Any other condition is not death of the body.

Chapter 3

Separate Body, Mind & Soul

True death of the body is death of the brainstem. But does death of the body also mean death of the mind? Many people believe the mind is somehow separate from the body, believing that death of the body and death of the mind are two different things. Furthermore, many people also believe the mind separates from the body upon death, to somehow continue living for eternity after the body dies. The thoughts, the speech, and the actions of people from untold millennia in the past to the present have been moulded by these beliefs. They have inspired people to deeds of great courage, to formulate philosophies whose fundamental truths have inspired generation after generation, or to build awe inspiring works and civilisations. These beliefs are so ancient, and so deeply embedded within the minds of most people, that many do not even question their truth. Indeed, the very persistence of these ancient beliefs may even mean they are true. So I could not ignore these beliefs in my investigation of the possibility of survival of the mind after death. But what are the origins of this belief in a difference between mind and body? What are the origins of this belief that the mind can separate from the body? And what are the origins of this belief in a life after death? These questions puzzled me, until one day I realised these beliefs are actually based upon sensations and experiences common to nearly all people. Many people undergo strange sensations and experiences seemingly proving all these things. When all these sensations and experiences are viewed collectively, it is not at all surprising that many people believe the mind is different from the body, that the mind can separate from the body, and that the mind continues to live after death. So what are these sensations and experiences?

To begin with, I cannot see, feel, smell, taste, touch, or measure the presence of the minds of living or dead people. No-one can do this. Yet each conscious thinking person has a mind, and everyone knows when the mind of a person is absent or present, even though the mind of each person is intangible and invisible. The mind is intangible and invisible, while the body housing the mind is tangible, visible, and corruptible. Furthermore, the mind may remain active and powerful even when housed within an injured, diseased, and failing material body unable to execute the commands of the mind housed within. So it is quite understandable that many people believe the mind to be an invisible, intangible, incorruptible, and immaterial something: something very different from the visible, tangible, corruptible, and material body.

Sometimes I feel surprised when I see my reflection in a mirror. I ask myself whether the reflection I see before me really is a reflection of my body. My reflection appears strange and unknown to me at these times. At such times I feel my mind is separate from my body, feeling at these moments as if I am observing my body as I move, eat, work, and perform other actions. Other people also experience these same sensations. Such sensations of apparent dissociation of mind and body make people feel that mind and body are somehow separate and different.

I often sense something has passed when I see a deceased person. I sense an emptiness, as if something is no longer present within the body of the deceased person, as if something has departed with the death of that person. I am not alone in this. This is a sensation experienced by most people. Such a sensation makes most people, including myself wonder if there is not something else besides the physical body that has died.

I remember a dream I had when a teenager. This was a dream in which I dreamed I was floating and flying above an unknown city and landscape. This dream felt very real to me at the time. I felt myself floating, flying, at times swooping low, and at other times ascending. I realised during the dream that it was not my body that was flying, but that my conscious mind was somehow flying outside my body. Strangely, this realisation did not disconcert me. It was a very vivid dream that I still remember. Many other people with whom I speak also say they have experienced similar flying dreams. Such dreams make most people, including myself, wonder whether the mind, or something that acts as the vehicle of the mind, can somehow separate from the body.

I am an anaesthesiologist. During my work I often administer drugs similar to curare to paralyse the muscles of people undergoing general anaesthesia. Such paralysis makes it possible for surgeons to safely perform many different types of operations. Curare paralyses all the muscles of the body, except for the muscles of the heart, the blood vessels, the urinary bladder, and the bowels. All this means that people paralysed with curare also cannot breathe, so during operations where curare is used as part of the anaesthetic technique, they are connected to machines that perform their breathing for them. People paralysed with curare are not unconscious, which means they can feel pain, see, hear, smell, taste, and feel everything normally. So when curare is used as part of an anaesthetic drug mixture, anaesthesiologists always administer other drugs to render people unconscious as well as insensible to all sensations and pain. But, very rarely, some people awaken during an operation, and feel the sensations and pain of the operation they undergo, in spite of the drugs that are supposed to render them unconscious and insensible to all sensations and pain. This is a horrible experience, like a nightmare. They are awake, they smell, they see, they hear, and they sense what is happening to their bodies, and about their bodies, and they may suffer pain from the operation they are undergoing. They may try to scream and shout, but paralysis of breathing and speech muscles means that no sound issues from their mouths. They may try to move to signal that they are awake, but despite the exertion of incredible will and energy, no movements occur, because all their muscles are paralysed. It is as if their conscious minds are locked inside their paralysed and helpless bodies. Reports of such experiences make many people think the mind is somehow separate and different from the body.

Occasionally someone tells me about unusual experiences undergone during a prior operation. A man once told me he found himself flying above the lawn outside the hospital at the same time he was undergoing an operation under general anaesthesia inside that same hospital.[1] This man said he knew his body was undergoing an operation inside the hospital, even as he flew outside above the hospital lawn. Curiously, he was not at all disconcerted by this fact at the time. A woman once related a similar experience. She told me she found herself awake, and standing next to her body at the same time as it lay upon the operating table under general anaesthesia. She heard the surgeon asking the anaesthesiologist whether he could begin the operation, and she heard the anaesthesiologist reply that the surgeon could begin. She tried to tell everyone she was still awake, only to discover she could neither speak nor move.[2] This woman also realised during her experience that her mind was somehow displaced outside her body. Reports of such experiences also make people feel the mind is somehow different from the body, because such experiences seem to prove the mind can separate from the body.

There are many stories told by people who underwent strange experiences while apparently dead, or near to death. Some of these people report seeing their bodies lying unmoving and apparently dead, while at the same time hearing a physician saying they were dead. Other people report passing through tunnels, seeing bright and wonderful lights, undergoing experiences in other worlds, meeting with deceased friends and relatives, or seeing gods and figures from their religion, while their bodies lay unmoving and apparently dead. Reports of such experiences also seem to indicate that the mind is somehow separate and different from the body, and that the mind can even separate from the body. Furthermore, such reports also seem to indicate that the mind separates from the body after death to continue living in a wondrous world populated by the dead.

Such sensations, experiences, and stories of dissociation of the mind from the body, all seem to indicate the mind is somehow separate and different from the body. These sensations and experiences also seem to indicate the mind can even survive bodily death. Such sensations, experiences, and stories are held by many people to be proof the mind is separate and different from the body, as well as proof of the reality of a life after death. These are not new sensations, experiences, ideas, or beliefs. Our ancestors had similar sensations, they underwent similar experiences, they heard similar stories, and they developed similar ideas and beliefs. Our ancestors believed in the reality of these sensations, experiences, and stories of separation of the mind from the body. So during the course of many millennia, our ancestors developed their belief in the reality of these sensations, and experiences, into a system of beliefs about the relationship between the mind, the body, and the nature of a possible life after death. And these same ideas and beliefs still permeate, and profoundly affect the collective thinking and structures of the societies in which we live.

For example, our ancestors could not see, touch, or sense the mind separating from the body. So they said this is proof the mind is invisible and immaterial, coexisting within the body, yet not part of the body. But they found it difficult to conceive of the mind as a separate entity. In addition, they knew from people who reported their experiences of mental separation, that these people often sensed movements, and sensations of flight at the same time as their physical bodies lay still and unmoving. Some of these people not only experienced separation from their bodies, but also told of meeting with deceased relatives and friends in a universe inhabited by the dead at a moment they themselves were apparently dead. So our ancestors developed the concept that each person has an invisible and immaterial body coexisting within the visible and material physical body. They called this invisible and immaterial body the 'soul'. And they believed this invisible and immaterial soul to be the vehicle of the mind, just as the body is the vehicle of the brain. They believed the soul could separate from the body, and they believed separation of the soul from the body explained all sensations and experiences of dissociation and disembodiment.

Our ancestors based their beliefs about the appearance of the soul upon the stories told by people who reported meeting their deceased relatives in the world inhabited by the souls of the dead. These people always reported that their deceased relatives had the same appearance as when they were alive. Furthermore, these people also reported that their deceased friends, and relatives, appeared to lead a life in the world inhabited by the souls of the dead very similar to that in the world of the living. So our ancestors eventually came to believe, and most people still believe, that the soul has the same appearance and size as the mortal body with which it is associated, and that the soul lives a life after death in much the same way as the body lived while alive. These are ancient beliefs. More than four thousand years ago these same beliefs were expressed in the ancient Egyptian Book of the Dead in which it is written:

> 'He[3] eats what the gods eat, he drinks what they drink, he lives as they live, and he dwells where they dwell; all the gods give him their food that he may not die. Not only does he eat and drink of their food, but he wears the apparel which they wear, the white linen and sandals; he is clothed in white, and he goeth to the great lake in the midst of the Field of Peace whereon the great gods sit; and these great and never failing gods give unto him (to eat) of the tree of life which they themselves do eat that he likewise may live. The bread which he eats never decays and his beer never grows stale.'[4]

Our ancestors could not see, touch, or sense the world they believed to be inhabited by the souls of the dead. So they said this world was also invisible and immaterial.

Our ancestors knew the material bodies of the dead do not live in the invisible and immaterial world inhabited by the dead. They knew this, because they observed that the material bodies of deceased people only lie still and decompose. So they developed the belief that it is the invisible, and immaterial soul that lives forever in this invisible, and immaterial world inhabited by the souls of the dead.

Our ancestors developed the belief that the immaterial soul is somehow located within the material and mortal body. This is a very reasonable belief. After all, during sensations and experiences of disembodiment, people sense their minds to be relocated from the usual location somewhere within their bodies, to locations outside their bodies, a fact apparently proving that the soul is normally located within the living body.

Our ancestors also came to believe the soul could temporarily separate from the body during sleep and disembodiment experiences, and that the soul departs permanently from the body at the moment of death. This latter belief was dramatically expressed more than fifteen hundred years ago by Saint Augustine[5]:

> 'Wherefore, as regards bodily death, that is, the separation of the soul from the body, it is good unto none while it is being endured by those whom we say are in the article of death. For the very violence with which body and soul are wrenched asunder, which in the living had been conjoined and closely intertwined, brings with it a harsh experience, jarring horridly on nature so long as it continues, till there comes a total loss of sensation, which arose from the very interpenetration of spirit and flesh.'[6]

Furthermore, our ancestors also developed the belief that the immaterial soul was not only immortal, but that the immortal soul never rests or sleeps. The reasoning behind this last belief is that dreams are apparently conscious mental experiences, and the soul is the vehicle of the mind. So our ancient ancestors said that dreams were remembered glimpses of the continued conscious mental activity of the immortal soul during periods the mortal body was resting and unconscious in sleep. Nearly two thousand years ago, an early Christian theologian called Tertullian wrote of this belief, saying:

> 'In like manner, the immortality of the soul precludes belief in the theory that sleep is an intermission of the animal spirit, or an indigence of the spirit, or a separation of the (soul's) connatural spirit. The soul perishes if it undergoes diminution or intermission. Our only resource, indeed, is to agree with the Stoics, by determining sleep to be a temporary suspension of the activity of the senses, procuring rest for the body only, not for the soul also. For the soul, as being always in motion, and always active, never succumbs to rest a condition which is alien to immortality: for nothing immortal admits, any end to its operation; but sleep is an end of operation. It is indeed on the body, which is subject to mortality, and on the body alone, that sleep graciously bestows a cessation from work.'[7]

These ideas of Tertullian about the nature of the soul were not new to people of his time. Greek and Roman philosophers preceding Tertullian went even further in their beliefs about the nature of the soul. They believed the human soul was limited by contact with the body, and that sleep and death actually allowed the soul to express its true nature by freeing it from the gross mortal body. The ancient Roman writer, statesman, and orator Marcus Tullius Cicero wrote of this belief:

> 'Again, you really see nothing resembling death so much as sleep; and yet it is when the body sleeps that the soul most clearly manifests its divine nature; for when it is unfettered and free it sees many things that are to come. Hence we know what the soul's future state will be when it has been wholly released from the shackles of the flesh.'[8]

In other words, not only did many of our ancestors believe the soul was immaterial and immortal, but they also believed that the soul was never-resting, eternally conscious, and possessed greater abilities than the mortal body with which it was associated. So it was, that our ancestors finally came to believe that each individual soul is an immaterial, immortal, never resting, superhuman version of the mortal body with which it is associated!

This belief of our ancestors that each person had a soul possessing these properties, was made all the more poignant by their continual confrontation with signs and evidences of their own mortality. Indeed, until as recently as 1700 CE, about half of our ancestors died before reaching the age of twenty years (see Appendix 1)! The infirmities afflicting so many of our ancestors, and the cruel transience of their lives, made our ancestors desperately hope for some form of life after death. Their holy people assured them of the reality of the belief that the soul would live eternally in a life after death. And stories of the experiences in strange and wonderful worlds told by those who supposedly arose from death appeared to confirm the promises of their holy people. So they believed in the words of their holy people and the apparent meanings of these sensations, experiences, and stories. To our ancestors, all these things were precious proof of the reality of a life after death.

The apparent proofs provided by their own sensations, their own experiences, as well as the wondrous stories of those who apparently rose from the dead, together with the words of their holy people, caused our ancestors to develop their belief in a life after death even further. They came to believe that this evanescent mortal life is no more than a preparation for an eternal life after death in a universe inhabited by the gods and the souls of the dead. Indeed, most of our ancestors maintained a desperately intense belief in the reality of all these things. This belief, this faith, comforted them, gave them a reason for living, and reconciled them to the bitter reality of their short and often harsh lives. Saint Paul, one of the founders of the Christian church, wrote of this faith in his 'Letter to the Hebrews' nearly two thousand years ago:

> 'Now faith is the substance of things hoped for, the evidence of things not seen.'[9]

Long before the founding of the Christian church, Marcus Tullius Cicero also wrote of the hope and the comfort contained within these beliefs, saying:

> 'And if I err in my belief that the souls of men are immortal, I gladly err, nor do I wish this error which gives me pleasure to be wrested from me while I live.'[10]

The words of Cicero are as true today as when he wrote this passage thousands of years ago. But does each person have a soul that is the vehicle of the individual mind? Or is this idea that each person has a soul only a belief so deeply rooted within the minds of people, that many people unquestioningly believe in the reality of the soul? This belief that each person has an invisible, immaterial, and immortal soul, raises fascinating questions about human nature and thought processes. But for me, the most interesting question was whether each person really does have an immaterial soul that continues to live after the body dies. If there is evidence each person has an immaterial soul, then there really is a possibility of a life after death. So I decided to learn whether each person has a soul.

But proving the reality of the human soul is not easy. After all, the soul is invisible and immaterial, which means it cannot be sensed with any human senses, nor detected with any known apparatus. I thought a long time about this problem of how I could somehow detect the presence of the human soul, or find some evidence proving the reality of the human soul. Finally, I decided there was no way I could directly detect or measure the presence of the soul. I could only determine the reality of the human soul by indirect means, by determining the reality of the soul with evidences provided by manifestations that could only be products of the presence of the soul. I found two such indirect methods of proving the reality of the soul. One method was to study experiences and sensations giving rise to the idea that the mind is separate from the body, because these are apparent proof of the reality of the soul. If each person really does have a soul, then a careful study of these sensations and experiences might yield proof that each person has a soul. The only other method I could think of to determine the reality of the soul was to study the truly vast body of knowledge about the human soul as revealed by holy people and prophets of all religions. This enormous body of knowledge could not be ignored, because it is a product of millennia of intense intellectual activity by countless clever and knowledgeable men and women. The very nature of this knowledge meant it might well contain proof that each person has a soul. I eventually decided to first study the properties of the soul as revealed by religion, because this enabled me to clearly define the basic properties assigned by believers to the human soul.

Chapter 4

Properties of the Soul

Many people believe in the reality of God. They believe God to be the all-powerful, all-knowing, and all-pervading creator of the universe. They also believe God instructs people through the medium of specially chosen holy people and prophets, who act as conduits revealing the reality, the instructions, and the intentions of God. Furthermore, they believe the revelations God made to these holy people, and prophets, are written in the holy texts of the religions and philosophies they expounded to their followers. These holy texts also contain many explicit and implicit descriptions of the properties of the soul. So I studied the properties of the soul as expounded in the holy books of major religions and beliefs. I hoped this knowledge of the properties of the human soul would clarify my thinking about the soul, and possibly even provide me with a way to prove the reality of the soul.

But I found it impossible to verify some of the properties of the human soul expounded in these holy books. This is not surprising, because the soul is invisible and immaterial. So the soul cannot be seen, touched, measured, detected, or sensed in any way by people or physical devices. Accordingly, it is impossible to determine the appearance of the soul, it is impossible to establish the way the soul is united with the body, it is impossible to confirm whether the soul never sleeps, and it is impossible to prove whether the soul is immortal. Fortunately, even though people believe the soul to be invisible, immaterial, as well as possessing all manner of other properties[1], all religious texts propagate the belief that the human soul possesses properties manifested by the material human body. Such manifestations of the presence of the soul can be detected, because the material human body manifests these properties of the soul. And if these properties of the soul cannot be explained by anything else except the presence of the soul, then it is very likely that each person does indeed have a soul. So I examined the texts of many holy books to determine, as well as to define properties of the soul manifested by the living human body.

One fundamental property of the soul agreed upon by nearly all religions is that of animation of the body by the soul. Saint Paul, one of the founders of the Christian religion, was one of many holy men through whom God revealed that each person has a soul. One of the revelations of God through Saint Paul expressing this belief was written in his first letter to the Corinthian church[2]:

'It is sown a natural body[3]; it is raised a spiritual body. There is a natural body, and there is a spiritual body.'[4]

This passage is very revealing. It says that each living body made of flesh and blood must have a soul. This is an understandable thought. After all, our ancestors understood that food, drink, and air, form and sustain the structures of the body. People eat lifeless plant material such as fruits, ve-getables, pulses, nuts, roots, and grains. People eat lifeless animal products such as milk, butter, and cheese. People eat dead animals, dead fish, and other lifeless creatures. People drink lifeless water, as well as other lifeless fluids. And people breathe lifeless air. So the flesh of the body is intrinsi-cally lifeless, because lifeless substances form and sustain the flesh of the body. This is why many people believe each person must have a soul, be-cause something must cause the body to live by somehow animating the intrinsically lifeless flesh forming the body. More than three thousand years ago, God confirmed this belief by inspiring Israelite prophets to write:

'And the Lord God formed man[5] of the dust of the ground, and breathed into his nostrils the breath of life; and man became a living soul.'[6]

The necessity for each living human body to be animated by a soul is a fundamental belief in nearly all religions. The terms used to express this belief vary from one religion to another, but the belief is universal. More recent writings by believers in the reality of an invisible and immaterial soul expound this belief more directly:

'We call ourselves physically alive, but in reality the material part of us is as dead as a door-nail. It is the energy behind the physical mechanism that is the real "live" thing. Nerves themselves are not alive – if they were, we have buried many a living body – it is the neuric[7] energy which animates, and the astral body[8] is the condenser of the nervous energy you are using right now.'[9]

These same believers developed this belief even further, writing:

'Without this "breath of life", man would really be nothing but the dust of the ground. The breath of life is the universal, the cosmic energy, condensed in the astral body which you are using every instant. You may think you are a living body, but you are, as said a living soul. It is the astral entity which is the real "You"; it is the universal energy that is the breath of life.[10]

All religions teach that the intrinsically lifeless flesh of each human body is animated by a soul. The converse is also true, because nearly all religions say the body dies when the soul separates from the body. The large body of Hindu holy books called the 'Upanishads'[11] clearly states this belief. The *Bhadaranyaka Upanishad* states that the 'life force' of a dying person is finally concentrated in the heart shortly before death, and then:

> *'After the apex of the heart becomes luminous, the Atman[12] pulls itself out of the body – sometimes though the eye, the skull, or another part of the body. When it pulls out, the life-breath[13] pulls out along with it; and when the life-breath departs, all organs cease to function.'[14]*

Stripped of all poetic verbiage, this passage simply states that the body dies when the soul separates from the body. Even so, many people believe that separation of the soul from the body does not always cause death. These people believe the soul can temporarily separate from the body during the several types of experiences of apparent separation of soul and body, such as out-of-body experiences, or astral travel. Furthermore, these people believe the soul is connected to the body by a sort of silver, or golden cord during such periods of temporary separation of body and soul. This cord acts as a sort of umbilical cord connecting soul and body, so that the soul can communicate with the body and sustain life within the body. And these people also believe the body dies when this cord is severed, because the soul is then permanently separated from the body.[15] This belief in a difference between temporary and permanent separation of body and soul is eloquently expressed in the Holy Koran[16]:

> *'God takes away men's souls upon their death, and the souls of the living during their sleep. Those that are doomed He keeps with Him, and restores the others for a time ordained.'[17]*

Many people still believe intensely in the reality of these same ancient beliefs, believing the body is alive because the immaterial soul animates the intrinsically lifeless flesh of the material body. So animation of the human body is a fundamental property of the human soul. It is also a fundamental property of the soul manifested by the body. But animation of the body by the soul is just one of the properties of the soul manifested by the body. Another important property of the soul is that of control exerted by the soul over the body.

All religions teach that the soul of each person is held responsible in an eternal life after death for the thoughts, speech, and deeds of that person while alive. This is a fundamental belief propagated by all ancient and modern religions. The ancient writers of the Egyptian Book of the Dead[18] described the judgement of the souls of the dead in the words:

> 'Thoth[19], the righteous judge of the great company of gods who are in the presence of the god Osiris[20], saith: "Hear ye this judgement. The heart of Osiris[21] hath in very truth been weighed, and his soul hath stood as a witness for him; it hath been found true by trial in the Great Balance[22]. There hath not been found any wickedness in him; he hath not done harm by his deeds; and he uttered no evil reports while he was upon earth." The great company of gods reply to Thoth, "He hath not sinned, neither hath he done evil against us. Let it[23] not be given to the devourer Amemet[24] to prevail over him."'[25]

Ancient Egyptians believed the soul of each person to be responsible for the thoughts, speech, and deeds of that person. This belief implies that the immaterial soul must interact with the material body to control every thought, word, and deed. If this were not so, the fate of the soul in an eternal life after death would not depend on the thoughts, speech, and deeds of the living material body. Ancient Israelites formulated much the same ideas, possibly because their ancestors were exposed to Egyptian religious thought during their period of exile in Egypt from about 1700 to 1250 BCE.[26] So ancient Israelite holy men wrote in the book of Ecclesiastes[27] that:

> 'For God shall bring every work into judgement, with every secret thing, whether it be good, or whether it be evil.'[28]

God also inspired the prophet Mohammed[29] to tell the world that the souls of each person that ever lived will finally be called before God to be judged on a final 'Day of Judgement'. This is why Moslems also implicitly believe the soul is responsible for the thoughts, speech, and deeds of the mortal body, believing that God knows and records every thought, word, and deed each person commits while they are alive. And it is written in the Holy Koran that on this day of judgement:

> 'The earth will light up with the effulgence of her Lord; and the ledger (of account) will be placed (in each man's hand), and the apostles and the witnesses will be called, and judgement passed between them equitably, and no wrong will be done to them. Each soul will be paid in full for what it had done. He[30] is cognisant of what you do.'[31]

The same idea permeates all holy books. All religions teach that the immortal soul is responsible for the thoughts, speech, and deeds of the physical body. Some people even believe each soul undergoes repeated cycles of birth, life, and death in a succession of physical bodies until spiritual development finally enables the soul to free itself from this cycle of repeated reincarnation. These people believe each soul is responsible for its individual level of spiritual development, and that some souls develop faster than others. Furthermore, those who believe in reincarnation also believe that the level of spiritual development of a soul determines the nature of the next reincarnation of that soul. Ancient Hindu prophets were inspired by their gods to write of this in the Upanishads, saying:

> 'For those who have lead a satisfactory life, the prospect is that they enter into a good, agreeable mother's womb, a Brahmana-womb or a Ksatriya-womb or a Vaisya-womb[32]; but for those who have lead an obnoxious life, the prospect is that they enter into an obnoxious mother-womb, into the dog-womb or the swine-womb or into the Candala-womb[33].'[34]

More recent writings by believers in the reality of an invisible, and immortal soul developed this belief in the control the body by the soul even further. They wrote:

> 'This may appear paradoxical to one who is accustomed to the idea that the conscious mind is a part of the physical mechanism. In fact, the material body has no mind at all, but clings over the astral, to speak symbolically, which is the real 'Ego' – through which the conscious mind really functions. It is erroneous to believe that the astral being has a supermentality[35]. It has not. The conscious mind, as you know it, is the mind of the astral body. Your normal, conscious mind – everything it contains – is the YOU, you the individual, now and throughout eternity, learning as it goes.'[36]

All these writings are unanimous. All these writings say that the thoughts, speech, and deeds of the living human body originate in the soul. In other words, these writings say that all properties of the mind originate in the soul. This belief means that either the soul is the vehicle of the mind, just as the body is the vehicle of the brain, or that the soul is the mind. But regardless of the exact nature of the mind, the influence of the mind is exerted through the soul. So the soul is responsible for all the thoughts, speech, and deeds of the body. But the mental activity required for purposeful control of the body is impossible without consciousness. Consciousness makes it possible to think, to have personality, to have emotions, as well as to perform purposeful actions. After all, an unconscious person does not think, manifests no personality or emotions, and performs no purposeful actions. Consciousness is the core of each individual being. This is why some religions teach that consciousness is also a property generated by the soul. Indeed, it is written in a Hindu holy book, the Bhagavad-Gita[37], that:

> '... , as the sun alone illuminates all this universe, so does the living entity[38], one within the body[39], illuminate the entire body by consciousness.'[40]

But thoughts, speech, and deeds require more than consciousness alone. Thoughts, speech, and deeds require other properties of mind, properties such as intellect, memory, personality, and emotions. These are properties of mind driving all purposeful conscious thoughts, speech, and deeds. Indeed, without intellect, memory, personality, and emotions, all conscious behaviour is only brutish reflex. This is why most belief systems teach that the soul is not only the generator of consciousness, but also the generator of all other properties of the conscious mind such as intellect, memory, personality, and emotions. These beliefs are ancient, and were expressed long ago by holy men who wrote in the Upanishads that:

> 'As speech, all names are poured in him[41], through the speech, he attains all names, as breath, all smells are poured into him, through breath he attains all smells, as eyes, all forms are poured in him, through the eyes he attains all forms, as ears, all sounds are poured in him, through the ears he attains all sounds, as Manas[42], all thoughts are poured in him, through Manas, he attains all thoughts; this is the penetration of all in Prana[43].'[44]

All these passages from different holy books say the same things about the soul. The soul is the mind of the body, because the soul generates consciousness, and the soul controls all conscious thoughts, speech, and deeds of the body. All these things mean that control of the body by the soul is also a fundamental property of the soul manifested by the body.

But how does the soul animate and control the body? If the body is animated and controlled by the soul, then the immaterial soul must somehow interact with the material body to animate and control the body. This is actually a very strange idea, because it means that somehow the immaterial soul can interact with the material body. Such an interaction between the immaterial and the material must occur. After all, if no interaction between the soul and the body occurs, then the body would neither be animated nor controlled by the soul. Accordingly, the immaterial soul interacts with the material body. This is another fundamental property of the soul manifested by the body.

The holy books of major religions and philosophies all say each person has a soul, and that each living body manifests these three fundamental properties of the soul:

1. the soul interacts with the body;
2. the soul interacts with the body to animate the body;
3. the soul interacts with the body to control the body.

These three fundamental properties of the soul have far reaching consequences for the functioning of the body, because they determine the functioning of the body. Knowledge of these fundamental properties of the soul made it possible for me to study the functioning of the body in relation to these properties of the soul, making it possible for me to determine whether each person has an immortal soul with these properties.

Chapter 5

Animation by the Soul

Nearly all religions teach that the body of each living person is alive because the soul interacts with the intrinsically lifeless flesh of the body to animate the body. Many people believe this to be a fundamental property of the human soul. Accordingly, the living human body is a manifestation of this fundamental property of the soul. So a study of the living human body should reveal whether the soul animates the body. And if animation of the body can only be explained by the soul, then this is possible proof of the reality of the soul.

But how is it possible for the soul to animate the body? I thought about this problem for a while, read books, and spoke with some people. I eventually came to the conclusion that there were actually only three ways the soul could animate the body. These are:

1 the soul may interact with the body through a single organ or tissue, animating the body by interacting with, and through this single organ or tissue;
2 the interaction of the soul with the body may somehow animate all organs and tissues within the body capable of living;
3 the soul may be no more than an animating life-force within each cell of the body.

These three different possibilities are amenable to accurate study because they manifest in the functioning of the body. I first decided to study the possibility that the soul animates the body through an interaction with a single body organ or tissue. I began with this possibility first because there is a vast amount of knowledge about the effects of destruction of different bodily appendages, tissues, and organs. This knowledge is a result of centuries of observation of the effects of operations, diseases, and injuries. I summarised this knowledge in a short list.

– A person can continue living after amputation of both arms and legs.
– A person can continue living after amputation of the lower half of the body.
– A person can continue living after removal or destruction of both kidneys.

- A person can continue living after destruction or removal of the entire digestive system.
- A person can continue living after destruction or removal of the pancreas.
- A person can continue living for a while after destruction or removal of the liver.
- A person can continue living after removal of the heart and lungs.
- A person can continue living after burns destroy more than one half of the skin.
- A fat person continues living after removal of tens of kilograms of fat tissue.
- A person can continue living after destruction or removal of the eyes, ears, and nose.
- A person can continue living after total spinal cord destruction.
- A person can continue living after destruction or removal of more than half of the brain.

A person can continue living after removal or destruction of any one or more of these organs and tissues. True, a person may be horridly crippled and mutilated after some of these organs and tissues are removed or destroyed, but they will still be alive. They may need intensive medical care to keep them alive, but they will still be alive. All these things mean that the soul does not animate the body through an interaction with any single one of these organs or tissues. But brain death, and in particular, death of the brainstem, always causes death of the body. Indeed, brainstem death is what defines death of the body. So is it possible that the soul animates the body by an interaction with the brainstem?

The brainstem is the most important part of the brain, because the brainstem is the generator of consciousness, as well as controlling breathing, circulation, and swallowing. Some unfortunate people suffer diseases or injuries causing massive brain, and brainstem destruction, or suffer diseases or injuries causing only brainstem destruction. Brainstem death is also called 'brain death'. A brain-dead person is unconscious, reacts to nothing, does not breathe, often has a failing circulation, and cannot swallow. Even so, it is possible to keep the body of a brain-dead person alive with intensive medical treatment: machines can take over the breathing, drugs and electrical devices[1] can sustain the circulation as well as heart action, and food and water can be poured through a tube inserted into the stomach to bypass the necessity for swallowing. The bodies of several brain dead people were once kept alive in this manner for several weeks.[2] After the bodies of these people finally died, a thorough examination of their bodies revealed something quite surprising:

'The consistency of the brain is always very weak and the weakening may proceed to such an extent that the brain substance is almost liquid. The colour[3] is a disgusting mixture of grey, green and brown.'[4]

Body tissues only decompose after death, and it takes many days before decomposing body tissues begin to liquefy. So the brains of these brain-dead people were dead, decomposing, and liquefying within their skulls, even though the rest of their bodies were still alive! Dead and decomposing organs are certainly not animated by a soul. Accordingly, the souls of brain-dead persons no longer animate their brains, because the brains of brain-dead persons are dead and decomposing. Furthermore, these studies of brain-dead people prove that the soul does not interact with the brain, or even with only the brainstem to animate the flesh of the body.

The conclusion of all these studies of the effects of surgery, injuries, and diseases of all body parts, organs, and tissues is very clear. The soul does not animate the body by interacting with any single body part, organ, or tissue.

So I examined the belief that the soul animates the organs and tissues of the body by a generalised interaction of the soul with the body. This belief means the soul does not animate the body by interacting with a single organ or tissue. Instead, it means the soul interacts with all the organs and tissues present within the confines of the body, animating those organs and tissues capable of living. This belief explains several problems raised by the belief in animation of the body by the soul. For example, this belief explains why it is possible to keep the bodies of horribly injured people alive. In the case of brain-dead people, their bodies contain organs and tissues capable of life, and application of the necessary medical treatments, makes it possible for the interaction of the soul with the body to continue animating those organs and tissues still capable of life.

Even so, there is a problem with this belief that the soul animates all viable organs and tissues within the confines of the body. It implies that all organs and tissues excised from the body will suddenly die, because after excision from the body they are no longer animated by an interaction with the soul within the body. Sudden death of organs and tissues after their excision from the body means that organ and tissue transplantation could never succeed. But organs and tissues transplanted from one body into another are nearly always obtained from deceased people, and these organs continue to live after removal from the deceased donor bodies, and they also continue to live after transplantation into living people. Indeed, organ and tissue transplantation are very successful medical treatments. This fact is proof that an interaction of the soul with the body does not animate individual viable organs and tissues. I examined specific examples from kidney transplantation to demonstrate the reality of this proof.

Kidney transplantation is a very successful type of organ transplantation. One way of acquiring kidneys is to excise them from the bodies of deceased people within several minutes after death. Most people believe the souls of the deceased depart from their bodies at the moment of death. So the souls of these dead people do not animate these kidneys before excision from their bodies, nor after excision from their bodies. Yet such excised kidneys do remain alive for several hours before transplantation into the bodies of living people, proving that animation of kidneys requires no interaction with a soul.

Consider another real situation with kidney transplantation. Both kidneys are removed from a man who has just died, after which his body is immediately cremated. All these things occur several hours before his kidneys are transplanted into other living people. No-one believes, or would claim, that the soul of this dead man animates his cremated ashes or his excised kidneys. Yet the kidneys of this dead man continued to live in the time between his death and their transplantation into the bodies of other living people. This is further proof that animation of kidneys requires no interaction with a soul.

The technique of living-donor kidney transplantation is yet another illustration of the absence of an interaction between the soul and the kidneys. A living person either sells, or donates one of his two healthy kidneys to a person whose kidneys no longer function. The donor is operated first. One of the two healthy kidneys of the donor is removed, and the living donor is aroused from anaesthesia. The recipient is then anaesthetised, and the excised donor kidney is transplanted into the living body of the recipient. The donor is alive and remains alive, so the soul of the donor remains within the donor. Similarly, the recipient is alive and remains alive, so the soul of the recipient remains within the recipient. Yet the excised kidney also remains alive in the period between excision and transplantation, even though it is severed from any contact with a living human body. This is proof that animation of kidneys requires no interaction with a soul.

The same principles apply to all transplantable organs and tissues. No single organ or tissue of the body requires an interaction with the soul to live, because when given the correct conditions, all organs and tissues of the body can live outside the body. Furthermore, not only can excised organs and tissues remain alive outside the body, they can even continue to function normally in organ preservation devices such as the 'Portable Organ Preservation System', a machine that first underwent trials with human organs excised from deceased persons in 2001 CE. This machine simulates the conditions of organs within the human body by maintaining excised organs at normal body temperature, pumping blood containing oxygen and nutrients through these organs, and removing waste products and carbon dioxide. Organs excised from living or deceased persons, and connected to Portable Organ Preservation System devices can live and function normally for more than one day: excised hearts continue to beat and pump blood, excised livers perform their normal functions of complex chemical transmutations and production of bile, while excised kidneys filter blood, remove waste products, and produce urine.[5] No-one proposes that an organ preservation device such as the Portable Organ Preservation System has a soul animating the living organ contained within, or that the souls of deceased persons still animate their excised organs contained within Portable Organ Preservation System devices, or that each organ has its own soul. Devices such as the Portable Organ Preservation System prove that human organs can live and function without the animating effect of a soul.

The reality of all these things proves that the animation and the functioning of individual organs and tissues within the body require no interaction with a soul. All these things are proof that the soul does not somehow animate all organs and tissues within the body that are capable of living. Organs and tissues awaiting transplantation are not the only body parts able to live outside the body. When viewed in a simple manner, all organs and tissues are no more than collections of many cells glued together to form specific organs and tissues. Cut an organ or a tissue out of the body, remove this special cellular glue, and all that remains is a collection of separated individual cells. These separated individual cells can live and function outside the body from which they were excised, as well as separated from the other cells to which they were once joined. This fact indicates the possibility that there is not single soul animating the body, but that there may be a wondrous 'life-force' animating each cell of the body.

But is a life-force within each cell needed to explain why the individual cells forming each organ and tissue of the body are alive? After all, chemical reactions build, sustain, and cause each cell to reproduce. The animating effect of a life-force within each cell may actually be no more than a product of myriad chemical reactions occurring within each living cell. So are cells animated by chemical reactions, or by a life-force? The times to damage and death of different human organs and tissues after cessation of breathing and heartbeat reveal answers to these questions.

- after breathing and heartbeat stop, brain damage occurs after three minutes, and the brain is dead after ten minutes;[6]
- after breathing and heartbeat stop, heart damage occurs after ten minutes, and the heart is dead after twenty minutes;[7]
- after breathing and heartbeat stop, spinal cord damage occurs after twenty-five minutes, and the spinal cord is dead after forty minutes;[8]

- after breathing and heartbeat stop, liver[9] and kidney[10] damage occur after thirty minutes, and these organs are dead after forty-five minutes;
- after breathing and heartbeat stop, muscle, skin and nerve damage occur after two hours, and these tissues are dead after somewhat more than four hours.[11]

These times to damage and death of different human organs and tissues are times measured when these organs and tissues are in people with a normal body temperature of 37 degrees Celsius. Times to damage and death of organs and tissues are shortened by high body temperature, and lengthened by low body temperature. This is a situation similar to preserving meat. Everyone knows that warm meat decays sooner than cold meat. These times to damage, and death of human organs and tissues at normal body temperature are facts confirmed by repeated measurement. Organ transplant surgeons excising organs and tissues donated by deceased persons must take these times into account, because the organs and tissues they excise must still be alive, otherwise they will not function after transplantation into a living person.

There are many different types of organs and tissues forming the human body. Each organ and tissue of the body is made of several different types of cells, and death of an organ or a tissue occurs when one or more of the different types of cells forming those organs or tissues die. So the time to death of any organ or tissue is the time taken for one or more of the different types of cells forming that organ or tissue to die. The different types of cells forming each organ and tissue die at different speeds after heartbeat and breathing stop. But if each cell of the body is animated by an immaterial life-force, why do the times to death of the different types of cells forming the organs and tissues differ after heartbeat and breathing stop? One way to explain this observation is to say that a different type of life-force animates each different type of cell in the body. This would mean there are as many different types of life-force animating the cells of the body as there are different types of cell in the human body. There is also another fact. Larger cells of each type of cell die more rapidly than smaller cells of the same type of cell. This would imply that larger cells of each type of cell have a different type of life-force than do smaller cells of the same type of cell. So this explanation implies that not only do different types of cell have a different type of life-force, but also that smaller and larger cells of the same type of cells have different life forces too! Such an explanation is very improbable. Why is there not just one life-force animating all cells of the body?

Body chemistry actually provides a better explanation of the speeds with which the different organs, tissues, and cells forming the body die after breathing and heartbeat stop. Breathing stops when the body dies, so no more oxygen enters the body after death. The heart also stops beating when the body dies, and no longer pumps oxygen-enriched blood around the body after death. Only a small amount of oxygen remains in each organ and each tissue of the body after breathing and heartbeat stop. The cells of the body need oxygen as an essential ingredient in the vital chemical reactions causing for each cell to function and live. Brain cells consume most oxygen, heart cells somewhat less, cells of the spinal cord even less, cells of the liver and kidneys even less still, the cells of the muscles and nerves even less, while the cells of skin and bone consume the least oxygen of all cells. Larger cells of each type of cell consume more oxygen than do smaller cells of the same type of cell. After death, the organs and tissues made of cells consuming a lot of oxygen, consume the remaining oxygen more rapidly than do organs and tissues made of cells consuming very little oxygen. So organs and tissues made of cells consuming a lot of oxygen die more rapidly than do organs and tissues made of cells consuming very little oxygen. And larger cells of each type die more rapidly than smaller cells of the same type. These differences in oxygen consumption explain the different speeds at which different organs, tissues, and cells die after death of the body. Accordingly, an unknown and wondrous life-force residing within, and animating each of the billions of cells forming the organs and tissues of the body, is not needed to explain why the cells of the body are alive and function. Body chemistry provides a better explanation. These are facts, and these facts mean there is no life-force animating each of the billions of cells forming the human body.

The differing times to damage and death of organs and tissues after death of the body also prove something else about the interaction of the soul with the body. Many people believe, and many religions teach, that each person has a single soul. Those who believe this, believe that a person dies when the soul departs from the body, because the soul then ceases to interact with the body to animate the organs and tissues of the body. If this is true, then why do not all organs and tissues of the body die at the same moment as the soul departs from the dying body? The very fact that different organs and tissues die at different times after death of the body, also proves that the organs and tissues of the body are not animated by an interaction with a single soul.

All these things prove that the body of each person is neither animated by a mysterious life-force, nor by any wondrous interaction of an immaterial soul with the material body. People are alive because their bodies are alive. So if each person has a soul, then the human soul has other properties.

Chapter 6

Control by the Soul

Thoughts, memories, emotions, and personality: all these things are properties of mind driving conscious movements, speech, actions, and deeds. Many people believe the mind is part of the soul, or that the soul is the vehicle of the mind, which is why they believe the soul controls all conscious movements, speech, actions, and deeds. This belief is also implied by all religions teaching that the soul of each person will be held responsible in a life after death for all thoughts, movements, speech, actions, and deeds of the living body. Indeed, this belief permeates the collective thought processes of nearly all societies. But does the soul interact with the body to control the body? This is an important question, because if the control exerted by the mind over the body can only be explained by a soul, then it is possible that each person really does have a soul, and that a life after death is possible. So I had to learn whether the living human body is controlled by a soul.

The soul is immaterial, which means the control exerted by the soul cannot be directly observed or detected. This is why it is only possible to study the control exerted by the soul over the body by examining the observable manifestations of this control: by observing movements, speech, actions, and deeds. One way of viewing such manifestations of the control exerted by the soul over the body, is to examine the analogous situation of the control exerted by a driver over an automobile. A driver controls an automobile through the mechanisms of the automobile. If the mechanisms of the automobile function normally, then the driver can exert normal control over the automobile. The automobile manifests this normal control by starting, moving, turning, and stopping in a manner determined by the driver. But changes in the functioning of the mechanisms of the automobile may render the control exerted over the automobile by the driver imperfect, as a result of which the automobile starts, moves, turns, and stops in an abnormal and uncontrolled manner. Malfunction or damage of the mechanisms of the automobile may be even be such that the driver is unable to exert any control over the automobile at all. All this means that the control exerted by the driver over the automobile is expressed through the mechanisms of the automobile, and the functioning of the mechanisms of the automobile express the control exerted by the driver. A study of the consequences of various types of malfunction of the mechanisms of an automobile will reveal the location of the driver, as well as the necessity for a driver to control the automobile.

The relationship of the soul to the body is similar to that of a driver and an automobile. The soul exerts control over the body through the mechanisms of the body, and the functioning of the mechanisms of the body express the control exerted by the soul. Accordingly, a study of how malfunction of the mechanisms of the body affect the control exerted over the body by the soul should reveal the location in the body where the soul exerts control over the body, as well as the existence of the controlling influence of the soul.

Those who believe in the reality of an immaterial and immortal soul believe the soul controls all movements, all speech, all actions, and all deeds. Bodily movements, speech, actions, and deeds are visible, audible, detectable, and measurable. Accordingly, this belief means that movements, speech, actions, and deeds are the visible, audible, detectable, and measurable manifestations of the control exerted by the soul over the body. Muscles are the mechanisms of the body causing all body movements, because muscle movements produce all speech, muscle movements produce all actions, and muscle movements produce all deeds. So if the soul initiates

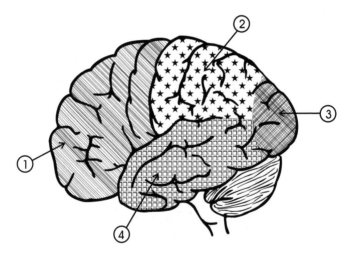

Figure 3   The brain, divided into lobes

A description of the surface of the brain is made easier by dividing it into lobes; a situation very similar to the division of the surface of our planet into continents and oceans. It makes the description of the any location on the brain surface much easier. There are four lobes on the brain surface.1 Frontal lobe. 2 Parietal lobe. 3 Occipital lobe. 4 Temporal lobe. The right hand side of the brain is a mirror image of the left hand side.

and controls all conscious movements, speech, actions, and deeds, then the soul initiates, as well as controls the movements of muscles generating movements, speech, actions, and deeds.

How are conscious voluntary movements generated? The idea of moving, speaking, performing an action, or performing a deed arises within the mind. The conscious idea, the will to do any of these things manifests as nerve activity within a part of the brain called the 'supplementary motor cortex' (see figure 4). The supplementary motor cortex transmits nerve signals to the appropriate sections of an adjacent part of the brain called the 'primary motor cortex' (see figure 4). The primary motor cortex translates the will to do these things into nerve signals activating specific groups of muscle movements. Nerve fibres conduct these nerve signals from the primary motor cortex into the spinal cord. Here these nerve fibres connect with other nerve fibres to form the nerves departing from the spinal cord to all parts of the body. These nerves make contact with the muscles of the

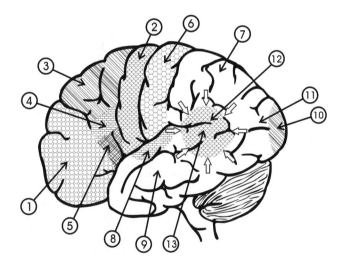

Figure 4 Drawing of the brain showing the functions served by the various regions of the cortex

1 Prefrontal lobe. 2 Primary motor cortex. 3 Supplementary motor cortex. 4 Frontal eye field (part of the supplementary motor cortex). 5 Broca's speech area, (part of the supplementary motor cortex). 6 Primary sensory cortex. 7 Associative sensory cortex. 8 Primary auditory cortex. 9 Associative auditory cortex. 10 Primary visual cortex. 11 Associative visual cortex. 12 General associative cortex. 13 Wernicke's speech area (part of the general associative cortex). White arrows around the general associative area indicate that nerve fibres from the associative areas associated with the specific senses all converge on the general associative area where information from these senses is integrated with other information.

body, transmitting nerve signals arising within the brain to these muscles, and these muscles respond, generating the intended movements, speech, actions, and deeds. This is how the conscious will to move, speak, act, or perform deeds finally manifests as the muscle movements generating the intended movements, speech, actions, and deeds. Furthermore, this is the chain of control of muscle movements, from the idea of moving, to the final execution of the movements.

So I decided to perform a step-by-step study of each level of this chain of control of muscle movement. This study revealed how changes in the functioning of nerves and muscles caused by injuries, diseases, and drugs affected the possible control exerted by the soul over bodily movements. This analysis enabled me to determine the possible places in the body where the soul exerts control over the body, and whether the soul actually exerts any control over the body at all.

An example of a low level of control exerted by the mind over muscles is manifested at the places where nerves make contact with muscles. Curare is a muscle-paralysing drug used as part of a standard combination of anaesthetic drugs. Curare causes muscle paralysis, but curare does not affect the muscle cells, nor does curare affect the brain, the spinal cord, or the nerves controlling and activating the muscles of speech, breathing, or voluntary movement. Instead, curare blocks the transmission of nerve signals controlling and activating the muscles of speech, breathing, and voluntary movements at the places where these nerves make contact with the muscles performing all these actions. This means that even though people are totally paralysed after administration of sufficient curare, they are still fully conscious and aware, even though they cannot speak, cannot breathe, and cannot move, no matter how hard they try.[1] The mind is supposed to be part of the soul, and the soul supposedly controls the body, yet the soul is unable to activate and move the muscles of the bodies of people to whom curare has been administered, no matter how hard these people may try to speak, breathe, or move. These effects of curare show that the soul must use the mechanisms of the body to control the body, as well as showing that the functioning of the mechanisms of the body affects the expression of any control exerted over the body by the soul. In addition, the effects of curare prove that the soul exerts no control over the body at the places where nerves make contact with muscles, nor does the soul directly control and activate the muscles themselves.

An example of a higher level of control by the mind over movements is manifested at the spinal cord. I administer a type of anaesthesia called 'spinal anaesthesia' to several patients every working day. The technique of spinal anaesthesia is simple. I insert a needle between the vertebrae of the back, and inject a local anaesthetic drug into the spinal canal between the nerves coming from the spinal cord. The local anaesthetic drug blocks the flow of nerve signals within the nerves inside the spinal canal at the point where the local anaesthetic drug is administered. This means that spinal anaesthesia blocks nerve signals transmitted from the brain to the muscles, as well as blocking the flow of sensory nerve signals from the body to the brain. The combined effect of these two things results in anaesthesia of the part of the body supplied by the blocked nerves. Spinal anaesthesia is often used to anaesthetise the lower half of the body. People are fully awake under spinal anaesthesia. They feel normal sensations in the upper half of their bodies, and can talk and breathe, as well as move their upper bodies. But they feel no sensations from the lower parts of the bodies, because the nerves transmitting sensory information from the lower half of their bodies are anaesthetised. They also cannot move the muscles of the lower half of their bodies, because the nerves activating the muscles of the lower half of their bodies are anaesthetised. Spinal anaesthesia effectively paralyses and removes all sensations from the lower half of the body. So when a leg of a person under spinal anaesthesia is lifted up, these people are often surprised. They cannot feel any sensations from their legs, and are surprised when they see their leg, often exclaiming: 'Is that my leg? It doesn't feel like my leg!' They often try to move their raised leg, but the anaesthetised leg does not move, no matter how hard they try to move it. Only after the effects of the local anaesthetic drug have disappeared, can these people feel sensations in their legs again, and move their legs again. The mind is supposed to be part of the soul, and the soul supposedly controls the body, but these effects of spinal anaesthesia show that the soul can only exert control over the body through the mechanisms of the body. If this were not so, then the control exerted by the soul could bypass those parts of the spinal canal where the conduction of nerve signals is blocked by the local anaesthetic drug. But this does not occur, which means that the effects of spinal anaesthesia show that the soul exerts no control over the body below the level of the spinal cord. In addition, the effects of spinal anaesthesia also show that the functioning of the mechanisms of the body affects the expression of any control exerted over the body by the soul.

An example of an even higher level of control exerted by the mind over the body is seen within the brain. The primary motor cortex is part of a larger section of the brain surface called the 'frontal cortex', or 'frontal lobe' (see figure 3 and figure 4). The primary motor cortex generates co-ordinated movements directed by conscious will. Damage or malfunction of the primary motor cortex causes paralysis of the muscles controlled by the damaged or malfunctioning regions of the primary motor cortex. People cannot move muscles controlled by malfunctioning, damaged, or destroyed regions of the primary motor cortex, no matter how hard they try to move these muscles. Malfunction, damage, or destruction of the left or right primary motor cortex manifests as the condition called a 'stroke'. Strokes affecting the left primary motor cortex cause paralysis of the right side of the body, while strokes affecting the right primary motor cortex cause paralysis of the left side of the body. A person who has had a stroke causing paralysis of one side of the body is unable to move his paralysed limbs, no matter how hard he tries to move his paralysed limbs. The mind is supposed to be part of the soul, and the soul supposedly controls the body, but the soul cannot arouse movements in the paralysed muscles of a person who has suffered a stroke. So the effects of primary motor cortex damage prove that the soul must use the mechanisms of the body to exert control over the body, and also prove that the functioning of the mechanisms of the body affects the expression of any control exerted over the body by the soul. In addition, the effects of primary motor cortex malfunction, damage, or destruction prove that the soul does not exert any control over the body outside the brain, or below the level of the primary motor cortex.

An even higher level of control within the brain exerted by the mind over movements is manifested by the supplementary motor cortex (see figure 4). The supplementary motor cortex is a part of the frontal cortex adjacent to the primary motor cortex. This region of the brain surface is responsible for actually initiating and planning movements. A person with a malfunctioning, damaged, or destroyed supplementary motor cortex, does not even think of moving those body parts controlled by the affected regions of the supplementary motor cortex. The very idea of moving these body parts does not even arise in the mind of an affected person! These effects of damage to this region of the brain show that a functioning supplementary motor cortex is required to express conscious will as manifested by voluntary speech and actions.[2] The mind is supposed to be part of the soul, and the soul supposedly controls the body. So these effects of supplementary motor cortex malfunction, damage, or destruction, show that the soul must use the mechanisms of the body to control the body, as well as showing that the mechanisms of the body affect the expression of the controlling effect of the soul. In addition, the effects of supplementary motor cortex malfunction, damage, or destruction prove that the soul does not exert any control over the body outside the brain, or below the level of the supplementary motor cortex.

Another level of control within the brain exerted by the mind over movements is manifested by yet another part of the brain. The effects of malfunction, damage, or destruction, of a part of the brain surface called the 'right parietal cortex' (see figure 3) are very strange. Malfunction, damage, or destruction of the right parietal cortex causes affected people to forget and to neglect the left hand side of their bodies. Stranger yet, when asked to draw a picture of their own bodies, affected people only draw the right hand sides of their faces and bodies, and do not draw the left hand sides of their faces and bodies. Likewise, when asked to draw a clock face, they only draw the right hand side of the clock face, and do not draw the left hand side of the clock face. Their left arms, and left legs appear paralysed, hanging limp and unused. Affected people do not even think of moving these limbs. Yet these limbs are not paralysed, because these people do move these apparently paralysed limbs in response to pain, or when forced to do so. People with right parietal cortex malfunction, damage, or destruction totally lack any insight into their condition, saying they are not paralysed and that there is nothing wrong with the functioning of their bodies.[3] The mind is supposed to be part of the soul, and the soul supposedly controls the body. The effects of right parietal cortex malfunction, damage, or destruction, also prove that the soul must use the machinery of the body to control the body, and also prove that the functioning of the body affects the expression of the controlling effect of the soul. In addition, the effects of right parietal cortex malfunction, damage, or destruction, also prove that the soul does not exert any control over the body outside the brain, or below the level of the right parietal cortex.

The mind is supposed to be part of the soul, and the soul supposedly controls the body. Yet these examples of the effects of anaesthesia, drugs, and disease at different levels of control exerted by the soul over movements, conclusively prove that any control exerted by the soul over the movements, speech, actions, and deeds of the body can only be exerted through the mechanisms of the body. They also prove that the functioning of the mechanisms of the body affects the bodily manifestations of any control exerted over the body by the soul. Furthermore, these examples also demonstrate that if the soul exerts any control over the body, then this control is exerted somewhere within the brain. In other words, if the mind is part of the soul, and the soul really does control the body, then somewhere within the brain, there is a part of the brain through which the soul exerts control over the body.

But the mind, which many people believe to be part of the soul, is more than just the idea of moving, the will to move, or the ability to move. Mind is more than just speech, movements, and deeds. Mind is the sum total of all consciousness, thoughts, intellect, memories, emotions, and personality. These aspects of mental function are what drive the conscious voluntary muscle movements generating movements, speech, actions, and deeds. So I studied whether brain malfunction, damage, or destruction revealed other evidences of the controlling influence of a soul.

Alcohol, other drugs, injuries, and diseases all alter the functioning of the brain. Brain injury, brain damage, brain cancers, brain diseases, and brain surgery also alter the functioning of the brain.[4] Altered brain function can cause profound changes in the thought processes, emotions, and personality factors driving conscious voluntary movements, speech, actions, and deeds. The story of Phineas Gage is the best-known example of mental changes caused by brain damage.

'Phineas Gage was a foreman in charge of a group of railway workers preparing the rail bed for a new railway line in the state of Pennsylvania in the United States of America. During the afternoon of 13 September 1848 CE, they found a rock obstructing the planned route of the railroad. This rock was too big to move, so they decided to blast it. Gunpowder was poured into a hole drilled in the rock, and Phineas Gage began to ram the gunpowder firmly into the hole with a 5.9 kilogram, 107 centimetres long, 3.2 centimetre thick iron staff. The powder exploded, driving the iron staff out of the hole, through the head of Phineas Gage, to land about fifteen metres away. The rod entered the head of Phineas Gage just under his left cheekbone, and emerged out of the top of his head above his left eye.

After a short period of unconsciousness, Phineas Gage awoke, and with bleeding head, was transported by ox-cart to his hotel room in a nearby town. He survived the injury, bleeding, and subsequent infection of his brain and head, but his personality was dramatically changed. Before his accident he was an efficient and capable worker, not given to using profane speech, friendly, and considerate of his fellows. After his accident, he became erratic and irreverent, at times using the grossest profanity, manifested no deference to his fellows, was impatient of advice and restraint when it conflicted with his desires, and while he made many plans, he was totally unable to remember or carry them out.

His friends all stated that he was simply not the same man as before the accident. His changed personality made it impossible for him to continue working at his previous occupation, and his employer dismissed him. Subsequently Phineas Gage toured the country as a carnival attraction, demonstrating his wounds, and the iron staff that caused them. After his death in 1868 CE, a detailed study of his body showed that the iron tamping rod and subsequent infection had caused extensive damage to the frontal lobes of his brain.'[5]

Throughout all the millennia of human belief in the reality of the soul, people have always believed the soul is unaffected by things affecting the body. This is a very understandable belief, because the body is material, as are the diseases and injuries affecting the body. But the soul is supposedly immaterial, so diseases and injuries affecting the material body should not affect the immaterial soul. Accordingly, those who believe in the reality of the soul do not believe that alcohol, other drugs, brain injury, brain infection, brain surgery, and other disorders can affect the immaterial soul. Indeed, the holy books of all religions also propagate the belief that the things affecting the body do not affect the soul. And the Hindu holy book called the 'Bhagavad Gita' expresses this belief very explicitly, saying:

> *'This individual soul is unbreakable and insoluble, and can be neither burned nor dried. He is everlasting, present everywhere, unchangeable, immovable and eternally the same.'*[6]

Another passage in the Bhagavad Gita further emphasises the fact that things affecting the material body do not affect the immaterial soul:

> *'That which pervades the entire body you should know to be indestructible. No-one is able to destroy the imperishable soul.'*[7]

All this means that the injury damaging the brain of Phineas Gage did not affect his soul, because his immaterial soul could not be affected by anything affecting his material body. According to the belief of many people, the soul is the vehicle of the mind, or the mind is a part of the soul. So the functioning of the mind of Phineas Gage should have been unaffected by the injury to his brain. But the injury to his brain did change the functioning of his mind, as was clearly manifested by his speech, actions, and deeds. There are two possible explanations for the changes in mental function manifested by Phineas Gage. One explanation is that changes in the functioning of his brain caused by his injuries affected the expression of the control exerted by his soul over his brain. Another explanation is that the mind is a product of the functioning of the brain, which is why the extensive brain damage suffered by Phineas Gage affected the functioning of his mind.

Everyone becomes sick at some time. Everyone knows from personal experience that disease and illness can change the intellect, personality, and emotions of sick people, as expressed by their movements, speech, actions, and deeds. Most sick people become passive. Others may become irritable. Sometimes sick people may even become unpleasant and unbearable. And some sick people may think, say, or do hurtful and evil things, even though these same people would never dream of thinking, speaking, or acting in these ways while in good health. There are two explanations for this observation. One explanation is that changes in brain function caused by illness alter the expression of the control exerted over the brain by the soul. Another explanation is that the mind is a product of the functioning of the brain, and so the altered intellect, personality, and emotions manifested by the speech, actions, and deeds of sick people are products of changes in brain function caused by illness.

People believe that alcohol, drugs, injuries, and diseases do not affect the immaterial soul. Yet if these things do not affect the soul, why is it that people who normally never think, speak, or act in an evil manner, sometimes do these things when the functioning of their brains is changed by alcohol, drugs, injury, or disease? Consider the following imaginary, but tragically real story.

> A man goes to a wine bar to meet his friends and drink some wine. They talk, drink a lot of wine, and have a wonderful time with each other. The man becomes very drunk. He realises vaguely that he is drunk. Yet even though he knows that drunken driving is dangerous, he still decides to drive himself home. He steps into his car and drives at a reckless high speed. Suddenly he sees a pedestrian crossing the road directly in the path of his car. But he reacts too slowly, and crashes at high speed into the pedestrian who is killed on impact.

This story is all too familiar. Each such event is deeply regrettable, senseless, and tragic. Yet such events do occur. If the mind is a part of the soul, and the soul is the vehicle of the mind, then the functioning of the mind of this man should not have been affected by the alcohol in his body. Nonetheless, alcohol did change his mental function. This a fact proven by the details of this story. We know this, because this man did decide to drive, even though he knew he was drunk, and even though he knew of the dangers of drunken driving. There are two possible explanations for the altered mental function of the man in this sad story. One explanation is that alcohol induced changes in the functioning of his brain that affected the expression of the control exerted over his brain by his soul. Another explanation is that the mind is a product of the functioning of the brain, and alcohol changed the functioning of the brain of this man, so changing the functioning of his mind.

Normal variations in body function also alter brain function. Sometimes these normal alterations in brain function may even cause people to think, speak, and act evilly or irrationally. The normal menstrual cycle of women is an example of normal changes in body function that affect mental function. About eight in ten women experience slight changes in mood and emotions several days prior to menstruation, and about one in fifty women experiences severe mental changes several days prior to menstruation. These severely affected women may experience symptoms such as depression, anxiety, sudden and dramatic mood swings, anger, and irritability. And these mental changes may result in these women having difficulties with their work and relationships prior to menstruation. Queen Victoria, queen of England from 1837 to 1901 CE, was subject to extreme mood and emotional changes in the days prior to menstruation:

> 'Once a month Queen Victoria would become unaccountably enraged at Prince Albert[8], screaming accusations and hurling any object that came to hand across the room. If the royal consort tried to reason with her, she would only shriek loudly and vituperatively. If he remained silent, he would be accused of insulting the royal presence. If he withdrew to his room, Victoria would pound on the door with her tiny fists.'[9]

Some severely affected women may think, speak, and behave in a hurtful or evil manner for several days prior to menstruation. Yet at other times these same women would never think of thinking, speaking, or behaving in this manner. The female menstrual cycle is a normal body function, exerting normal changes upon the functioning of the material body that should not affect the immaterial soul. So if the mind is a part of the soul, or the soul is the vehicle of the mind, then the changes occurring in the bodies of women prior to menstruation should not affect their mental function. But the mental function of many women, as manifested by their speech, actions, and deeds, does change for several days before menstruation. There are two possible explanations for these normal cyclical changes in mental function. One explanation is that changes in brain function during the normal female menstrual cycle alters the expression of the control exerted by the soul over the brain. Another explanation is that the mind is a product of brain function, so the cyclical, hormone induced changes in brain function during the normal female menstrual cycle, cause these cyclical changes in mental function.

There is another important aspect to control of the body by the soul. People must be conscious to have conscious thoughts, or conscious will, as well as to consciously express their thoughts, emotions, and personality, by their speech, actions, and deeds. Many people believe consciousness is a property of the soul, believing that the soul generates the phenomenon of consciousness in the mortal body. Nonetheless, the soul must use the mechanisms of the body to generate consciousness. The effects of injuries as well as the effects of general anaesthetic drugs prove this.

I administer general anaesthesia to many people each week. Often I induce unconsciousness by injecting drugs directly into a vein in an arm or hand. Everyone is unconscious twenty to forty seconds after I inject these drugs. All such general anaesthetic drugs induce temporary unconsciousness by causing temporary malfunction of those brainstem functions generating consciousness. Some people struggle, and try their utmost to resist losing consciousness to the effects of these anaesthetic drugs, but no-one ever succeeds, everyone loses consciousness. There are two possible explanations for the loss of conscious resulting from brainstem malfunction caused by these anaesthetic drugs. One explanation is that such brainstem malfunction proves that any control exerted over the body by the soul is expressed through the mechanisms of the body, and that the functioning of the mechanisms of the body affects the expression of any control exerted over the brain by the soul. Another explanation is that the functioning of the brainstem generates consciousness, which is why brainstem malfunction induced by anaesthetic drugs causes unconsciousness.

These are a few examples of the effects that malfunction, damage, or destruction of different parts of the body have upon control exerted over the body by the mind as manifested by movements, speech, actions, and deeds. Everyday experience, everyday observation, and repeated experiment, prove these things again and again. These observations are facts. All these observations show that if the mind is part of the soul, and if the soul does indeed control the body, then the soul only exerts control over the body through the mechanisms of the body, in addition to which the functioning of the mechanisms of the body alters the bodily manifestations of the control exerted over the body by the soul. But this is quite different to what many people believe, and quite different to what is taught by most religions. After all, many people believe, and most religions teach, that the control exerted by the soul over the body is unaffected by the functioning of the mechanisms of the body.

These are two clear and indisputable facts about the control exerted over the body by the soul – any control exerted by the soul over the body is exerted through the mechanisms of the body, and any control exerted by the soul over the body is affected by the functioning of the mechanisms of the body – these two facts raise the question of whether the soul exerts any control over the body at all. After all, it is possible to explain all these observations of the effects of changes in body and brain function by saying that the mind is an expression of the functioning of the brain. This would mean that the soul is not the vehicle of the mind, but that the brain is the generator and the vehicle of the mind. Accordingly, if the mind is a product of the functioning of the brain, then changes in the functioning of the brain and the body will certainly alter the functioning of the mind, as well as all observable manifestations of the control exerted over the body by the mind, such as conscious movements, speech, actions, and deeds. Indeed, to explain mental activity as being a product of brain function, explains all observed facts with something provable, whereas to explain the expression of mental activity as being due to control exerted over the body by the soul through the mechanisms of the body, is to explain the expression of mental activity with something that is impossible to prove. So it is far more likely that the mind is a product of the functioning of the brain. Even so, the examples and arguments in this chapter are not conclusive proof that there is no soul, just as these examples and arguments also do not prove that the body is controlled by the soul. It is still possible that the soul exerts some sort of very indirect unconscious control over the body, or that the soul manifests in other ways. So I searched for other ways to determine whether each person has a soul, and I found there are perceptions and experiences seemingly indicating that each person has a soul, as well as seemingly indicating the existence of other invisible and immaterial aspects to the world. For example, there are perceptions and experiences such as paranormal senses, the perception of a human aura, experiences of separation of the mind from the body, as well as experiences of contact with immaterial entities. Accordingly, I decided to study these perceptions and experiences to find whether they were direct, or indirect evidence for the reality of a human soul.

Chapter 7

Paranormal Senses

Many people hear of, read about, or actually undergo inexplicable experiences, seeming wonders, or apparent miracles. Often these events and experiences cannot be explained by tangible material events. They appear to result from something originating outside the physical and material world. So they are called 'paranormal', 'paranormal phenomena', 'paranormal events', or 'paranormal sensations'.

Our ancestors believed intensely in the reality of the paranormal. They were especially fascinated by paranormal sensory abilities, because such abilities gave them apparent control over a world they perceived as dominated by incomprehensible and uncontrollable forces. Paranormal sensory abilities held the promise of being able to learn about distant events, to be able to read the thoughts, and understand the emotions of other people, to influence, and to gain power over others, to influence the outcome of wars and conflicts, or simply to gain wealth. Notwithstanding this ancient belief in the reality of paranormal sensory abilities, such sensory abilities remain very fickle, often yielding inaccurate information. Yet this has never deterred people from consulting those believed to possess these abilities to a greater degree than others, such as soothsayers, seers, palm readers, clairvoyants, sorcerers, magicians, wizards, alchemists, necromancers, shamans, or witches. Indeed, most past and present societies have always held apparently successful practitioners of these arts in high esteem. Nonetheless, even though the ability to apparently successfully use paranormal sensory abilities to acquire information has always been held in high esteem, the God of the Jewish and Christian religions forbids the use of paranormal senses, saying through the words of the ancient Israelite prophets that:

> *'A man also or woman that hath a familiar spirit, or that is a wizard, shall surely be put to death: they shall stone them with stones: their blood shall be upon them.'[1]*

Most people reporting information acquired by apparently paranormal means do not purposefully try to obtain information by these means. Instead, they spontaneously undergo experiences during which they acquire this information by means of apparently paranormal sensations.

Surveys made in various countries during the late twentieth century revealed that paranormal experiences are very common, even though they manifest only occasionally during an individual lifetime. These surveys revealed that about 25% to 85% of people have undergone at least one apparently paranormal experience during their lives.[2] These are widely varying incidences, but for practical purposes it means that as many as eight in ten people have undergone at least one apparently paranormal experience. Such experiences just happen, and the occasional accuracy of information acquired during these paranormal experiences forms the basis of this ancient belief in the reality of paranormal sensory abilities.

Many people say that paranormal sensory abilities must be real if so many people have experienced them, and believed in their reality for so many millennia. But such experiences, and such beliefs, no matter how ancient, and no matter how deeply ingrained in the human psyche, are not proof of the reality of paranormal sensory abilities; they only indicate the possible reality of paranormal sensory abilities. The possible reality of paranormal sensory abilities has profound consequences. If paranormal sensory abilities do indeed exist, then it is possible that other immaterial aspects to the universe also exist, such as an immaterial soul coupled to the body of each person. So I decided to examine the evidence for immaterial aspects to the universe as revealed by paranormal sensory abilities. I began by studying reports of spontaneous paranormal events.

Many spontaneously occurring paranormal sensory events are warnings of injuries, illness, or death of family members or friends. A good example is the dream of a woman about one of her brothers who was serving as a soldier in the German army fighting in Russia during World War Two, (1939 to 1945 CE). She reported:

> 'We did not receive news from my youngest brother for quite some time during the war. I then dreamed as follows: I stood before a high painting that was hidden by a curtain. I opened the curtain by pulling a cord. There, life-size, was a picture of my brother in full uniform. A delicate cloud of smoke rose from his left hand. The next morning, I told my mother, "Willy has probably suffered a slight wound in his left hand". Shortly afterwards, we received a postal card from my brother. He had scribbled on the margin, "I have been slightly wounded in the left hand."'[3]

Many Germans knew from their own family members, or from conversations with others, that the Russian Front was an exceptionally savage and bloody campaign. Mid-year German troop strength on the Russian Front from 1941 to 1944 CE, was about three million soldiers during each of these four years, and about one in two of these soldiers was killed or wounded.[4] So the anxious dreams of family members of German soldiers fighting in Russia at this time were often true, sometimes even occurring at about the same time as the family member was killed or wounded. This means these dreams or visions were not necessarily paranormal perceptions, instead they were very likely no more than chance synchronous events.

Indeed, many apparently paranormal sensations and perceptions are no more than chance synchronous events. Most people have dreams or visions, hear sounds, smell odours, or have thoughts and feelings bearing no relationship to events in their lives. Such dreams or visions, sounds, odours, thoughts, and feelings, are usually dismissed or ignored. They are seldom remembered. But dreams or visions, sounds, odours, thoughts, and feelings, occurring just before, or at about the same time as the related events, are remembered and reported. They arouse a sense of wonder in most people. Nonetheless, they are no more than chance synchronous events, and are not proof of the reality of paranormal sensory abilities.

Nearly everyone has had such experiences. Sometimes you think of writing a letter to a far friend or family member, and on that day, to your great surprise, you receive a letter or message from that person. Or you wish to telephone a friend or family member, and just as you are about to telephone them, they telephone you. Such events are not examples of paranormal phenomena, but are examples of two events occurring synchronously. Each person has a circle of family members, friends, and others with whom they regularly communicate, and who regularly communicate with them. So there is always a chance that both parties will try to communicate with each other at the same time. Such occurrences are rare, but have nothing to do with paranormal phenomena. They are manifestations of chance synchronous events.

Interactions between people also provide examples of apparently paranormal sensations. For example, some people are extremely adept at understanding the thoughts and emotions of others. This is an unconscious ability present to a greater or lesser degree in all people, enabling people to understand the thoughts and emotions generating the facial expressions, body positions, body movements, and body odours they observe in other people. This ability is highly developed in some people, but is not a manifestation of paranormal sensory abilities. An example of this is the communication between two lovers. The involvement of the two lovers with each other is so intense, that each can interpret the moods, emotions, and thoughts of the other without speaking, because each lover unconsciously perceives, and understands, the meaning behind the ever changing facial expressions, body odours, body positions, and movements of their loved one. This same ability also explains the non-verbal communication between identical twins which some people believe to be paranormal[5], as well as between parents and children which many people also believe to be paranormal.[6]

The experiences of the dying are another source of spontaneous paranormal sensory experiences. Tradition has always endowed the dying and the nearly dead with paranormal perceptive abilities, because people have always believed that the proximity of the dying and the nearly dead to an immaterial life-after-death enhances such sensory abilities. Indeed, some dying persons, and those who nearly die, do report obtaining information by means that appear to be paranormal.[7] There are two categories of paranormally acquired information reported by the dying and the nearly dead.

There is information about local events, which are events occurring within the range of the physical senses of the body. This is called 'local information'. The second type of paranormally acquired information, is information about distant events, which are events occurring beyond the range of any of the physical senses of the body. This is called 'distant information'. The story of a man who underwent an out-of-body experience while being resuscitated is a good example of a report of local information. After recovering consciousness, he reported:

> 'I could feel myself leaving my body from the headward portion, detaching and floating in the air without any sensation of falling. Then I was lightly standing on my feet watching the nurses pushing down on my chest. Two more nurses came in and one was wearing a rose on her uniform. Two more nurses came in and one orderly and then I noticed that they had gotten my doctor back from his visits in the hospital. He had seen me earlier. When he came into the room, I wondered why he was here. I felt fine! Then my doctor took off his coat to relieve the nurse pushing on my chest. I noticed that he had on a blue-striped tie. The room started getting dark and I had the sensation of moving rapidly down a dark corridor.'[8]

The heart of this man had stopped beating, which was why the nurses applied heart massage. Yet even though his heart no longer beat, efficient heart massage applied by a nurse generated a flow of blood through his brain sufficient to sustain consciousness long enough for him to observe all that occurred in his vicinity with his physical senses. He was conscious, but unable to move, and this is why he appeared unconscious to the people resuscitating him. After all, a person who does not breathe, has no heartbeat, and does not move, certainly appears to be unconscious. The report of this man is a report of events he observed happening to his body, and around his body with his physical senses while he was being resuscitated. It is a report of local information.

People sometimes report acquiring distant information. They perceive this distant information at a time that they were physically incapable of observing the things they later reported. An example of this is the report of a man who acquired distant information during a period he was undergoing resuscitation for heart problems. He reported:

> 'I was terribly ill and near death with heart problems at the same time that my sister was near death in another part of the same hospital with a diabetic coma. I left my body and went into the corner of the room, where I watched them work on me down below. Suddenly, I found myself in conversation with my sister, who was up there with me. I was very attached to her, and we were having a great conversation about what was going on down there when she began to move away from me. I tried to go with her but she kept telling me to stay where I was. "It's not your time," she said. "You can't go with me because it's not your time." Then she began to recede off into the distance through a tunnel while I was left there alone. When I awoke, I told the doctor that my sister had died. He denied it, but at my insistence, he had a nurse check on it. She had in fact died just as I knew she did.'[9]

This man perceived everything that happened to his body and around his body during his out-of-body experience. This is local information. At the same time he learned of the death of his sister in a distant room in the same hospital. This is distant information. He was being resuscitated for heart problems at the same time his sister died, so he was in no condition to learn of her death at that moment. Some people might say this man learned of the death of his sister by means of paranormal sensory abilities. But paranormal sensory abilities are not needed to explain how he learned of the death of his sister. This man knew his sister was near to death in a diabetic coma[10] in the same hospital, and people in a diabetic coma often die.[11] He needed no paranormal senses to predict the death of his sister, because he was very likely to have been correct. The fact his sister died at about the same time as he was being resuscitated was no more than coincidence. So his apparently paranormal sensations and experience were a combination of his own sensations, together with a statement of a likely event.

But the explanation of some other reports is not so easy. This is certainly so for the story told by a woman called Maria. Maria was admitted into hospital for heart problems, and her heart suddenly stopped beating. She had an apparently paranormal experience during the subsequent resuscitation, and reported her experience to a social worker called Kimberly Clark who wrote the following passages about the experience of Maria:

'She[12] said: "The strangest thing happened when the doctors and nurses were working on me: I found myself looking down from the ceiling at them working on my body."'[13]

This is a typical example of perception of local events during an out-of-body experience. But then Maria made an even more surprising statement to Kimberly Clark:

'... Maria proceeded to describe being further distracted by an object on the third floor ledge on the north end of the building. She "thought her way" up there and found herself "eyeball to shoelace" with a tennis shoe, which she asked me to find for her.'[14]

Kimberly Clark did just that. She found the tennis shoe at the location described. This is surprising. How could this woman have known of the presence of the tennis shoe at such an inaccessible location? A common problem with this type of story is that all the circumstances surrounding such an event are seldom told. It is possible that Maria was an employee of the hospital in which she had her cardiac arrest, and had seen the tennis shoe on the ledge during her work. Maria may have visited someone in hospital at some time, and seen the tennis shoe on the ledge. Someone may once have told Maria about the tennis shoe on the ledge. Many explanations are possible, but this report provides insufficient information to decide whether the perceptions reported by Maria really were paranormal, or were derived from prior knowledge.[15] The story of Maria is but one of many such stories. There are many other stories for which only paranormal explanations seem possible, and such stories have been reported since the dawn of human history.

Studies of such reports of spontaneous paranormal experiences have never yielded absolute proof of the reality of the paranormal. They only provide an indication of the possibility of the paranormal. Even so, these reports do arouse a sense of wonder. It would be wonderful if everyone could consistently employ paranormal sensory abilities. Unfortunately, paranormal sensory abilities are very fickle, because although they are sometimes present, they are mostly absent. However, two facts about paranormal sensory abilities are certain. If paranormal sensory abilities are real, then people who perceive paranormal sensations must posses paranormal sensory abilities, otherwise they would be incapable of perceiving these things. Furthermore, paranormal experiences are common, because as many as eight in ten people have undergone at least one apparently paranormal experience, a fact fuelling the widespread belief that each person possesses latent, but largely unused paranormal sensory abilities. But if paranormal sensory abilities are so widespread, their reality should be easy to prove. So is there any evidence for the reality of paranormal sensory abilities?

Scientific societies were founded to investigate claims of paranormal events and sensory abilities, as well as to stimulate scientific studies of these phenomena. The first such society, was the Society for Psychical Research founded in London in England in the year 1882 CE. Similar societies were subsequently founded in other countries. These societies all stimulated scientific study of paranormal sensory abilities, resulting in many careful investigations of paranormal sensory abilities being conducted over a period of more than one hundred years. But the results of more than a century of careful scientific study of paranormal phenomena are disappointing, because there is still no real proof for the reality of paranormal sensory abilities.

Card-guessing experiments are typical examples of studies designed to determine whether people can use paranormal sensory abilities to detect something in the present. For example, individual playing cards are sealed into numbered, but otherwise identical thick, totally opaque envelopes. A person is asked to guess which playing card is in each envelope. These guesses are recorded for each envelope. At the end of the experiment, all the envelopes are opened, and the number of correct guesses are recorded. A person is said to have paranormal sensory abilities if more cards are guessed correctly than would be expected by chance. A person is also said to have paranormal sensory abilities if fewer cards are guessed correctly than would be expected by chance. There are infinitely many variations upon this type of experiment. Cards and envelopes do not have to be used. Pictures, objects, electronic devices, or anything where a choice is made between several different possibilities selected according to chance are all that is required. Many dedicated and capable researchers have performed such experiments for more than one hundred years, but they have never consistently and conclusively proven the reality of paranormal sensory abilities with such experiments.

The absence of conclusive proof from such studies is why many researchers attempted to enhance the manifestation of paranormal sensory abilities. Studies were performed to determine the mental states during which paranormal sensory abilities are most likely to manifest. These studies revealed that meditation, mental relaxation, and sensory deprivation techniques all seem to enhance paranormal sensory abilities.[16] Calm and relaxed people appeared to manifest more paranormal sensory abilities than did anxious and tense people.[17] Believers in the reality of paranormal sensory abilities apparently manifested more paranormal sensory abilities than those who did not believe. People with a warm and spontaneous outgoing character manifested more paranormal sensory abilities than those with a cool, withdrawn, and isolated character. Many experiments were performed under conditions believed to enhance paranormal sensory abilities, and with people most likely to possess paranormal sensory abilities. Yet, notwithstanding several decades of careful experimentation performed by many capable and motivated investigators, none of these experiments ever provided any consistent, and conclusive proof of the reality of paranormal sensory abilities.[18] The conclusion to more than a century of work by many dedicated investigators is disappointing; the only evidence for the reality of paranormal sensory abilities are the reports of people who spontaneously underwent apparently paranormal sensory experiences. This is not only a disappointing conclusion, it is also a very strange conclusion when one considers that up to as many as eight in ten people might be expected to possess paranormal sensory abilities. But if paranormal sensory experiences are so common, why has the reality of paranormal perceptive abilities never been conclusively demonstrated during more than one hundred years of dedicated scientific endeavour? One possible answer to this question is that paranormal sensory abilities might not manifest in the artificial environments of scientific experiments designed to demonstrate their existence. So I decided to search for evidence of paranormal sensory abilities in life situations where paranormal sensory abilities could be expected to manifest. There are actually several life situations where people would be expected to develop, and to use any latent paranormal sensory abilities. Consider the situations of people who become deaf or blind, and even worse, those people who become both deaf and blind. It is common knowledge that deaf and blind people develop the use of their remaining sensory abilities to compensate for their disabilities. Accordingly, if there was a possibility that deaf or blind people could overcome their disabilities by developing any latent paranormal sensory abilities, then they would certainly do this. Up to as many as eight in ten people may possess latent or developed paranormal abilities, so if paranormal sensory abilities really do exist, then many deaf, blind, or deaf-blind people should manifest paranormal sensory abilities.

There are many different causes of blindness. But these many causes may be divided into blindness caused by disorders affecting the eyes, or blindness caused by disorders affecting the brain. Throughout the whole world, the most common causes of blindness are eye diseases or eye injuries. People blinded by eye diseases or eye injuries were once able to see normally. Blindness caused by eye diseases or eye injuries does not damage the brain, or affect any other senses. So even though people blinded by eye diseases or eye injuries cannot see anything around them, they are still able to see in their dreams, see their visual hallucinations, see their visual fantasies, and see their visual memories.

Likewise, there are also many different causes of deafness. These many causes may also be divided into deafness caused by disorders affecting the ears, or deafness caused by disorders affecting the brain. Throughout the whole world, the most common causes of deafness are ear diseases and ear injuries. People deafened by ear diseases or ear injuries were once able to hear normally. Deafness caused by ear diseases or ear injuries does not damage the brain, or affect any other senses. So even though people deafened by ear diseases or ear injuries cannot hear anything around them, they can still hear their auditory hallucinations, hear remembered sounds, and have dreams in which they hear sounds.

There are actually a lot of deaf and blind people in this world. There are more than seven million totally blind people, and more than thirty million partially blind people now alive on this world (see Appendix 2). There are more than four million totally deaf people, and more than twenty eight million partially deaf people now alive on this world (see Appendix 2). There are more than five hundred thousand totally deaf-blind people, and more than fourteen million partially deaf-blind people now alive on this world (see Appendix 2). Uncounted millions of blind people, deaf people, as well as deaf-blind people have lived and died in the past.

The plight of those who are deaf-blind is the most extreme, because they can neither hear nor see. Yet those who are deaf-blind can still sense much of what occurs in their vicinity with their physical senses. Each person can experience this for themselves. You can 'blind' yourself with a blindfold, and become 'deaf' by inserting earplugs. While blinded and deafened in this way, you are still able to sense much of what occurs around your body. You know the position and orientation of your body in relation to your surroundings, and you can sense the positions of your limbs and other body parts in relation to each other and your surroundings. If someone stealthily approaches you while you are blinded and deafened in this way, you are often able to sense their coming, their presence, and their going. You may sense minute vibrations in the ground caused by their footsteps and movements. You may sense slight turbulence in the air as they move. You may feel their body warmth. You may smell their body odours. You sense all these things. And sensing all these things, either consciously or unconsciously, you are able to perceive the presence of other people. You may even develop your senses to such a degree, that you can identify people by their individual body odours, their individual patterns of movement, and their individual manners of approaching and touching you. You are able to derive all this information by using your physical senses of position, movement, vibration, touch, smell, and temperature. These are not paranormal sensory abilities. They are physical senses possessed by everyone.

People who are deaf-blind can neither see nor hear. Everyone knows that people who are deaf-blind train and develop their remaining senses as much as possible, compensating with these remaining senses to some degree for being deaf-blind. This is common knowledge learned from ages-old observation of blind and deaf people. As many as eight in ten people have undergone at least one paranormal experience, which means that about eight in ten people may well possess latent, or undeveloped paranormal sensory abilities. If this is true, then most of those who are deaf-blind could be expected to develop their latent, or undeveloped paranormal sensory abilities, so compensating for their lost hearing and sight. Indeed, it would even be common knowledge that many deaf-blind people possess paranormal sensory abilities. But the untold millions of deaf-blind people who have lived in the past are not known to have possessed any paranormal sensory abilities. The more than five hundred thousand totally deaf-blind people, as well as the more than fourteen million partially deaf-blind people now alive, are also not known to possess any paranormal sensory abilities. None of the deaf-blind people now alive can 'see' without seeing, or 'hear' without hearing, and none of these deaf-blind people possess paranormal sensory abilities aiding them in their interactions with the world. Ages-old common knowledge about the sensory abilities of deaf-blind people, attributes them only with being gifted in the use of their remaining physical senses, but not that they possess any paranormal sensory abilities.

Some people may ask what I mean by the term 'ages-old common knowledge'. Each person can answer this question by asking himself what his reaction would be upon hearing that a loved family member, such as a father, a son, or a brother, has suddenly become deaf-blind. Would you ever say; 'Joyous news! Oh happy day! He has been doubly blessed: blessed with deafness, and blessed with blindness. Now he will be able to develop his latent paranormal senses, and these will enable him to hear without hearing, and to see without seeing. He will be unhindered by the gross material senses of hearing and sight. He will be able to perceive people as they really are, to learn and to understand the motives underlying their every word, and their every action. He will be able to perceive the world around him as it really is. He may even be able to perceive the future. Oh lucky, lucky man! Let us feast and celebrate!' Such a reaction is unheard of. No-one throughout all history, or in any known human society has ever reacted to such news in this way. The normal reaction upon hearing such news is of pity, of sorrow, and of compassion for the enormity of the calamity afflicting the loved family member. Becoming deaf-blind is not regarded as a wonderful opportunity to develop latent paranormal sensory abilities. No-one expects a deaf-blind person to develop paranormal sensory abilities, even though paranormal sensory abilities are common. Instead, to become deaf-blind is regarded as a profound personal tragedy, because everyone knows that the afflicted family member will be severely handi-capped for the rest of their life. And the afflicted family member, living in his now dark and silent world, almost totally dependant upon help from others, knows this best of all. This is ages-old common knowledge about the effects of becoming deaf-blind, and this ages-old common knowledge teaches that deaf-blind people live in a dark and silent world. Their infor-mation about this world, and their perceptions of this world, are derived only from their remaining physical senses, modified by their memories of the world as they experienced it when they still possessed the ability to see and hear.

The same is true for those afflicted only with blindness or only with deaf-ness. Ages-old common knowledge teaches that the blind and the deaf de-velop the use of their remaining senses. But there is no ages-old common knowledge attributing the blind or the deaf with any special paranormal sensory abilities. If blind and deaf people did develop their paranormal sensory abilities, then many of the untold millions of blind and deaf peo-ple who lived in past ages would certainly have developed these abilities to compensate for their inability to see, or their inability to hear. But in past ages, the blind were only known to be unable to see, and the deaf were only known to be unable to hear. There are more than thirty seven million blind people, and more than thirty two million deaf people now alive on our world. Many of these tens of millions of living blind, and deaf people, would also be expected to develop any latent paranormal sensory abilities to compensate for their lack of sight, or their lack of hearing. But the blind and deaf people who are now alive, are not known to possess any paranor-mal sensory abilities compensating for their inability to see, or their inabil-ity to hear. Blind and deaf people only develop, and train their remaining physical senses, so as to compensate for their disabilities. They never train themselves in the use of any paranormal sensory abilities, even though as many as eight in ten people may possess paranormal sensory abilities. The only common knowledge that everyone has about the sensory abilities of blind and deaf people, is that those who are blind are blind, and that those who are deaf are deaf.

Many millions of blind, deaf, and deaf-blind people on this world live in wealthy countries. People living in the wealthy countries of Western Eur-ope and North America are highly literate, and live in societies with good communications facilities. Hundreds of books about the paranormal are published each year in these countries. Hundreds of television and radio programs about the paranormal are transmitted each year in these coun-tries. Many millions of people living in these countries are even obsessed with the paranormal, believing wholeheartedly in the reality of paranormal sensory abilities. The millions of blind, deaf, and deaf-blind people now living in these countries also share these beliefs. Yet even though as many as eight in ten people may possess paranormal sensory abilities, the millions of blind, deaf, and deaf-blind people living in these countries are not known to possess any paranormal sensory abilities. There is ages-old knowledge that these people intensively train, and develop, the use of their remaining physical senses, but there is no ages-old knowledge that these people intensively try to train, and develop, the use of any latent paranormal senses. Furthermore, if blind, deaf, and deaf-blind people possessed paranormal sensory abilities, rapid communications in these countries would ensure that everyone living in these wealthy countries would know these people possessed paranormal sensory abilities. But all everyone in all these countries knows about these people is, that the blind are blind, that the deaf are deaf, and that the deaf-blind are deaf-blind. All these things prove that blind, deaf, and deaf-blind people have no paranormal sensory abilities.

As many as eight in ten people could be expected to possess manifest, or latent paranormal sensory abilities. So many, or most, blind and deaf people should be able to regularly utilise paranormal sensory abilities. But blind and deaf people are no more able to regularly utilise paranormal sensory abilities than are people who can see and hear. I pondered possible reasons why the blind and the deaf manifest no paranormal sensory abilities. I spoke to other people about this problem. Some of these people told me reasons explaining why blind and deaf people manifest no paranormal sensory abilities. I will discuss three of the reasons some of these people told me as to why blind, and deaf people manifest no paranormal sensory abilities where one would expect them to be present.

1   Some people say that affliction with blindness and deafness is actually necessary for the spiritual development of the souls of the blind and the deaf.

Accordingly, people stricken with blindness and deafness do not develop paranormal sensory abilities to compensate for their sensory deficits, because otherwise no spiritual development would result from being blind or deaf. I can illustrate the ridiculous nature of this explanation with an example of another situation, a situation where fate places people in a dreadful position. Consider the plight of helpless survivors trapped underneath the rubble of a collapsed building. Is it not possible that entrapment underneath the rubble of a collapsed building is necessary for the spiritual development of these survivors? If this is true, then we should not rescue these people. After all, to rescue these people might shorten a necessary period of spiritual development, or even totally eliminate the spiritual development resulting from entrapment, and slow death underneath piles of rubble. Or should we rescue these people? We see the answer to these questions all about us. Of course we rescue people trapped underneath the rubble of collapsed buildings. To accept that adversity is necessary for the spiritual development of afflicted persons is to lose all free will. To accept the consequences of such an argument is to lose the power to do anything, except starve and die.

2 Some people say that blind, deaf and deaf-blind people do not experience their disabilities as unpleasant or as a hindrance, which is why they do not develop any latent paranormal sensory abilities.

This is a ridiculous argument. Everyone knows this by asking themselves whether they would 'enjoy', or not 'mind' being blind, deaf, or deaf-blind. No-one wants to be blind, deaf, or deaf-blind. Those afflicted with these conditions feel exactly the same way. They hate being blind, they hate being deaf, and they certainly hate being deaf-blind. Blindness and deafness are unpleasant, and definitely a hindrance. These people may appear content with their disabilities, but the sad truth is that those afflicted with deafness, blindness, or both, must often simply accept and endure these conditions. After all, at this time there are only a few curable types of blindness and deafness. All afflicted people can do, is accept their condition with all the fortitude they can muster, and try to develop the use of their remaining senses as much as possible. And these people do develop their remaining senses, but they never develop any paranormal sensory abilities.

3 Some people say that paranormal senses are not intended to be used for selfish or personal purposes.

I personally find this argument very strange. No-one can tell me who says these powers are not to be used for selfish or personal purposes. Is it God, or simply the 'laws of the universe'? They cannot say. In addition, those people giving this as a reason seem to forget that spontaneous manifestations of paranormal sensory abilities are nearly always for so-called selfish, or personal purposes. After all, most spontaneous occurrences of paranormal perceptions are warnings of danger, of illness, and of matters concerning the persons themselves, or those near and dear to those reporting these perceptions. Every day, blind and deaf people experience many problems, and dangers due to their disabilities. Yet, are such problems and dangers of less value than those experienced by people who can see and hear normally? I do not think so. Nonetheless, this belief that paranormal perceptions are not supposed to be used for selfish or personal reasons is amazingly persistent. I can illustrate the ridiculous nature of this belief with two examples.

Sometimes I catch a train at the busy central railway station in the city where I live. This station is frequented by pickpockets, as well as being infested by many other denizens of amazingly suspicious appearance and demeanour, just hanging around, watching, and waiting. Posters warn people of the presence of thieves and pickpockets, and my ears are regularly assailed by loud warnings about thieves, and pickpockets over the public announcement system. Imagine three well dressed handicapped men travelling with each other. They want to catch a train at this station. One is blind, one is deaf, while the third is blind and deaf. One cannot see the thieves, one cannot hear any suspicious movements, and one cannot see or hear anything. They are targets, easy to rob, ideal prey for the waiting pickpockets, and immediately noted as such. Their wallets will disappear from their pockets in an instant as they join the jostling mass of people on the station platforms. Yet if these blind and deaf people had the use of paranormal sensory abilities, they would be able to perceive, and avoid the unwelcome attentions of these thieves. This is an example of a very selfish and personal use of paranormal sensory abilities by blind and deaf persons. True, this is a theoretical example, but in 1950 CE, a certain Professor Tenhaeff received a letter from a man who reported a real paranormal experience he underwent several years earlier. This man wrote:

> *'During September 1939, I was an engineer on board one of the Shell Petroleum company ships in the harbour of Curacao. I was writing in the engine-room logbook in my cabin. Suddenly I clearly saw the face of my wife and that of an unknown man, and I heard my wife scream several times: "I couldn't help it". I fixed the face of this unknown man in my memory. At that time I had been separated for two years from my wife who lived in Rotterdam. Six months later, my contract was finished, and I returned to Holland. I told my wife about my vision, and she confessed to committing adultery on that very evening in September. And the man with whom she had sex had the same appearance as the man in my vision, a fact I later personally confirmed.'*[19]

A jealous husband voyaging far away from home for more than two years, and a lonely wife longing for love and attention; a stereotype recipe for adultery. Nothing could be more selfish, or more personal, than this last manifestation of paranormal sensory abilities. These two examples illustrate that the problems resulting from being deaf, blind, or both, are just as selfish, and just as personal, as are other things to which people who can hear and see normally are exposed. So this idea that paranormal senses are not intended to be used for selfish or personal purposes, can be discarded as mere foolish superstition.

Such explanations of why blind and deaf people manifest no paranormal sensory abilities, are only reflections of personal belief systems, not logic. One thing is certain, the people most motivated to develop any latent para-normal sensory abilities, are the many millions of blind, deaf, and deaf-blind people on this world. But these people only develop their remaining physical sensory abilities. They never develop or manifest any paranormal sensory abilities.

Everything taken into account, there is only one conclusion possible. Para-normal sensory abilities enabling people to sense events occurring in the present do not exist. The ancient, and almost universal belief in the reality of such paranormal sensory abilities is no more than an ages old delusion. So this aspect of the paranormal is not indirect evidence of any immaterial, or spiritual aspects of the universe, such as the human soul. Even so, there are other types of possibly paranormal sensations.

Chapter 8

Dreams & Visions

The last chapter discussed paranormal perceptions of things and events occurring in the present. Yet this is only one aspect of an ancient, widespread belief in the reality of paranormal sensory abilities. Many people also believe paranormal sensory abilities are independent of space and time, believing that those gifted with paranormal sensory abilities are able to sense what has happened in the past, what is happening in the present, as well as what will happen in the future. An ability to sense the past, the present, and the future by means of a paranormal sensory ability independent of space and time is a wonderful idea. It hints at the possibility of a grand interconnectivity of all things in the universe independent of distance, or location in the past, the present, or the future. Such a grand interconnectivity might at times allow the occurrence of omens, at other times arouse dreams in the sleeping, induce visions in the awake, generate emotions of déjà vu, or even permit people to sense the presences of entities elsewhere in the universe, in the past, the present, or the future. Nonetheless, even if such a wondrous grand interconnectivity does exist, this does not mean people sense these things by means of paranormal sensory abilities. After all, there is not a shred of evidence for the reality of a paranormal ability to sense things in the present. Even so, many people do believe in the possibility of a paranormal sensory ability to foretell the future. They call this ability 'precognition'. Precognitive experiences are actually quite common. Up to as many as six in ten people have experienced at least one apparently paranormal experience foretelling the future, such as a premonition, a vision, a dream predicting the future, or have undergone a déjà vu experience.[1] Paranormal experiences foretelling the future often make a deep impression on those undergoing them, which is why many people have an intense, almost visceral belief in the reality of a paranormal ability to sense the future.

A paranormal ability to foretell the future may also be a manifestation of immaterial aspects of the universe, such as an immaterial human soul able to sense these things. So prediction of the future by all manner of paranormal sensory abilities, such as premonitions, omens, dreams, visions, déjà vu, sensed presences, may all be aspects of human experience providing indirect evidence of the reality of an immaterial human soul. If these experiences can only be explained by paranormal phenomena, then there is a possibility that an immaterial human soul really does exist. Accordingly, I decided to investigate the reality of a paranormal sensory ability to foretell the future. Unfortunately, these phenomena are immaterial, and cannot be investigated directly. So all I could do was to offer alternative, but provable physical explanations. I reasoned that if all these supposedly paranormal perceptions can be explained with provable physical phenomena, then these perceptions are not necessarily proof of paranormal perceptive abilities. And this would mean these supposedly paranormal phenomena are not indirect proof of the reality of the human soul.

Our ancestors really believed witches, augers, soothsayers, shamans, seers, and oracles could foretell the future.[2] The services of the more successful practitioners of these arts were in great demand. Even now, people flock in great numbers to Tarot card readers, palmists, numerologists, and astrologers to hear what the future may hold in store for them. But the fact that people throughout untold millennia have always believed these people could predict the future, is no proof of the reality of a paranormal ability to foretell the future. So I examined the results of experimental studies of prediction of future events.

An example of a typical experiment to detect an ability to foretell the future is an experiment whereby people predict the results of dice throwing. Their predictions, as well as the resulting numbers on the thrown dice are recorded. After a number of throws of the dice, the results of the predictions are checked against the numbers shown by the thrown dice. A person is said to have a paranormal sensory ability to foretell the future if more throws of the dice are predicted correctly than would be expected by chance. A person is also said to have paranormal sensory abilities if fewer throws of the dice are predicted correctly than would be expected by chance. There are many variations upon this type of experiment. Dice do not have to be used. Cards, electronic devices, or anything where a choice is made between several different possibilities selected according to chance are all that is required. Many capable researchers have conducted such experiments during the last one hundred years, but none of these experiments has proven the reality of a paranormal ability to foretell the future. Repetition of these experiments with highly motivated people with personality characteristics conducive to manifesting paranormal abilities, and under circumstances conducive to manifesting paranormal abilities, have also never demonstrated the reality of a paranormal ability to foretell the future.[3]

It might be said such experiments are artificial, and that an ability to foretell the future could not manifest under such circumstances. So I searched for real life situations where people are highly motivated to use any existent paranormal abilities to predict the future. Gambling is just such a life situation. Gamblers try to predict the outcomes of throws of dice, of coins, of bones, of roulette wheels, or of anything producing a chance outcome. Gamblers wager their money, their possessions, their clothing, their freedom, and at times even their lives. Gamblers are highly motivated, because they really do want to win. Gamblers are often superstitious. Many truly believe they are lucky, sometimes even believing themselves to possess an ability to predict the outcomes of the games of chance they play. Consider games where a gambler tries to predict a purely random outcome generated by a machine, by dice, or a random number generator. Even if only a few gamblers possess an ability to foretell the future by paranormal means, this would be evident in the results of such games, because the outcomes of such games would be correctly predicted more often than would be expected by chance alone. So do such games of chance provide evidence for paranormal abilities?

Gambling casinos nearly always offer their customers the chance to play roulette, a mechanical game of chance generating a truly random outcome. Roulette is played upon a table at one end of which is a large, well balanced, horizontally mounted wheel, whose upper surface is divided into thirty seven slotted sectors. There are thirty six sectors numbered from one to thirty six, and these are equally coloured black or red. The remaining sector is coloured green or white, and numbered zero. The roulette table is run by a representative of the casino called a croupier. Participating gamblers place their wagers at marked places on the table, wagering upon one or more numbers, a colour, or a combination of colour and numbers. Eventually the croupier calls a halt to placing wagers, sets the roulette wheel in motion, and throws a ball into a gutter on the edge of the rotating wheel in a direction opposite to the direction of rotation. The wheel eventually stops turning, and the ball slows down to roll into one of the slotted sectors of the wheel. This slot is the winning number and colour. The croupier pays the winners out at a fixed rate for each correctly guessed number, or combination of numbers and colours, but always at a rate that yields the casino an average profit of $1/37 = 2.7\%$ of all money wagered. All the money wagered by the losers is collected by the croupier and goes to the casino. Modern, well run casinos continually monitor each roulette table to eliminate cheating, as well as to check whether the roulette wheels truly do generate random numbers.

Roulette players are just as motivated to win as are all other gamblers. There is an aspect to roulette making it an ideal form of gambling to investigate the reality of an ability to foretell the future. If two or more people gamble against each other, and each gambler possesses some ability to foretell the future, the paranormal advantage possessed by each gambler will be eliminated by the paranormal abilities of the other gamblers. But roulette players do not play against each other, instead they wager upon a mechanically generated random outcome. So any paranormal ability to foretell the future, no matter how slight, will manifest at the roulette table. Accordingly, if even only some people possess a paranormal ability to predict the future, then one would expect that a preponderance of roulette players will choose winning colours, numbers, or combinations. This preponderance might not be large, but it would be clearly evident after many millions of roulette games. A rate of correct predictions slightly above normal means that casinos would not collect the 2.7% they expect. It might even mean that casinos would lose money to successful roulette players, because the losses of the losing roulette players would no longer be sufficient to pay out the winnings of the winning players. But the earnings of casinos on roulette wheels are precisely what chance predicts, which is why gambling casinos earn handsome amounts of money from roulette players. The fact that roulette wheels generate a percentage income for casinos precisely equal to that predicted by chance alone, together with the commercial success of the game of roulette, clearly demonstrate the absence of any human paranormal ability to foretell the future. The same is also true for the other mechanical and electronic games of chance in casinos, such as poker machines.[4]

More than one hundred years of dedicated scientific research, as well as the resounding commercial success of poker machines, and roulette in gambling casinos, provide clear proof people do not possess an ability to predict the future by paranormal means. Nonetheless, despite these facts, people still believe in the reality of some sort of paranormal ability to foretell the future, in dreams, omens, portents, astrology, the meaningfulness of their sensations of déjà vu, visions, sensed presences that comfort, and even warn them of dangers. People who believe, experience, and report these things are not insane, nor are they reporting wild and sickly fantasies. They are normal people reporting what for them are profound personal experiences. But how can such experiences arise if paranormal sensations and paranormal prediction of the future do not exist? So I examined various manifestations of this apparently paranormal sensory ability to foretell the future.

I began by examining predictions of the future revealed by dreams. Studies of many thousands of spontaneous, apparently paranormal experiences revealed that half of these experiences were predictions of the future. Furthermore, these studies revealed that one half of all spontaneous paranormal experiences occurred as dreams.[5] Most people sleep about eight hours a day, and about one quarter of this time is spent dreaming.[6] If one half of all spontaneous paranormal experiences occur during dreaming, which is a state of mind present during only two of the twenty four hours in a day, this means that dreaming is a mental state during which people are more sensitive to paranormal sensory perceptions. This is no new idea. John Bunyan expressed these same ideas in a sermon on the soul several hundred years ago, quoting texts out of the book of 'Job' in the Holy Bible as evidence for the truth of this idea.

> 'Can the body hear? hath it ears? so hath the soul (Job 4:12,13). It is the soul, not the body, that hears the language of things invisible. It is the soul that hears God when He speaks in and by His Word and Spirit; and it is the soul that hears the devil when he speaks by his illusions and temptations. True, there is such an union between the soul and the body, that ofttimes, if not always, that which is heard by the ears of the body doth influence the soul, and that which is heard by the soul doth also influence the body; but yet as to the organ of hearing, the body hath one of its own, distinct from that of the soul, and the soul can hear and regard even then, when the body doth not nor cannot; as in time of sleep, deep sleep and trances, when the body lieth by as a thing that is useless. "For God speaketh once, yea twice, yet man, (as to his body) perceiveth it not. In a dream, in a vision of the night, when deep sleep falleth upon men, in slumberings upon the bed; then he openeth the ears of men, and sealeth their instruction," etc. (Job 33:14-16). This must be meant of the ears of the soul, not of the body; for that at this time is said to be in deep sleep; moreover this hearing, it is a hearing of dreams, and the visions of the night.'[7]

This belief was ancient even when the book of Job was complied sometime between 1000 to 350 BCE. And just like our ancestors countless millennia ago, most people still regard dreaming as a strange, even wondrous mental state. Observers see dreamers as asleep and unconscious people; yet at the same time, these dreamers are undergoing all manner of conscious experiences in an unseen world within their minds. So are dreams experiences undergone by the immaterial soul while the body rests? Do dreams reveal paranormally acquired information? If these ancient beliefs are true, then proof of paranormal perceptions during dreaming is certainly a form of indirect evidence of the reality of the immaterial human soul.

One thing is certain; dreams do not reveal paranormally acquired information about events in the present, because paranormal perception of events in the present simply does not occur. So what about paranormally acquired information about future events? Many studies have been made of precognitive information revealed in dreams, but such studies only confirm that dream reports provide no evidence for the reality of a paranormal ability to predict the future.[8] However, some people would question the validity of such studies, saying they are so artificial, so rigid, and so critical, that paranormal sensory abilities could not manifest under such conditions. These people would quite correctly say that one fact is certain, people do report dreams foretelling the future, and the content of some of these dreams corresponds exactly with a future event. An often cited story is one told in 1906 CE by the American author Samuel Clemens, (better known by his pen name, Mark Twain) . During 1858 CE, both his brother Henry and he were crew members on a Mississippi River steamboat called the 'Pennsylvania'. One night Samuel Clemens had a dream:

> *'In the morning, when I awoke I had been dreaming, and the dream was so vivid, so like reality, that it deceived me, and I thought it was real. In the dream I had seen Henry a corpse. He lay in a metallic burial-case. He was dressed in a suit of my clothing, and on his breast lay a great bouquet of flowers, mainly white roses, with a red rose in the centre. The casket stood upon a couple of chairs. I dressed, and moved toward that door, thinking I would go in there and look at it, but I changed my mind. I thought I could not yet bear to meet my mother. I thought I would wait awhile and make some preparation for that ordeal. The house was in Locust Street, a little above 13th, and I walked to 14th, and to the middle of the block beyond, before it suddenly flashed upon me that there was nothing real about this – it was only a dream. I can still feel something of the grateful upheaval of joy of that moment, and I can also still feel the remnant of doubt, the suspicion that maybe it was real, after all. I returned to the house almost on a run, flew up the stairs two or three steps at a jump, and rushed into that sitting-room – and was made glad again, for there was no casket there.'*

Several weeks later, the steam boiler of the 'Pennsylvania' exploded, his brother Henry was fatally injured, and subsequently died. Samuel Clemens related what occurred after the death of his brother:

> *'I think he died about dawn, I don't remember as to that. He was carried to the dead-room and I went away for a while to a citizen's house and slept off some of my accumulated fatigue – and meantime something was happening. The coffins provided for the dead were of unpainted white pine, but in this instance some of the ladies of Memphis had made up a fund of sixty dollars and bought a metallic case, and when I came back and entered the dead-room Henry lay in that open case, and he was dressed in a suit of my clothing. He had borrowed it without my knowledge during our last sojourn in St. Louis; and I recognised instantly that my dream of several weeks before was here exactly reproduced, so far as these details went – and I think I missed one detail; but that one was immediately supplied, for just then an elderly lady entered the place with a large bouquet consisting mainly of*

white roses, and in the centre of it was a red rose, and she laid it on his breast.'[9]

This is a dramatic story. It is a story apparently proving the reality of dreams predicting the future. Yet this was a story told nearly fifty years after the events occurred, and for which there was no independent verification. Furthermore, Samuel Clemens admitted that he had told, and retold this story many times before it was finally recorded on paper. So it is possible he had unwittingly embellished, and re-embellished this story by unconsciously introducing non-factual elements, which he eventually came to believe were true after re-telling this story so many times. Even so, how could such a dream, so accurate in all details, occur without the reality of a paranormal ability to foretell the future?

I thought about this problem for a while. Finally I realized the answer lay in the enormous number of dreams experienced by each person during a lifetime. Everyone dreams four to six times each night[10], and there are 365 days in a year. This means that each person has about 1,400 to 2,000 dreams each year, and has as many as 98,000 to 140,000 dreams during a 70 year life-span. If dreaming is not a state of mind making people more receptive to paranormal perceptions of the future, then the relationship of dream content to future events is purely chance. Accordingly, it is only to be expected that the content of one, or more, of the many tens of thousands of dreams experienced by each individual will correspond to some degree with future events. This is why many people have had dreams whose content bore some relation to subsequent events. However, dreams corresponding exactly in almost every detail with subsequent future events are very rare, and the dream of Samuel Clemens is an example of just such a rare dream. Accordingly, people recognise such dreams as rare events, often regarding them with awe, telling, and retelling them. This statistical explanation of dreams foretelling the future explains all their properties, such as: the fact that dreams foretelling future events are uncommon, the fact that many people have had at least one dream corresponding to some degree to a future event, and the fact that dreams corresponding exactly to future events are very rare. So precognitive dreams, no matter how emotionally changed, no matter how personally profound and meaningful, are really no proof of an ability to predict the future by paranormal means. Instead, they are most likely mere products of chance.

Major disasters illustrate the chance nature of precognitive dreams. After each major disaster in the world, there are always people who come forward saying they dreamed that particular disaster would occur, or that they dreamed a disaster was imminent. Yet it is only after the disaster has actually occurred, that these people say they realised the meaning of their prior dreams of disaster, and come forward to report their dreams. Reporting such prior dreams of disaster in this way is no proof of the precognitive nature of these dreams. It is merely a retrospective imposition of meaning to dreams that by chance happened to correspond to a subsequent event. After all, there is always someone on the world who will have a dream corresponding to a future event.

Each night, each of the six billion people now inhabiting our world will have four to six dreams, making a total of twenty four to thirty six billion dreams occurring on our world during each twenty four hour period. However, not all dreams are remembered, not all people are educated adults with an interest outside their own communities, and not all people living on the world have access to communications such that they can relate the content of their dreams to events elsewhere in the world. For example, babies and small children cannot express themselves clearly. There are also the sick, the demented, the oppressed, the impoverished, the enslaved, the dispossessed, the homeless, the itinerant, outlaws, outcasts, beggars, and peasants living in isolated communities. Who hears the dreams of these people? Such people often have little interest in the world outside their small communities, or think only about their next meal, and a place to sleep. They do not report precognitive dreams of disasters that later occupy the thoughts of people all over the world, such as dreams of wars, or dreams of the Hindenburg disaster, or dreams of the attack on the World Trade Centre. And such people form a very large proportion of the world population. So assume that out of the six billion people now inhabiting this world, there are only fifty million educated, and articulate adults with access to modern communications, as well as an interest in matters outside their own communities. Furthermore, because most people remember only very few of their dreams, make the assumption that these people remember only one in every one thousand of their dreams. This means that worldwide, these fifty million educated and articulate adults will remember two, to three hundred thousand dreams during every twenty four hour period. Chance dictates that the content of some of these dreams will eventually correspond with a future disaster somewhere in the world. So dreams of disasters are very likely no more than chance dreams: chance dreams awaiting corresponding future disasters to attain precognitive significance.

It is only when people find a relationship between a dream and a real event, that the dream attains precognitive significance, and is remembered. This is human nature. After all, what of the countless anxious dreams, dreams of tragedy, dreams of disaster, dreams of luck, dreams of happiness, and dreams of wonderful things where no corresponding future event ever occurred? These dreams are forgotten. This is fact confirmed by daily experience. So while dreams provide each dreamer with wonderful imagery, and powerful emotions, they are no more accurate in predicting the future than is chance.

There are other types of apparently paranormal perceptions of future events, such as awake visions, premonitions, and déjà vu. Consider awake visions of future events. An example of such visions was reported by an Englishman called Michael Bentine. Michael Bentine served as an intelligence officer in the English Air Force during World War 2. One of his tasks was to brief aircraft crew prior to their undertaking bombing missions over Germany. During these briefings he would sometimes see visions:

> 'Occasionally, he would see the face of a young flier turn into a skull and would know that it would be the young man's last flight.'[11]

A woman I know very well once told me she experiences similar perceptions. She perceives darkness, or coloured lights around photographs of those who soon become seriously ill and die. She says she knows of other people with similar abilities and perceptions. Such stories made me ask myself how it was possible for such visions or perceptions to occur, if paranormal prediction of the future is only fantasy. Eventually I came to the conclusion that the key to these visions lies in the fact they occur in fully conscious individuals, who are able to directly perceive the persons who subsequently become sick or die. After all, people observe each other continuously. Each person continuously makes conscious and subconscious observations of people in their surroundings. These conscious and subconscious observations provide surprising amounts of information about the sex, race, income, education, social standing, personality, mental state, and health of the persons being observed.

The eyes are the most evident organs of observation. Many people have an acute sense of human behaviour in relation to the context in which the people they observe find themselves. People observe the clothing and grooming of people in their surroundings, their speech, whether they are perspiring, their skin colour, and skin reactions, as well as their gait and movements. All these observations provide information about sex, race, income, education, social standing, personality, mental state, and health. Many people also consciously and subconsciously observe the eyes of other people, regarding eyes as 'windows of the mind'. They observe the subtle play of muscle movements around the eyes, the rate at which a person blinks, the level of the eyelids, the volume of tears round the eyelids, the colours of the whites of the eyes, the colours of the iris, and the directions a person is looking. Furthermore, pupil size also influences the reactions of people to each other. For example, a person with narrow pupils is often regarded as hard and unfriendly, while a person with wide pupils is regarded as a warm and friendly. Most people do not say people possess these attributes because their pupils are narrow or wide, instead they say a person has 'hard eyes', 'unfriendly eyes', 'warm eyes', 'friendly eyes'.[12] All these visual observations provide enormous amounts of information about individuals. But the eyes are not the only senses with which people observe each other.

Hearing is another sense with which people observe each other. People make sounds as they move, as they breathe, and as they speak. The noise a person makes while walking, and moving, reveals information about their health and state of mind. A sick and unhealthy person makes different sounds than a healthy and active individual. Breathing sounds tell much about the health of a person. For example, the sounds of coughing, sneezing, wheezing, puffing, rapid breathing, and shortness of breath are all manifestations of health, and sometimes of mental state. Voice not only transfers information as speech, but also reveals much about the origins, sex, race, education, social standing, health, and mental state of a person. This is why each person consciously and subconsciously observes the way others speak, their choice of words, their tone of voice, as well as the presence of stuttering or pauses between words and sentences. But vision and hearing are not the only senses used to observe others, smell is also important.

Each individual produces a complex chemical signal, a product of the many different volatile substances released into the air by the body. The body releases volatile substances into the atmosphere from two basic sources: in exhaled air, and from the body surface. This complex chemical signal is very revealing, and is sensed both consciously and subconsciously by each person. Everyone recognises the smells of garlic, of onions, of spices, of peppermint, of eucalyptus, and of many other things eaten by our fellows. All these odours are volatile chemicals released into exhaled air from the skin and lungs of those who eat these things. Body metabolism changes during disease, often changing the types and quantities of the many volatile substances each person normally exhales with each breath. This is why the breath of sick people smells different to that of healthy people. Typical examples are the musty smell of rats on the breath of people with severe liver disease, the acetone odour on the breath of people suffering from severe unregulated diabetes or hunger, the sweet stench of pus and decay on the breath of someone with a severe infection of the lungs, throat, or sinuses. Body odours also originate from the skin. These are the consciously and unconsciously perceived odours of sweat, urine, faeces, dirt, and volatile substances originating from foods such as cheese, garlic, or strong smelling meats. In addition to all these odours, there are also the consciously, as well as unconsciously perceived odours of substances secreted by special apocrine sweat glands in the pubic area and in the armpits. The apocrine glands of women secrete a different profile of chemicals than do the apocrine glands of men. This is why women and men have different body odours. Exercise and physical exertion also determine body odour. Genetic makeup also determines the types, and quantities of volatile substances emitted in exhaled air and by the skin. All these things combine to make the chemical signal emitted by each person unique to that person. This is why siblings, babies, and mothers can recognise each other by smell alone. Mood, emotion, and psychiatric illness also change the body odour emitted by an individual. This is why many people can consciously, or subconsciously perceive the reek of despair, the smell of fear, the odour of exhaustion, or the scent of sexual attractants. Some psychiatrists even say they can smell a typical body odour originating from people with schizophrenia. People can consciously and subconsciously detect all these things by smell alone, although this ability is more pronounced in some people than in others.[13]

The normal senses possessed by each of us generate a flood of information about others in our surroundings. So people reporting visions of the impending deaths of others due to sickness, may actually be unconsciously integrating a multitude of visual, auditory, and olfactory indicators of the health of these other persons. They subconsciously register the changed total profile of all these factors, unconsciously integrate these observations into a conclusion, subsequently converting them into conscious visions of darkness, changed aura's, or other changes in the ways they see these people, or their pictures. In this way they say they can predict the impending deaths of these people. Michael Bentine probably did just this. He consciously saw the heads of doomed young fliers as skulls, while actually subconsciously perceiving their deadly exhaustion, fear, and desire to cease the seemingly unending horror, stress, and danger of bombing missions. If all these things were present to a higher degree than normal, these fliers would probably make more mistakes than usual, so that they were more likely than others to die on a bombing mission. When viewed in this way, an ability to predict the future of some people, is no more than a product of the integration of a totality of conscious, and subconscious perceptions. Paranormal perception of the future is not required to make such predictions.

Yet why is it that these people actually see such visions? Michael Bentine saw skulls, and this woman I know saw aura's. Furthermore, why are such visions sometimes accompanied by a powerful sense of an unseen external presence, or by actual visions of someone, or something? This type of paranormal prediction of the future is often reported in the Holy Bible. Prophets saw, or sensed the presence of God, and either heard God speak, or were instructed by the presence of God to foretell the future. Isaiah was an example of just such a prophet. One day he saw God, and God chose him as a prophet:

> 'In the year that king Uzziah died I saw also the LORD sitting upon a throne, high and lifted up, and his train filled the temple.
> Above it stood the seraphims: each one had six wings; with twain he covered his face, and with twain he covered his feet, and with twain he did fly.
> And one cried unto another, and said, Holy, holy, holy, (is) the LORD of hosts: the whole earth (is) full of his glory.
> And the posts of the door moved at the voice of him that cried, and the house was filled with smoke.
> Then said I, Woe (is) me! for I am undone; because I (am) a man of unclean lips, and I dwell in the midst of a people of unclean lips: for mine eyes have seen the King, the LORD of hosts.
> Then flew one of the seraphims unto me, having a live coal in his hand, (which) he had taken with the tongs from off the altar:
> And he laid (it) upon my mouth, and said, Lo, this hath touched thy lips; and thine iniquity is taken away, and thy sin purged.
> Also I heard the voice of the Lord, saying, Whom shall I send, and who will go for us? Then said I, Here (am) I; send me.
> And he said, Go, and tell this people, Hear ye indeed, but understand not; and see ye indeed, but perceive not.
> Make the heart of this people fat, and make their ears heavy, and shut their eyes; lest they see with their eyes, and hear with their ears, and understand with their heart, and convert, and be healed.
> Then said I, Lord, how long? And he answered, Until the cities be wasted without inhabitant, and the houses without man, and the land be utterly desolate,
> And the LORD have removed men far away, and (there be) a great forsaking in the midst of the land.'[14]

Isaiah was inspired by God to foretell of the coming invasion, plundering, and enslavement of the land of Israel by the powerful neighbouring Babylonian kingdom in 722 BCE. He really did have these visions, he really did feel that hot coal on his lips, and he really was convinced and inspired by God. He truly experienced all these things. But regardless of these experiences and visions, Isaiah also knew such an invasion was not just likely; he knew it was a certainty. He knew of the Babylonian lust for territorial expansion and plunder. He heard these things in the market place, from conversations with others, and from rumours. Such things were the talk of his day. Furthermore, Isaiah had even more knowledge, because the then current king of Israel, King Hezekiah, once told Isaiah he had recently exhibited all his treasures and wealth to a group of visiting Babylonian ambassadors.

> 'At that time Berodach-baladan, the son of Baladan, king of Babylon, sent letters and a present unto Hezekiah: for he had heard that Hezekiah had been sick.
> And Hezekiah hearkened unto them, and showed them all the house of his precious things, the silver, and the gold, and the spices, and the precious ointment, and (all) the house of his armour, and all that was found in his treasures: there was nothing in his house, nor in all his dominion, that Hezekiah showed them not.
> Then came Isaiah the prophet unto king Hezekiah, and said unto him, What said these men? and from whence came they unto thee? And Hezekiah said, They are come from a far country, (even) from Babylon.
> And he said, What have they seen in thine house? And Hezekiah answered, All (the things) that (are) in mine house have they seen: there is nothing among my treasures that I have not showed them.
> And Isaiah said unto Hezekiah, Hear the word of the LORD.
> Behold, the days come, that all that (is) in thine house, and that which thy fathers have laid up in store unto this day, shall be carried into Babylon: nothing shall be left, saith the LORD.
> And of thy sons that shall issue from thee, which thou shalt beget, shall they take away; and they shall be eunuchs in the palace of the king of Babylon.'[15]

So the Babylonian invasion really was a certainty. This incredibly naive king had shown these Babylonian ambassadors just what the plunder-hungry nobility of Babylon wanted to see, and where they could collect it. Isaiah needed no paranormal powers to predict a Babylonian invasion after he heard what Hezekiah had done. He knew the Babylonians would come; it was only a matter of time. This is one prophecy of which we know all the details. However, Isaiah did have a real and powerful sense of the presence of God, and he really did have visions. Such visions and predictions still occur, only they are rather more mundane warnings of danger, of seen and unseen presences, and of guardian angels. There are many such stories. Consider the story told by a woman skier:

> 'A young woman was skiing down a ski slope that was new to her. Eager to get going, she missed a sign that would have directed her safely down the

hill. As she turned a corner, suddenly a man dressed all in black, stood right in her line of vision and directed her in a different direction. She told me that there was no way to not obey him and she wondered what a man dressed all in black without skis or boots would be doing up on the hill in the middle of nowhere.

His sudden appearance made her fall. And although she was bruised and bumped, she was not seriously hurt. When she looked up to speak to him, she saw that he had disappeared. Not only had he disappeared but there were no tracks in the snow indicating that he had ever been there. When she examined the spot and looked to where she had been headed, she saw that if he had not distracted her when he had, she would have skied right over an outcropping high enough to seriously injure or even kill her. It occurred to her later that this angel must have worn black so that she would see him clearly against the snow white background of the ski hill. There was no doubt in her mind after seeing no tracks and the sudden disappearance that he was an angel.'[16]

Superficially, this is a wonderful story of a vision in which a guardian angel warned of impending possible disaster. Yet this woman needed no paranormal sensory abilities to know of the dangerous rock outcropping. As someone who has occasionally skied, I know each skier unconsciously adjusts their skiing to the possible conditions of the terrain ahead, on the basis of experience gained while skiing. Such unconscious information processing is necessary, otherwise you simply cannot ski very fast, or with any ease. So it was very likely this woman subconsciously perceived a potentially dangerous change in the terrain ahead of her. Only, instead of stopping because of a conscious suspicion of a potentially dangerous change of terrain, she had a vision of a man in black who caused her to fall before she encountered the danger ahead. But how could such a vision occur? Other people also have visions whose meaning they do not understand at the time, but which they later experience. During this later experience they are overwhelmed by a powerful sense of déjà vu; they feel they have already seen and experienced that which they are undergoing. An example of this type of experience was told me by a woman I have known nearly all my life. In this vision or dream she saw herself seated at a dining table together with her two small boys, the house and table were different from that in which she lived at the time, the boys were older, and her husband was not present. Several years later, she was divorced and living with her two boys in a different country. One day she was sitting at the dining table with her two boys. Suddenly she was overwhelmed by the sense she was re-living an episode in her life, and remembered her vision. She had seen, and lived this episode before.

Many people have experienced similar sensations of familiarity, or equally powerful sensations of déjà vu. Such sensations are very common. For example, in the story of the woman above, the situation of sitting at a dining table with her two boys was one which had repeated itself many, many times. And in this situation, a powerful sensation of déjà vu could well have created a false memory. Nonetheless, why did this woman have such an overwhelming sense of the reality of her vision, and of déjà vu? How could this happen?

Visions, memories, sensations of seen and unseen presences, visions of guardian angels, and overwhelming sensations of déjà vu are seemingly disparate sensations and experiences. Yet this difference is only superficial. Studies of people with epilepsy originating within the structures of their temporal lobes, studies of people with tumours in their temporal lobes, and studies of electrical stimulations of the structures of the temporal lobes, indicate that these seemingly disparate sensations and experiences are all generated within the temporal lobes of the brain (see figure 3).[17]

But most people reporting prophecies, sensations of seen and unseen presences, experiences of déjà vu, and perceptions of visions are usually not sick, they have no temporal lobe epilepsy, nor do they have brain tumours. So how can the seemingly healthy brains of healthy people generate such sensations and experiences?

The answer lies in the terms anatomical and functional variation. Human bodies basically have an identical structure and function, and this is evident in the reasonably small range of anatomical, chemical, and functional variations between people. Even so, there are differences between people. There are men and women, the young and the old, the short and the long, the fat and the thin, the muscular and the weak, as well as many different races. Together with these obvious differences, there are also some differences in anatomy and function between people. These differences are due to a complex interaction between individual genetic constitution, anatomy, diet, and many other factors. These same considerations are also true for brain structure and function. Brain structure and function is on average the same in all people, but there are variations between individuals.

Among these variations, there is a small percentage of perfectly healthy people who manifest short periods of increased electrical activity within the temporal lobes of their brains. These short periods of increased electrical activity are very similar to the electrical activity of epilepsy, but do not cause any evident convulsions, falling, or other manifestations of temporal lobe epilepsy.[18] These episodes of temporary, unusual, epilepsy-like electrical activity in the temporal lobes are called 'temporal lobe transients'. And people with temporal lobe transients are known to regularly experience déjà vu, to sense seen and unseen presences, to have visions, and to be

greatly interested in religion and the paranormal.[19]
Experimental studies show that external factors can induce changes in temporal lobe function. For example, application of rapidly changing weak, one microtesla magnetic fields to the brain can cause changes in the electrical activity of the brain.[20] Indeed, application of such rapidly changing, weak magnetic fields to the temporal lobes of many people arouses sensations of déjà vu, of sensed presences of entities, and visions[21], especially in those people known to have temporal lobe transients.[22] No experimenter has ever reported seeing the presences and visions sensed by people undergoing applications of rapidly changing weak magnetic fields to their brains. This means these visions and presences were only present within the minds of these people, and not real physical events, otherwise everyone could see these things.

One microtesla magnetic fields are actually thirty to sixty times weaker than the magnetic field of the earth, a fact indicating that the brains of some people are very sensitive to their electromagnetic environment. Everyone is continually exposed to changing magnetic fields. We are all immersed in the magnetic field of the earth, the strength of which changes due to normal movements of the earth's crust at fault lines, volcanic activity, and the effects of solar flares. Furthermore, our electromagnetic environment is influenced by rainfall and electrical storms, as well as by the proximity of electrical power lines, electrical machinery, and electrical apparatus. If powerful enough, rapidly changing electromagnetic fields induced by all these things can arouse paranormal sensations, the sensed presences of entities, of gods, of hauntings, and of memories generating déjà vu experiences[23], especially in those with temporal lobe transients. It is even possible that the ever-increasing quantity of electrical devices, and machinery in our environment, may cause such phenomena to occur more frequently now, than in the past.

So are people with temporal lobe transients, the blessed few whom in past ages would have been called prophets, holy men, or holy women? Temporal lobe transients are a form of excessive nervous activity within the structures of the temporal lobes very similar to epilepsy. And just as in epilepsy, the privations, exposure, exhaustion, metabolic disorders caused by bad food, drugs, dehydration and sunstroke in hot deserts, or cold and oxygen starvation in high mountains, to which many prophets, holy men and holy women were exposed, might well have activated increased temporal lobe nervous activity within their brains. These people certainly had a profound sense of the presence of gods and other entities. They sensed something greater and more important than themselves. They certainly had visions. They had a sense of universal familiarity with the past, present, and the future, because a profound sense of déjà vu made them feel familiar with all things. And if these people were not known as prophets, holy men or holy women, they might well have been known to be gifted as seers, augers, oracles, soothsayers, necromancers, witches, wizards, fortune-tellers, witch-doctors, or shamans. But the days of many of these professions are past. Now we would simply call such people spiritual, deeply religious, or psychically gifted.

All these things mean there is absolutely no evidence for the paranormal nature of dreams foretelling the future, for visions, for paranormal explanations of the presences sensed by some people, or for paranormal explanations of déjà vu sensations. Such experiences are no more than products of chance, and the functioning of the body. True, they are wonderful experiences, but they are still no more than products of chance, and the functioning of the brain, coupled with a deeply rooted human desire to be part of a world more wondrous, and more fantastical than that experienced with the physical senses.[24] In my opinion, these things explain all these phenomena. Furthermore, they explain these phenomena with provable physical facts.

However, all these explanations do not conclusively exclude the possibility of a paranormal ability to sense the future. After all, an ability to somehow sense the future by paranormal means may exist, although there is no real evidence for precognitive abilities of any sort. This sounds inconclusive, but it does mean that because apparently precognitive abilities may be products of chance, or generated by the functioning of the body, I could not regard them as indirect evidence for the reality of an immaterial human soul. So I continued my search for direct and indirect evidences for the human soul.

Chapter 9

The Aura

Paranormal sensory abilities almost certainly do not exist. Even so, there is another possibly immaterial aspect of the body. This is the multicoloured halo of light that some people say they see surrounding the body of each person. They call this multicoloured halo of light the 'aura'. One man wrote of this aura of light he saw surrounding each person, saying:

> 'The human aura is both an energy field and a reflection of the subtle life energies within the body. These energies make us what we are and in turn, are affected by our surroundings and life style. The aura reflects our health, character, mental activity and emotional state. It also shows disease – often long before the onset of symptoms.
> Close to the skin is the etheric aura. It is a pale, narrow band that outlines the body and is usually no more than half an inch wide. It looks like milky smoke clinging to the body.
> The main aura is banded around the body – strata like. Imagine a person with thick, coloured hoops of light dropped over them and you get the idea. These colours emanate from the psychic centres (or chakras). Basic energy is drawn up from the planet through the feet and fed into the chakras, much like a plant does with water. Each chakra is a transformer that generates energy of a different type and colour. The strength, activity and colour tone of each chakra, depends on the person's character, personality, emotional state and life style. Together they generate the dominant hue of the aura.
> The aura is photosensitive and expands to many times its normal size in sunlight. The aura chakra system can be likened to a tree. Energy/nutrient is drawn up through the feet/roots and fed through the body/trunk to the chakras/leaves. The aura also absorbs energy from other energy sources around us, like sunlight and ozone, plants and other people.'[1]

Another writer described the human aura with these words:

> 'Bagnall[2] reports that the aura cannot be dispersed by a current of air but that it is attracted to a magnet held close to the skin and that, like the electrical field around a charged conductor, it extends farthest from a projection such as a finger or the tip of the nose. He describes the aura as being composed of a hazy outer layer and a brighter inner layer, in which there seem

to be striations running out at right angles to the skin. Bagnall and other aura watchers say that every once in a while a much brighter ray 'reaches out from the aura like a searchlight' and extends several feet away from the body before vanishing again.'[3]

Many people believe the aura is a manifestation of 'a basic energy underlying all matter'.[4] They say animals, plants, and lifeless objects also have an aura. Perhaps the soul is also a manifestation of this 'basic energy underlying all matter' in the universe. So a study of the human aura may reveal whether such an immaterial aspect of the human body exists. And if such an immaterial aspect of each human body does exist, then each person may indeed possess an immaterial soul. So I decided to study the nature of the human aura.

My first question was to ask how people could see this aura. Much has been written about the human aura, and all these writings teach that the aura is seen with the eyes. But the human eye only responds to light in the seven colours of the visible spectrum: violet, indigo, blue, green, yellow, orange, and red.[5] Black and darkness is the absence of light and colour. The colour white, and white light is the combination of all seven colours of the spectrum. All other colours are products of the mixture of different amounts of the seven different colours of light forming white light. So if people can see an aura of light surrounding the human body with their eyes, this means one of two things. Either the human body emits light, so forming an aura of light around the body of each person. Or the energy generating the aura affects light near the body, changing the nature, or the colours of the light near the body, so forming an aura of light around the body of each person.

Only a few gifted people are ever able to see the human aura. One possible reason for this is that most people cannot see the aura because it is too faint to be seen against a background of normal lighting. Darkness is one way of eliminating background light, in addition to which, darkness also increases the sensitivity of the human eye to light. Indeed, after remaining in total darkness for an hour, the sensitivity of the human eye to light increases by as much as twenty five thousand times.[6] Darkness is an experience every living person undergoes for several hours every night. But even after remaining in total darkness for more than an hour, people still cannot see an aura of light surrounding other people standing in the dark. This may mean that the light emitted by the human body is too faint to be seen by most people. So perhaps the eyes of those who say they can see the aura are much more sensitive to light than the eyes of most people. Photographic apparatus and photographic film are much more sensitive to light than are human eyes. Thousands of millions of people have been photographed since the development of practical photography in 1839 CE by William Henry Talbot.[7] And each year, many more thousands of millions of photographs are made of people. Yet in all this time, no-one has ever photographed an aura of light surrounding the body of each person in the dark. All that can be seen on photographs of people made in darkness with extremely sensitive photographic film, are the people being photographed. The fact that the human aura can neither be seen, nor photographed in the dark, proves that the human aura is not caused by light emitted by the human body.

Another possibility is that the aura is caused by an effect of the soul upon light in the vicinity of the body. This would explain why the aura can neither be seen nor photographed in darkness. This would also explain why the colours of the aura are affected by the colour of the ambient light, the colour of the surroundings, as well as the colour of any clothing worn. This would also explain why the human aura increases in size, brightness, and intensity in bright sunlight. Ambient light is needed for all these properties. Nonetheless, extremely few people can see the human aura, even though the aura of light surrounding each person becomes brighter in bright sunlight. Vast experience with photography teaches that if something can be seen, then it can be photographed. Yet during all this time, during which thousands of millions of photographs have been made of people standing in bright sunlight, photographs never reveal an aura of light surrounding the body of each person. This is conclusive proof the human aura is not caused by something affecting light in the vicinity of the human body.

Very few people can see the human aura, and the human aura cannot be photographed. These two facts mean that the aura of light surrounding each human body has nothing to do with light seen with the eyes. After all, if the aura was produced by emission of light, or by an effect upon light illuminating the body, then the aura could be seen and photographed by everyone. Even so, these facts do not mean that the aura is an illusion. After all, some people are very adamant that they can see an aura of light surrounding each person. They say they do not see the aura with their eyes, otherwise everyone could see and photograph the aura. Instead, they say they see the aura as an image in their minds by means of a paranormal sense called the 'third eye'. And many people believe each person has such a third eye. But is this true? Intense study of human anatomy during the past four hundred years has never revealed a third eye in humans. So perhaps this third eye is not a physical part of the body, but a property of the soul. Furthermore, if the third eye is immaterial, then it cannot be seen or sensed in any way. How can the possibility that people see the human aura with a possibly paranormal third eye be proven?

One way of determining the existence of this third eye is to question people blinded by eye diseases. Eye diseases only affect the eyes. Blindness caused by eye diseases does not affect the brain, does not affect other sense organs, does not affect any paranormal senses, and certainly cannot affect any immaterial aspects of the body. The senses and the brains of people blinded by eye diseases develop normally, and function normally until they become blind. Everyone knows that blind people always try to develop their remaining senses to compensate for their blindness. This means they will also consciously, or unconsciously, try to develop any latent or existing paranormal senses, such as vision through the third eye. Indeed, blindness would be no great handicap to blind people with the ability to see with a paranormal third eye, because they would be able to see the auras of all the objects, animals, and people about them with their third eye. This would be almost as good as normal light. So if a third eye exists, then many of the countless millions of blind people who have died in the past would have developed the ability to use this third eye. In addition, if a third eye exists, then many of the more than seven million totally blind people, and the more than thirty million partially blind people now alive[8] would also be able to use this third eye. If the blind could see with this third eye, there would also be ages-old common knowledge attributing the blind with an ability to see auras, and many of the countless millions of blind people who lived in the past would have said they could see the human aura. But there is no ages-old common knowledge that the blind can see auras. The more than thirty seven million blind people now alive, also never say they can see auras. All that is known about blind people is that they are blind. They certainly see nothing with their eyes, they see nothing with their third eye, and they only learn what is happening in the world about them with their remaining senses. Furthermore, the only training blind people ever receive to help them in their daily lives, is to develop the use of their remaining physical senses. They never receive training in the use of the third eye. So the aura of light supposedly surrounding each human body is not a paranormal phenomenon seen by people with the ability to use an immaterial, or paranormal third eye. In fact, the reality of an immaterial, or paranormal third eye is extremely doubtful.

An aura of light surrounding each person cannot be seen by most people, cannot be photographed, and cannot be seen by any paranormal sense such as a third eye. So the claims of people who say they can see auras may be no more than wishful fantasies. But if the aura is only a fantasy, why do some apparently perfectly normal people still claim they can see an aura of light surrounding each person? A chance remark made by a woman I know revealed another possibility. She said that she knows a man who can see auras. And as proof that this man was not subject to wild fantasies, she added that his son also sees auras. This immediately made me think that the ability to see auras is due to inherited abnormalities in the functioning of the human eye.

My son confirmed this a few days later. He told me he always saw coloured lights around people and objects for a short time after swimming underwater with his eyes open. The local swimming pool where he used to swim is filled with chlorinated fresh water. Opening the eyes while swimming in chlorinated fresh water causes temporary swelling of the surfaces of the eyes. This swelling changes the optical properties of the eyes, and these changes enabled him to see auras for a short time after swimming underwater. This also explains why some people can see auras better than others. The shapes of the different parts of the eye differ slightly from one person to another, and some people are born with different degrees of optical distortion in their eyes than other people. This explains why some people can see an aura of light surrounding each person. People see auras because of optical distortions in their eyes.

Indeed, a study of the optical properties of human eyes reveals why this is so. But before I discuss the optical distortions allowing people to see auras, I first want to carefully define the properties of the human aura. These properties are derived from a number of sources.[9] And any explanation of why the optical properties of the eyes permit people to see the human aura must explain these properties of the aura. These properties are:

- the aura cannot be photographed;
- there is a milky coloured mist called the 'etheric aura' close to the surface of each person;
- the aura is composed of multiple bands of coloured light surrounding each person, and often has a predominant colour;
- sometimes, jets, streaks, swirls, and bands of many colours are seen in addition to the aura;
- the colours of the clothing, the skin, the light, and the surroundings all affect the colours of the aura;
- the aura disappears in the dark, is barely visible in dim light, and increases in size with increasing light intensity.

These are the properties of the aura of light some people say surrounds the body of each person. But how do the optical properties of the eyes enable people to see such auras? A short description of the structure and function of the human eye makes an explanation of these properties more obvious. The function of the eyes is to focus images of what is seen upon the light sensitive membrane at the back of each eye called the 'retina'. Light focussed upon the retina by the optical system of the eye generates nerve signals that are conducted into the brain along the sensory nerves. The optical system of the eye is actually the cornea, the fluid in the front chamber of the eye called the 'aqueous humour', the lens, and the jelly-like fluid in the rear chamber of the eye called the 'vitreous humour'. The cornea is the transparent part of the eye in front of the iris and pupil, and performs about seventy-five percent of the focussing of light upon the retina. But the cornea cannot adjust focus for objects at different distances. This is the function of the lens. The lens is soft, and small muscles surrounding the edge of the lens of each eye cause the lens to become flatter or thicker. Pupil size also affects the functioning of the optical system of the eye. Changes in the thickness of the lens changes the focal distance, while changes in pupil width affects depth of focus, and both effects enable people to clearly see near and far objects. But the human eye is not a perfect optical instrument. It is subject to several types of optical distortion, such as spherical aberration, chromatic aberration, and coma. All these things affect the properties of images focussed upon the retina[10], and explain the genesis of the aura.

To begin with, the cornea and lens of each eye function like magnifying glasses. They are a type of lens called spherical lenses, which means that they have a spherical shape. A problem with spherical lenses is that not all the light passing through such lenses is focussed onto the same point. The centre of a spherical lens focuses light at a point further from the lens than does the edge of the lens. This is called spherical aberration. Everyone can see this phenomenon with a cheap large magnifying glass. I specifically mention a cheap large magnifying glass, because cheap magnifying glasses are nearly always spherical lenses, simply because spherical lenses are cheaper to produce than other types of lenses. Hold such a cheap large magnifying glass in front of your eyes, and look through it at an object about one half to one metre from your eyes. Move the magnifying glass forwards and backwards. At one point you will see that the image in the centre of the magnifying glass is sharp, while the edges of the image are blurred. The centre of the image is in focus, while spherical aberration causes those parts of the image near the edge of the magnifying glass to be out of focus. At another point you will see that the whole image is blurred, and that the edges of the image are indistinct and surrounded by a pale mist. Spherical aberration causes all these effects. The human eye is also subject to spherical aberration, which is why images seen out of the corners of the eyes are less distinct than those seen in the centre of the visual fields.

Pupil size also influences these effects of spherical aberration by affecting the focal depth of the optical system of the eyes. Small pupils increase the depth of focus of the eyes, so that near and far objects are seen clearly.

Wide pupils reduce the depth of focus of the eyes, so that only objects upon which the eyes are focussed are seen clearly, while everything else is blurred.[11]

I read the instructions given by one man to learn how to see the aura. These instructions made it clear to me that changes in pupil size, together with spherical aberration, explain how people can see that part of the aura called the 'etheric aura', or 'etheric body'. This man first asked his readers to practice with an object such as a book. He wrote:

> *'Close your eyes, take a few deep breaths and relax. When you are calm, look at the book. Focus your eyes on nothing, just a little to the side and a foot or two[12] behind it. Hold and get used to that focus but don't strain your eyes or tense your forehead. Concentrate! You need a gentle, steady un-focus, just like daydreaming. It is crucial your eyes are really relaxed and dreamy while you hold the unfocus. After a while you will see a pale milky aura coming from the object. Keep looking steadily at it and a bright yellow or green aura will start building up from the object. Don't change focus and look directly at it or the aura will disappear.'[13]*

The writer of this passage instructs the person to relax and unfocus their eyes while looking to one side of the objects they are viewing. Such relaxation of the eyes relaxes the lens in each eye and widens the pupils. Widened pupils mean that light can enter the eyes from the sides of the corneas, and this light is more affected by spherical aberration. Pupil widening decreases the depth of focus, while relaxation of the lens in each eye means that nothing is in focus. All these things mean that all objects viewed in this way are out of focus, and affected by spherical aberration. This is the cause of the pale milky aura around objects, and this pale milky aura around people is called the etheric aura. So a person who sees the etheric aura, is really seeing an out of focus image resulting from a combination of reduced focal depth, and spherical aberration.

But how do people see colours in the aura? Simple uncorrected spherical lenses like the cornea, the lens in the eye, or a cheap magnifying glass do not bend different colours of light equally. An uncorrected spherical lens bends violet light more than indigo, more than blue, more than green, more than yellow, more than orange, more than red light. This effect is least evident for light passing through the centre of a lens, and is most evident for light passing through the edge of a lens. This is the cause of the rainbow coloured edges of images seen through some lenses. It is an effect called 'chromatic aberration'.

Everyone can see examples of chromatic aberration by looking at objects through a cheap magnifying glass in bright sunlight. Move the magnifying glass nearer and further from your eyes. At certain points you will see that objects in the centre of the magnifying glass are reasonably in focus, while at the edge of the magnifying glass, the images are out of focus, and surrounded by bands of different coloured light. These coloured bands are larger near to the edge of the magnifying glass, and are smaller in the middle of the magnifying glass. Experiment some more with different coloured objects and backgrounds, and you will see that the colours of these bands of light depend upon the background colours, and the colours of the objects. For example, you will see a yellow haze around the head of a person with dark coloured hair who is standing in front of a white background.

The cornea and lens in each human eye are uncorrected spherical lenses, which means they are also subject to chromatic aberration. And just like the example of looking through a cheap magnifying glass, chromatic aberration is greatest when looking at objects out of the corners of the eyes. Indeed, many instructions for viewing auras require people to view images through the corners of their eyes, while relaxed and not focusing on anything.[14] This is just the right way to achieve the most chromatic aberration in the image seen. So chromatic aberration explains the different colours seen in auras.

A beam of light passing through the centre of a cheap magnifying glass is relatively unaffected. But when a beam of light passes at an angle through the edge of a cheap magnifying glass, the image is smeared out into an elongated form like a comet with a tail. This effect is called 'coma'. And when the light beam contains more than one colour, the image is smeared out into a multiply coloured jet of light. Everyone can also observe this effect of optical coma by looking at objects through a magnifying glass held at an angle to the direction of sight. Move the magnifying glass backwards and forwards. At certain points you will see jets, bands, and streaks of light emanating from objects near the edge of the magnifying glass. This is the effect of coma.

The human eye is also subject to coma, and instructions given for viewing auras require people to view images through the corners of their eyes while relaxed, and not focussing on anything.[15] This is not only the correct way to achieve the most chromatic aberration, but also the right way to achieve the most optical aberration due to coma. This is why people see rays, jets, bands, and streaks of light in auras.

When you look at objects through a cheap magnifying glass, you notice that these layers, rays, jets, bands, and streaks of light surrounding everything are larger, and brighter in bright sunlight than in dim light. This is because bright light provides a brighter image that visibly spreads over a larger area. The same is also true for human eyes. This explains why the size of the human aura increases in bright sunlight. It also explains why the size of the human aura decreases in dim light, and disappears in the dark.

Just looking through the corners of relaxed and unfocussed eyes enables people to see an aura of light surrounding other people. Relaxation of the eyes causes the pupils to widen, allowing light to enter the eyes from nearer the edges of the corneas. The resulting images on the retina of each eye are out of focus, and subject to all manner of optical distortion, such as spherical aberration, chromatic aberration, and coma. This is how people can see an aura of light surrounding each person. The ability to see an aura surrounding the body of each person is not a paranormal ability. Instead, people see auras because they utilise the normal optical distortions present in all human eyes.

I checked the truth of this idea by going to a paranormal fair where many people displayed, and employed their paranormal sensory abilities. Once there, I looked in the section where people able to see auras were seated. I observed these people. I saw that some of these people viewed auras by looking through the corners of their eyes. Others quite evidently relaxed their eyes, staring at a point in the distance, far behind the person at whose aura they were looking. These observations confirmed my idea that the ability to see the aura was no more than conscious, or unconscious utilisation of the optical distortions present in every human eye. Theory and practice became one. I now knew that the ability to see an aura of light around each person was not a paranormal ability. Instead, the ability to see an aura of light surrounding each person is something most people can learn by teaching themselves to look at others in such a way, that the images they see undergo distortion by the optical system of their eyes.

But not everyone needs to learn how to do this. Corneal shapes, and curvatures, differ slightly from one person to another. The optical system of some people's eyes have such a degree of optical distortion, that they are able to see an aura of light around each person without any conscious effort on their part at all. Their children may inherit the same abnormalities, and so may also be able to see auras. This is why some people are born with the ability to see auras. In particular, those people born with nearsighted eyes are most likely to be able to see auras.

Nearsightedness is actually a very common visual defect. About one in four adults in the United States of America is nearsighted, while more than seven in ten Chinese and Japanese adults are nearsighted.[16] And as many as one in every two hundred people descended from Western European races is extremely nearsighted.[17] Normally, the optical system of the human eye focuses images of what is seen quite precisely upon the retina in the back of each eye. The eyeball of a person with normal sight is shaped like a ball, but the eyeball of a nearsighted person is shaped like an egg, with the longest axis in the front to rear direction. So the eyeball of a nearsighted person is longer than the eyeball of a person with normal sight, and this means that images of distant things are focussed at a point in front of the retina. Such images are seen as an unfocussed blur. Nearsighted people can only clearly see those things held close to heir eyes, hence the term 'nearsighted'. All the effects of spherical aberration, chromatic aberration, and coma are exaggerated in nearsighted eyes, because the length of a nearsighted eyeball is longer than normal, which means that the distorted image is spread over a larger area of the retina than in a normal eye. This is why nearsighted people are more likely to see auras than are normally sighted people.

Nearsightedness is a curious condition. Usually a person is nearsighted because they inherit this condition from their parents. But nearsightedness can also develop in the otherwise normal eyes of young people. This is because the development of the eyes in young people is affected by the way they use their eyes. Children and teenagers who do a lot of reading, study, or fine handiwork, often become nearsighted, because their eyes lengthen in response to the necessity to focus upon objects close to their eyes.[18]

In past ages, the only people who had the leisure, as well as the ability to read and write for prolonged periods of time were usually priests, monks, and other religious people. They lived and worked in rooms dimly lit by the guttering light of candles, oil lamps, or fires. In such chambers they studied the holy texts of their religions, and they wrote dissertations and books about the God-given glories of their religious beliefs. They strained their eyes for long periods of time to see what they were reading, and to see what they were writing. Reading and writing for long periods of time in dim light causes long-lasting deformation of the lens, and vitreous humour within each eye, resulting in temporary and permanent nearsightedness, even in older people.[19] But people had no glasses to correct their nearsightedness in ancient and mediaeval times. So the more these ancient and mediaeval scholars studied, and the more they wrote, the more nearsighted they became. And as their eyes become more nearsighted, they noticed they could see an aura of light surrounding each person when they looked out of the corners of their eyes. They saw a golden glow surrounding the heads of some people, and sometimes they even saw wonderful coloured lights surrounding the bodies of people. They told others of the auras of light they saw surrounding the body of each person, and learned that no-one else could see these things. So they, and all other people, came to believe God had rewarded them for their piety with the ability to see a glorious spiritual aspect of the human body. People believed this was further proof of the reality of God, and further proof of the reality of an immaterial and spiritual aspect of the human body. Mediaeval painters also learned of these auras of light, and painted golden aureoles around the heads of holy people as evidence of their holiness.

Everyone can reproduce the effects of nearsightedness by holding a cheap large magnifying glass in front of their eyes. Do this, and move the magnifying glass closer to, and further away from your eyes. At some points, you will see an aura of light surrounding all people and objects, and near the edges of the magnifying glass you will see jets and streaks of light. Look through the magnifying glass at the head of a dark-haired person standing in front of a white background, and you will see a golden-yellow aureole surrounding their head. This is the golden aureole seen by our mediaeval ancestors. This simple experiment demonstrates why nearsightedness was most likely to be the reason our ancestors could see golden aureoles of light surrounding the heads of people.

People see auras because distortions in the optical system of their eyes affect the images they see. This also explains why it is impossible to photograph auras. The optical systems of cameras are designed with great care so as to be free of all optical distortions, which is why photographic cameras make photographs free of auras surrounding each person. However, holding a large magnifying glass in font of a camera lens reproduces the same optical distortions in the optical system of a camera as does nearsightedness in a human eye. When the lens is moved closer to, or further away from the camera lens, a point is eventually found at which photographs can be made which are identical to the auras drawn by those people with the ability to see auras.[20] This is further evidence that the ability to see auras is caused by optical distortions in the eyes of people with the ability to see auras.

All these things taught me that the ability to see the human aura is no fantasy. Some people really do see an aura of light surrounding each person. But this ability is nothing mystical, magical, or spiritual. People see an aura of light surrounding each person because of optical distortions in their eyes. This means the aura is not proof of anything immaterial associated with the human body, as well as proving that the aura is not indirect proof of the reality of the human soul. So I proceeded to study other experiences and perceptions indicating the possible existence of the soul.

Chapter 10

Disembodiment Defined

The human body is not animated by a soul. The soul does not exert any direct control over the body. Neither paranormal sensory abilities, nor an aura of light surrounding the body exist. None of these things provides any direct, or indirect evidence for the reality of the human soul. But this does not mean the human soul is a fantasy. There are other sensations and experiences apparently indicating the reality of the soul. One such experience is the 'out-of-body experience'. This is an experience during which people perceive their minds to be displaced outside their bodies. The report of a woman who underwent an out-of-body experience during childbirth is one example of such an experience:

> 'When the dilation had neared completion, the birth agony was nearly driving me out of my mind. And maybe that was just what happened. I felt a strange and whirling sensation, like I was a propeller on an aeroplane. It seemed to go faster and faster and then ...pop! I was floating over the bed in the labour room looking down on my body and the nurse who sought to ease my pain. I was shocked to see how contorted my facial features were. At first I thought I must have died, but then the body on the bed thrashed wildly and let out a terrible cry of pain. I was baffled. That was me down on the bed writhing in what was obviously awful agony, but it was also me up near the ceiling watching the scene below and feeling absolutely no pain at all.'[1]

This woman saw her body from a vantage point outside her body, an observation apparently indicating that her conscious mind was displaced outside her body. Many other people also report undergoing similar experiences during which they suddenly found their conscious minds displaced outside their bodies. Such experiences sound strange and quite improbable, but are actually very common, because about one in three people reports having undergone at least one out-of-body experience.[2] Even though out-of-body experiences are strange experiences, they are nonetheless real experiences. Furthermore, they are apparent proof that the mind is separate from the body, because the mind apparently separates from the body during out-of-body experiences. Many people believe the soul is the vehicle of the mind, which is why these experiences may be proof of the reality of a human soul. This meant I had to study out-of-body experiences to learn whether they really are due to separation of the mind from the body, and by doing so, indirectly prove the reality of the human soul.

Out-of-body experiences are very intangible experiences, because the apparent separation of the mind from the body occurring during these experiences cannot be seen, sensed, photographed, or measured. This intangibility meant that the only way I could learn the true nature of out-of-body experiences was to examine the reports made by those who underwent these experiences. So I examined reports of out-of-body experiences, and these reports revealed properties shared by all out-of-body experiences. The derivation of these shared properties was quite extensive, so I devoted this chapter to a careful definition of these properties. This was my first step in learning the likely nature of out-of-body experiences.

The first property of the out-of-body experience is very evident; the out-of-body experience is a conscious experience. The very fact that people can see their bodies, as well as observe what is happening to, and around their bodies, means they are conscious. So even though the bodies of people undergoing out-of-body experiences may appear unconscious and unresponsive to observers, the minds of these people are definitely conscious, and undergoing conscious experiences, as well as making conscious observations. After all, unconscious people are just that, unconscious, with no thoughts, and no perceptions, nothing at all. So the first shared property of all out-of-body experiences is that they are conscious experiences.

The situations during which out-of-body experiences occur are another property of these experiences. Many studies show out-of-body experiences usually occur during sleep. Indeed, many people, including myself, have had at least one dream during which they dreamed they were flying outside their bodies. One man reported just such an out-of-body experience. He wrote:

> 'Last Thursday night, I went to bed feeling really stressed and hoping to have interesting dreams as sort of a "poor man's vacation". I think my desire to escape the events of the day may have been the catalyst for what happened next.
>
> I must have drifted off for a while, but then awoke suddenly. My entire body was vibrating intensely. I layed there awake while the vibrations increased. From reading about out-of-body experiences I recognised the sensations and wasn't scared. I had full choice to either stop it or let it continue. The vibrations escalated until I felt I could leave my body if I wanted to. In my eyes, I saw flashes of blue light the colour of static electricity. As I was laying on my left side, I rotated clockwise and gave myself a mental "push" out.
>
> I floated up and looked down to see my body on the bed and my dog still

sound asleep next to it. I wouldn't have recognised the body as mine ... it was white and featureless. The "me" that was out of my body was everything I identified as myself, but no vibrations. I don't remember trying to look at my new form, but was puzzled as to how I could see without physical eyes.

I recalled I should have the ability to pass thru the bedroom to go outside the house. The thought of safely trying to go thru the glass window concerned me, so I went up to the solid wall. I felt a slight resistance but pushed and went thru with the sensation of wet soft cardboard. I floated to roof level and travelled about a half a mile to the house I grew up in. Travel time seemed instantaneous.

I entered thru the garage roof and exited out the front wall with the same sensations of soft wet cardboard. I headed home and the next I knew I was back in my body. Another out-of-body experience happened that same night and I don't remember where I went. But the initial "launch" was identical.'[3]

Out-of-body experiences also occur during many other situations. For example, extreme mental excitement caused by terror, excitement, or severe pain, can induce out-of-body experiences. An example of such an experience was given in the beginning of this chapter. The dying, and the nearly dead, may also undergo out-of-body experiences. A woman, who nearly died of massive internal bleeding after an operation to remove her womb, reported undergoing a typical out-of-body experience while being resuscitated. She wrote:

'I remember coming round from the anaesthetic and then drifting off and finding myself out of my body, over the bed looking down at my carcass. I was aware only of being a brain and eyes, I do not remember having a body. The next thing I realised was that I was neither a woman nor a man, just pure spirit. I could see the doctors and nurses round my bed frantically trying to give me a blood transfusion. They were having difficulty finding a vein in my arm. I was amused at all this fuss going on with my body as it did not concern me a bit.'[4]

Out-of-body experiences also occur during many other mental states and bodily conditions. One study of out-of-body experiences showed that only about one in ten out-of-body experiences occurs during conditions perceived as near-death states. Nearly all out-of-body experiences actually occur during states of mental relaxation such as dreaming, meditation, fatigue, cardiac arrest, or general anaesthesia. Only relatively few out-of-body experiences occur during states of mental excitation, such as during extreme

pain, childbirth, automobile and other accidents, or sexual orgasm.[5]
The disembodied mind is invisible. This may seem self-evident, but it is
worthwhile examining the evidence for this property of out-of-body experiences. To begin with, people reporting their out-of-body experiences only
ever say that observers paid attention to their apparently unconscious
bodies. They never, ever say that observers saw their apparently displaced
minds. Observers of people who undergo out-of-body experiences also
never report seeing the minds of these people displaced outside their
bodies. Furthermore, people have been intensively photographed since William Henry Talbot first developed practical photographic apparatus and
techniques in 1839 CE. Yet during all these many years since the discovery
of photography, and after many billions of photographs have been made of
people in many different conditions, no-one has ever succeeded in photographing the mind separating from the bodies of people undergoing out-
of-body experiences. All these things prove that the disembodied minds of
people undergoing out-of-body experiences are invisible.
The disembodied mind is immaterial. People reporting their out-of-body
experiences sometimes say their disembodied minds passed through solid
objects, such as walls and roofs. A solid object cannot pass through another solid object like a wall or a roof. Only an immaterial substance can
pass though a solid material object. In addition, people cannot see, sense,
measure, or photograph the disembodied minds of people undergoing out-
of-body experiences. All these things indicate the immaterial nature of the
disembodied minds of people undergoing out-of-body experiences.
People undergoing out-of-body experiences report perceiving many different types of sensations. They perceive their minds to be displaced outside
their bodies. They really do sense they are separated from their bodies, because they perceive their bodies from positions outside their bodies, and
they may even perceive themselves to be floating and flying. This sense of
disembodiment is not the only sensation that people perceive during out-
of-body experiences. The disembodied minds of people undergoing out-of-
body experiences are also capable of perceiving sensations such as sight
and hearing. This is why the disembodied minds of people undergoing
out-of-body experiences can accurately observe what occurs around their
bodies. They can 'see' what is happening to their bodies, and around their
bodies. They also often 'hear' what people say in the vicinity of their
bodies, as well as 'hearing' all other things occurring in the vicinity of their
bodies. This is why many people reporting their out-of-body experiences
can accurately relate what occurred in the vicinity of their bodies during
their experiences. Sometimes these reports even contain details that could
apparently only have been observed from positions outside their bodies.
But the sensations perceived during out-of-body experiences are curiously

selective. People undergoing out-of-body experiences can 'see' and 'hear', and they perceive sensations of displacement, floating, flying, or movement outside their bodies. Yet when reports of out-of-body experiences are care-fully analysed, no other sensations are ever reported. People never report feeling pain during out-of-body experiences occurring in situations where they would normally feel pain. In fact, they always say they 'felt no pain'. People never report feeling other people touching their bodies during out-of-body experiences, even when these other people were busy moving their bodies, touching their bodies, or doing other things to their bodies. They always say they 'felt nothing'. The out-of-body experience reports in this chapter give examples of all these things. This phenomenon of selective sensation is very strange. Why can people 'see' and 'hear' during out-of-body experiences, yet not perceive other sensations such as pain and touch? Nonetheless, despite the strangely selective nature of these percep-tions, these reports do show that the disembodied mind is capable of con-scious sensory perception.

The minds of people undergoing out-of-body experiences are unable to arouse their bodies to speak or move. Reports of people who tried speaking and moving during out-of-body experiences prove this. An example of this is the story of a woman who had an out-of-body experience caused by mas-sive internal bleeding after an operation. During her out-of-body experi-ence, she indignantly tried to tell the physicians resuscitating her to stop doing a venal cut-down that was needed to administer a life-saving blood transfusion[6]:

> *'I was brought back to my room after surgery[7] and was speaking to my nurse,' she reminisced in 1979, 'when a strange separated feeling between my body and my brain occurred. High above my body I floated wondering why so many doctors were around my bed and why they were doing a venal cut-down when I told them not to.'[8]*

This woman was surprised about all the fuss and people around her bed. A venal cut-down is a procedure during which an incision is made in the skin to find a vein through which a blood transfusion can be administered. Venal cut-down is performed without any form of local anaesthesia during life-threatening emergency situations, such as reported in this experience. It is a painful procedure when performed without local anaesthesia, yet this woman did not report feeling pain. She did try to tell the doctors per-forming the venal cut-down to stop. But apparently no-one heard her speak, they did not respond to her attempt to speak, and they did not stop. So it is very likely that none of the people around her bed heard anything. Her attempt to speak was no more than an unsuccessful attempt to speak.

There are many other reports of out-of-body experiences during which people made unsuccessful attempts to speak or to move. All these reports indicate that the condition of the bodies of people undergoing out-of-body experiences is such, that the displaced minds of these people cannot exert
any conscious control over their bodies.

The properties of the displaced mind during an out-of-body experience are
identical to those of the conscious mind. The disembodied minds of people
undergoing out-of-body experiences are no more intelligent than their conscious minds, have the same personalities as their conscious minds, and
have the same interests as their conscious minds. Indeed, all reports, and
all stories of out-of-body experiences show that the personality, emotional
structures, intellect, will, initiative, as well as all other properties of the disembodied mind are the same as those of the conscious mind. The out-of-
body experience of the woman undergoing childbirth demonstrates this.
She was understandably concerned about her predicament, as well as the
pain her body was apparently undergoing, but she gave no indication in
her report of changed intellect, emotional, or personality structure. Another
example is the woman who underwent an out-of-body experience due to internal bleeding after an operation. She did not understand what was happening. She proved this, because she wondered why so many doctors were
clustered about her bed, and also because she told them to stop performing the venal cut-down necessary to save her life. In fact her report gives
no indication that her disembodied mind had superhuman intellect, understanding, changed personality, or emotional structure, during her out-of-
body experience. These are only two examples among many such stories
and reports. But all these reports reveal the same thing; the out-of-body experience changes none of the properties of the conscious mind.

Reports of out-of-body experiences are always reports of remembered experiences. People never tell observers they are undergoing an out-of-body
experience during the experience itself. People undergoing out-of-body experiences are nearly always in an abnormal state of consciousness, and are
unable to speak, or exercise any form of bodily control during their out-of-
body experiences. So they are only able to tell others about their out-of-
body experiences after regaining consciousness and the ability to speak.
This means that people must remember their out-of-body experiences,
otherwise they cannot tell others about their experiences. The reports of
people observing individuals undergoing out-of-body experiences also confirm this. People observing the bodies of people undergoing out-of-body experiences see nothing except unresponsive, or unconscious individuals.
They cannot see, photograph, or film the minds of these people separating
from their bodies. It is only after these people recover the ability to speak,
and can tell of their experiences, that observers learn these people under-

went out-of-body experiences. This is the normal situation with out-of-body experiences. However, there is one exception to this rule, the rare situation of brain operations performed upon awake persons under local anaesthesia. During such operations, the patients are awake, co-operative, and can speak. Out-of-body experiences can be aroused in these people by electrical stimulation of parts of the general association cortex (see figure 4), and these people tell their physicians they are outside their bodies during their out-of-body experiences.[9]

This completed my list of the properties of the disembodied mind during out-of-body experiences. I made a summary of this list to clarify my thinking:

- the out-of-body experience is a conscious experience;
- the disembodied mind is displaced outside the body;
- the disembodied mind is invisible;
- the disembodied mind is immaterial;
- the disembodied mind is the same as the conscious mind of the person undergoing the out-of-body experience;
- the disembodied mind is unable to control the body;
- the disembodied mind is capable of detailed, but very selective perceptions;
- the out-of-body experience is a remembered experience.

These are the properties of the disembodied mind during out-of-body experiences. Many people believe the soul is the vehicle of the mind. If this is true, then these properties of the disembodied mind are actually properties of the disembodied soul during the out-of-body experience. These properties of the disembodied mind, or soul, during out-of-body experiences are not proof that disembodiment of the mind or the soul actually occurs. Instead, they are merely a description of the properties of the disembodied mind or soul during out-of-body experiences. Any explanation of the genesis of out-of-body experiences must be able to explain and predict these properties. But having learned these properties of the out-of-body experience, I realised that I still could not begin with any further study of the out-of-body experience. It was first necessary to clearly define, and understand how the conscious mind perceives what happens within the body, to the body, and in the world around the body.

Chapter 11

Sensation, Body & Mind

Mind is the intangible sum total of all intellect, personality, emotion, memory, and behaviour patterns. The mind of each person defines that individual. But the individual mind is not something isolated and intangible, nor is it without any relationship to the body or the world. The mind interacts with the body and the world to control the body, to perceive what is happening within the body, to the body, and in the world around the body. And the mind learns what is happening within the body, to the body, and in the world around the body through the senses.

These things may appear self-evident, but they require rigorous definition, because the relationships between the body, the mind, and the sensations perceived by the mind, are not always clear. Many people believe the mind is something separate, different from the material body, and that the soul is the vehicle of the mind, just as the body is the vehicle of the brain. But if this is true, how can the mind perceive sensations from the material world? How can the mind perceive sensations during out-of-body experiences, or at other times when the mind is not apparently disembodied? Are sensations conveyed to the mind through the senses of the body? Or, if the soul is the vehicle of the mind, are sensations conveyed to the mind through the senses of the soul?

Some people believe the mind can perceive what is happening within the body, to the body, and outside the body through the medium of paranormal sensory abilities. These people give examples of paranormal sensory abilities, such as the ability to see the human aura, the use of a mythical sense organ called the 'third eye', as well as many other paranormal perceptive abilities. But paranormal sensory abilities do not exist, which means that the mind only acquires sensory information through the physical senses of the body.

Physical senses are the known senses of sight, smell, hearing, taste, touch, position, weight, movement, and others. Physical sensations are sensed by sense organs, and sense organs are present in almost all body tissues and organs. The eyes sense light. The ears sense sound. The nose senses smell. The tongue senses taste. Muscle spindles sense movement, weight, and position. Naked nerve endings distributed throughout the whole body sense pain, touch, and movement. Pacinian corpuscles sense touch and movement. Golgi tendon organs sense stretch. There are many other special sense organs, but regardless of their structure, and regardless of the senses they subserve, all sense organs do the same thing, they convert the sensations they detect into sensory nerve signals conducted along sensory nerves. These sensory nerves ultimately all converge on the brain, an organ formed of 1200 to 1500 grams of soft, jelly-like nerve tissue, enclosed within the protecting confines of the hard bones of the skull that isolate, and shield the brain from the outside world. Sensory nerve signals conducted into the brain by these sensory nerves end in different parts of the brain. These different parts of the brain process, and interpret these sensory nerve signals, and the mind perceives these processed and interpreted sensory nerve signals as sensations.

This description of how the conscious mind perceives sensations has been proven again, and again during centuries of intense study of the human body. All these studies prove that the intangible mind only acquires information about what is happening within the body, to the body, and in the world outside the body, by means of the physical senses. The description of how the mind consciously perceives sensations, reveals that conscious perception of sensations by the mind goes through several links in what can be called the 'chain of perception'. These links in the chain of perception are:

- the 'stimulus' or sensation which activates the sense organs.
- 'sense organs' located just about everywhere within the body detect the stimulus, and generate sensory nerve signals.
- 'sensory nerves' conduct the sensory nerve signals from the sense organs into the brain.
- the 'brain' processes sensory nerve signals from the sense organs.
- the 'mind' somehow uses processed sensory nerve signals from the brain to perceive the sensation.

These links in the chain of perception are the mechanisms of the body through which the mind perceives sensations. Perception of light by the mind is one example of this chain of perception for a particular sensation. Light enters the eyes, and is focussed upon the retina at the back of each eye. Special nerve cells in the retina convert these light signals into sensory nerve signals. Sensory nerves going from each eye to the brain conduct these sensory nerve signals into the brain. The brain processes and interprets these sensory nerve signals in various ways. Somewhere after this last link in the chain of perception, the mind perceives light, colours, objects, and movements. But does this very material, and very physical chain of perception really exist? One way to determine this is to perform a step-by-step thought experiment to study the effects of conditions affecting each link in the chain of perception of light.

The 'stimulus' is the first link in the chain of perception of light by the mind. Blindfold yourself to remove the sensory stimulus of light. No light enters your eyes, your eyes function normally, the sensory nerves going from your eyes to your brain function normally, and your brain functions normally. Yet your conscious mind perceives no light, because no light enters your eyes to generate sensory nerve signals which are interpreted by your mind as light. Paranormal senses do not exist, which means your mind sees no light with any paranormal sensory ability. So you see no light at all. This indicates that a stimulus must be present to activate sense organs, otherwise the mind will not perceive anything. Light is the stimulus in this situation. Light must enter your eyes to activate the sense nerves leaving your eyes, and at the end of the chain of perception your mind perceives this light entering your eyes. This example demonstrates that the mind only perceives light through the mechanisms of the body.

The 'sense organs' are the second link in the chain of perception, and the eyes are the sense organs of light. Diseases such as 'retinitis pigmentosa', 'macular degeneration', or 'retinal detachment' destroy the functioning of the retina. Nerve cells in the retinas of people afflicted by these disorders generate no sensory nerve signals in response to light. So light enters the eyes of people afflicted with these disorders, is focussed upon the retina as normal, the sensory nerves going from the affected eyes to their brains function normally, and their brains function normally. Yet the conscious minds of these people perceive no light, because the diseased retinas of people afflicted with these disorders no longer generate sensory nerve signals in response to light. Paranormal sensory abilities do not exist, which means that the minds of these afflicted people see no light with any paranormal senses. People see no light through eyes afflicted by these disorders. This example also demonstrates that the mind only perceives light through the mechanisms of the body.

The 'sensory nerves' are the third link in the chain of perception. In the case of light, sensory nerves from the eyes conduct sensory nerve signals from the eyes to the brain. Many eye operations are performed under local anaesthesia. One standard technique of local anaesthesia is to inject a local anaesthetic drug just behind the eyeball. The effect of this is to block conduction of all sensory nerve signals along the sensory nerve going from that eye to the brain. A person undergoing this type of local anaesthesia sees nothing through the anaesthetised eye. The anaesthetised eye is blind. In this situation, light enters the anaesthetised eye normally, is focussed normally upon the retina, and the retina generates normal sensory nerve signals in response to the light. These sensory nerve signals are conducted along the sensory nerve going from the eye to the brain. But these sensory nerve signals are conducted no further than that part of the sensory nerve where the local anaesthetic drug blocks conduction of sensory nerve signals. Accordingly, these sensory signals do not enter the brain, and the mind of this person perceives no light through the anaesthetised eye. There are no paranormal sensory abilities, which means that this person also sees no light with any paranormal sense. This means the mind can only perceive light after sensory nerve signals generated by light enter the brain. This example also demonstrates that the mind only perceives light through the mechanisms of the body.

The 'brain' is the fourth link in the chain of perception. Sensory nerves conducting sensory nerve signals from the eyes end in various regions of the brain. A complex situation arises when one or more of these brain regions is damaged or malfunctions. The effects caused by these things range from total blindness, to strange phenomena such as 'blindsight', (a condition where a person cannot see light but is able to localise moving objects). The brain is the last link in the chain of perception of the sensation of light. Perception of light signals by the brain is always affected by damage, or malfunction of those parts of the brain interpreting sensory nerve signals from the eyes. No paranormal senses ever compensate for changes in vision caused by damage, or malfunction of those parts of the brain involved in sight. This is a fact. All studies of people with damage or malfunction of those parts of the brain involved in sight, prove again and again, that those parts of the brain processing sensory nerve signals from the eyes must function normally for the mind to see normally. The mind can only consciously perceive light and images formed by light, after the brain has correctly processed sensory nerve signals from the eyes. These studies also demonstrate that the mind only perceives light, and images formed by light, through the mechanisms of the body.

The 'mind' is the fifth and last link in the chain of perception. The brain processes nerve signals from the eyes in various ways, and somehow the mind perceives these processed sensory nerve signals coming from the eyes as conscious perceptions of light, of colours, of images, and of movements. Exactly how the mind actually perceives these processed nerve signals, and transforms them into conscious perceptions is as yet poorly understood. No-one knows exactly how this happens, and no way of looking at this problem explains how this happens. All that is known is that the mind perceives processed sensory nerve signals from the eyes as light, colours, images, and movements. I can only imagine two possible mechanisms for the transfer of processed nerve signals from the brain to the mind. If the mind is a product of the functioning of the brain, then the transfer of processed sensory nerve signals to those regions of the brain whose functioning generates conscious mind is a logical next step. A second possibility is that the mind really is an immaterial something, quite separate from the physical brain. If this is true, then the transfer of processed sensory nerve signals from the brain to the mind is something quite wondrous. Somehow processed nerve signals from the material brain are transferred into the immaterial mind. I cannot even imagine how such a transfer of measurable physical signals, into immeasurable signals in the immaterial mind could happen.

Having read all this, some people will quite reasonably say: 'Ah, but some people see images and lights aroused by memories, daydreams, dreams, visions, and hallucinations. No light, and no chain of perception are needed to generate these visual images perceived by the mind.' This is only partly true, because when the brain activity of people experiencing a visual memory is measured, those areas of the brain processing visual images are as active as if the eyes were viewing these same things.[1] The same is also true for visual hallucinations seen by people with brain diseases such as schizophrenia.[2] In these, and other similar situations, increased nervous activity in those parts of the brain concerned with processing the sensation of light, manifests as daydreams, visual dreams, visions, visual hallucinations, and visual memories. Electrical stimulation of some parts of the brains of conscious people undergoing brain surgery under local anaesthesia, can also generate visual imagery, or arouse visual memories. All this means that the mind perceives visual hallucinations, perceives daydreams, perceives dreams, and perceives visual memories, through the same brain mechanisms as images seen through the eyes. These facts also prove that the mind only perceives light, and images formed by light, through the mechanisms of the body.

This is a discussion of perception of light by the mind, but the same principles apply to all other sensations. The perception of all other sensations by the mind can also be analysed step by step in this same manner. All such analyses reveal the same thing; the intangible mind only perceives what is happening within the body, to the body, and in the world around the body, through the medium of the chain of perception. Furthermore, the brain must function normally, otherwise the mind will not perceive these sensations normally. This chain of perception of sensations by the mind is a fact. And this chain of perception indicates that perception of all sensations by the mind only occurs through the mechanisms of the body. The mind only knows what is happening within the body, to the body, and in the world about the body from sense information entering the brain. This means that changes in normal function, or malfunction, of any link in the chain of perception will affect the way the conscious mind perceives sensations. Experiments and observations of illusions aroused by abnormally functioning sense organs, sensory nerves, spinal cord, and brain all prove this. I will give some examples of the effects of abnormal function at each different level in the chain of perception.

The first example is the well-known experience produced by turning around and around and suddenly stopping. This is a wonderful example of how abnormal sense organ function deceives the mind. Stand on a soft surface in case you fall. Turn yourself around and around for about ten seconds. Stop turning, close your eyes, and hold on to something. You feel your body is still turning, or that the world is turning around your body. This is a sensation aroused in your brain by the functioning of the sense organs. Turning your body causes movement of fluid within 'semicircular canals' embedded within your skull next to your ears. Movement of fluid within these semicircular canals, stimulates sense organs within these semicircular canals to generate sensory nerve signals indicating that the body is turning. But the fluid in these semicircular canals keeps moving for a short time after you suddenly stop turning, causing sense organs within the semicircular canals to generate sensory nerve signals indicating your body is still turning. So your brain receives false sensory nerve information indicating that your body is turning. Your brain processes this sensory information, and your mind is tricked into perceiving that your body is turning. This means the mind perceives an illusion aroused by abnormal sense organ function. The fact that the mind perceives the body is turning, also means that the mind cannot directly sense the true situation. This is another example demonstrating that the mind uses the senses of the body to determine what is happening within the body and to the body.

Another example is that of a local anaesthetic injection administered by a dentist. The effects of such local anaesthesia are a good example of how abnormal sensory nerve function deceives the mind. Many people receive an injection of a local anaesthetic around the sensory nerves of their teeth prior to undergoing painful dental treatments. These injections often anaesthetise part of the face as well as the teeth being treated. After leaving the office of the dentist, many people notice a curious effect of the local anaesthetic injection; sensations of touch on the partly anaesthetised cheek feel very strange, and people sense that the partly anaesthetised part of their face feels massively swollen. But when they look in a mirror, they see that their face is not swollen at all. Yet even after seeing that their face is not swollen, their conscious mind still senses that their face is swollen. This is an illusion generated by abnormal sensory nerve function caused by the local anaesthetic drug. This illusion only occurs when the effects of the local anaesthetic drug start to wear off, which is why most people usually only notice this illusion after leaving the dentist's office. In the period when the effects of the local anaesthetic drug start to decline, some nerves are still anaesthetised, others are partly anaesthetised, and others have regained their normal function. The total effect of all these things is

that these partly anaesthetised sensory nerves conduct an abnormal mix of
sensory nerve signals into the brain, so generating these sensations, and
this illusion. This example also proves that the mind uses the senses of
the body to determine what is happening within the body, and to the body.
Spinal anaesthesia provides an example of how abnormal spinal cord function deceives the mind. I often administer spinal anaesthesia to people undergoing operations on their legs, hips, and operations in the lower abdomen. I insert a needle between the vertebrae of the spine, and inject a
small amount of a local anaesthetic drug into the fluid surrounding the
spinal cord, and the nerves coming out of the spinal cord. The local anaesthetic drug blocks conduction of nerve signals going from the brain to the
muscles of the whole of the body below the navel, as well as blocking conduction of sensory nerve signals going from the whole of the body below
the navel to the brain. A few minutes after injection of a local anaesthetic
drug, people cannot move any of the muscles in their bodies below their
navels, and their minds cannot perceive any sensations from the whole of
their bodies below the navel. They have no idea of the positions of the
anaesthetised parts of their bodies, often even forgetting the existence of
the anaesthetised parts of their bodies. This is beautifully illustrated by
raising a leg of a person undergoing spinal anaesthesia so that they can
see it. People undergoing spinal anaesthesia are always surprised when
they see one of their anaesthetised legs, and they almost always ask: 'Is
that my leg?' They also often exclaim: 'It certainly doesn't feel like my leg!
I can't even feel my legs!' These things indicate that their minds cannot
sense their legs without using the mechanisms of their bodies. This is a
third example that the mind uses the senses of the body to determine
what is happening within the body, and to the body.
Brain operations performed under local anaesthesia provide yet another example of how abnormal brain function deceives the mind. People undergoing some types of brain operation must be awake and co-operative during their operations. Many thousands of people have undergone brain operations while conscious under local anaesthesia. Such operations are
usually done to remove abnormally functioning parts of the brain, and
these abnormally functioning parts of the brain are usually found by administering small electrical shocks to the brain. Normal parts of the brain
also receive small electrical shocks during such operations, and the effects
of these small electrical shocks reveal the functioning of those parts of the
brain. People smell something when small electrical shocks are administered to regions of the brain concerned with smell. People see lights,
flashes of light, patterns of light, or even complete visual hallucinations
when small electrical shocks are administered to regions of the brain concerned with sight. People hear sounds, speech, or even music when small

electrical shocks are administered to parts of the brain concerned with the sense of hearing. People sense movements, touch, or changes in body weight, when small electrical shocks are administered to parts of the brain concerned with these sensations. Their minds only perceive the sensations aroused in their brains by the small electrical shocks, and their minds do not directly sense the true situation. Many more examples are available, and they all show the same thing; the mind perceives sensations aroused in the stimulated parts of the brain. This is a fourth example showing that the mind uses the mechanisms of the body to determine what is happening within the body, and to the body.

All these examples of the normal chain of sensation, as well as all these examples of what happens during various conditions affecting the chain of sensation, make the relationship between sensation, body, and mind very clear. It is irrelevant whether the mind is a product of the functioning of the brain, or whether the mind is something immaterial. There are no paranormal sensory abilities, so the mind only perceives physical sensations, and the mind only perceives these physical sensations at the end of a chain of perception whose functioning is based upon the mechanisms of the body. Experiment, and observation confirm the truth of all these things. This is the relationship between sensation, body and mind, and clarification of this relationship finally made it possible for me to investigate the out-of-body experience.

Chapter 12

Disembodied Feelings

People see their bodies from a vantage point outside their bodies during out-of-body experiences, actually viewing their bodies as an observer would. It is as if their minds were relocated outside the confines of their bodies during these experiences. Sometimes their displaced minds even travel from one room to another, from one place to another, from one part of the world to another, sometimes even to distant planetary and stellar systems. Many people believe the soul is the vehicle of the mind, and say that out-of-body experiences are proof of this belief. They believe these experiences truly are evidence of a temporary separation of the soul from the body. Indeed, out-of-body experiences are apparent evidence for the reality of the human soul. This meant I had to learn the nature of these experiences, so as to learn whether each person has a soul.

Out-of-body experiences are very intangible. The apparent separation of the soul from the body during these experiences cannot be seen, sensed, photographed, or detected in any manner. In fact, we only learn that people undergo out-of-body experiences, because these people tell us they underwent these experiences. Furthermore, the only apparent proof these people underwent out-of-body experiences, are the verifiable details of what they say happened to their bodies, and around their bodies during their experiences. But these things are always remembered details, because out-of-body experiences are remembered experiences. After some thought, I finally decided the only way I could learn the nature of out-of-body experiences, was to determine whether the mechanisms of the body could generate these experiences. My reason for using this method was to provide an alternative, provable explanation for these experiences. After all, if the physical mechanisms of the body can generate out-of-body experiences, then out-of-body experiences are not proof of the reality of an immaterial human soul.

My first step to determine whether the body could generate out-of-body experiences, was to define the properties of these experiences. This definition of the properties of out-of-body experiences did not prove that the soul actually separates from the body during out-of-body experiences, nor did it prove that the mechanisms of the body generate these experiences. Nonetheless, definition of the properties of out-of-body experiences did focus my study of the nature of these experiences, because any explanation of how the body could generate these experiences had to explain these properties of out-of-body experiences. My second step to determine the nature of out-of-body experiences was to examine how the mind perceives sensations. After all, the fact that people sense themselves floating, or moving outside their bodies, or perceive actual sensations of disembodiment, as well as hearing and seeing things during their out-of-body experiences, means they must sense these things in some way. The way the mind perceives sensations determines what the minds of people undergoing out-of-body experiences can sense, as well as the range across which the minds of these people can sense these things. Careful definition of all these things made it possible for me to study whether the mechanisms of the body could generate out-of-body experiences.

An understanding of how people perceive their bodies is also crucial to any understanding the nature of out-of-body experiences. Each person has a detailed mental image of their body within their mind, and continually refreshes this personal mental body image. Such a mental image of the body is essential for normal movements and actions, because when disease, injury, or illusions disturb this body image, people can no longer move normally, or perform normal actions.[1] The reality of this personal, mental body image can be illustrated with a simple exercise.

Close your eyes and think of your body. Think of how your body appears. You can visualise the appearance of your body within your mind: your clothing, hair, face, make-up, hands, feet, shoes, and so forth. You can picture the relative positions of your body, and your limbs within your mind, as well as the relative positions of your limbs, and body in relation to your surroundings. All these things form an image of your body and your surroundings in your mind. Your mind adjusts this mental image of your body as you move, speak, and breathe, continually refreshing your mental image of your body, and your body parts in relation to each other, as well as the relationship of your body, and body parts to your surroundings. You regularly refresh this image with the experiences you undergo at every moment of the day, what you see when looking at your reflection, as well as from comments made by other people about your appearance. Your mental image of your body continually changes. For example, move one of your arms. At any moment, without opening your eyes, you can accurately sense how fast your arm is moving, the direction your arm is moving, as well as the new positions of your arm in relation to your body and your surroundings. Furthermore, you can even sense how the position of your clothing on your body changes as you move your arm. Not only can you sense all these things, but you can also visualise all these things within your mind. This is an example of how your mind forms, and continually adjusts your mental image of your body.

Sensory nerves connecting sense organs in all parts of the body with the brain, conduct sensory nerve signals generated by these sense organs into the brain, continually feeding the brain with sense information about the body and its surroundings. The internal mental image of the body within the mind of each person is a product of the way the mind interprets this continual stream of sensory information. So at every moment, the mind has exact knowledge of the appearance of the body, the relationship of each body part to the body and its surroundings, as well as the relationship of the body to its surroundings.

Sometimes, mental diseases, bodily malfunction, or changes in normal bodily function, generates a copy of this internal body image which is seen by an affected person as a wraithlike twin of their own body. This twin, or double, is identical in every way, wears exactly the same clothing, and mimics their every action. Most people view this double at a distance, but never from a distance greater than two to three metres. Curiously, no-one ever reports feeling a sense of dismay, or consternation upon realising they are viewing a double of their own body. Instead, most people say they feel calm, dispassionate, or even indifferent when viewing such a double of their own bodies. Germans call such a double a 'Doppelgänger'. Affected people really see their doppelgängers, but no-one else except for these affected people can see them, no-one else can photograph them, and no-one else can detect them. Doppelgängers exist only in the minds of the people who see them. They are also known as 'autoscopic hallucinations', because they are hallucinatory images of oneself.[2] A physician once published the report of a woman who had autoscopic hallucinations containing all these elements. He wrote:

'Mrs. A., a retired schoolteacher, aged 56, had experienced autoscopic hallucinations since her husband's funeral. When she returned home from the cemetery and opened the door to her bedroom, she immediately became aware of the presence of somebody else in the room. In the twilight of the late afternoon she noticed a lady in front of her. Mrs. A. lifted her right hand to turn on the light. The strange lady made the same movement with her left hand, and thus their hands met. Mrs. A. felt cold in her right hand and experienced a sensation as if all blood ran out of her hand. Under the electric light she noticed that the stranger wore an exact replica of her own coat, hat, and veil. In spite of this unusual situation, Mrs. A. was neither surprised nor afraid. She 'felt deprived of any feeling,' and, without bothering any more about the intruder, she began to undress and took off her veil, her *hat, and her coat. The lady in black did exactly the same. Only then looking into the stranger's face, did Mrs. A. become aware that it was she herself staring at herself, as if in a mirror, and mimicking her own movements and gestures. It occurred to her it was her 'double,' her 'second self,' looking at her. She felt that it was more alive and warm than she was herself. Feeling extremely tired and weary, she lay down on her bed. As soon as she closed her eyes, she lost sight of her apparition. Almost at once she felt stronger, as if 'the life of this astral body' was coming back into her own body.'[3]*

These are the properties of autoscopic hallucinations. But what about out-of-body experiences? Many people quite reasonably say that autoscopic hallucinations are very different from out-of-body experiences. After all, during autoscopic hallucinations people perceive images of their bodies from a vantage point within their physical bodies, a perception very similar to how people viewing reflections of their bodies in mirrors perceive their bodies. This is quite different to how people undergoing out-of-body experiences perceive their bodies. People undergoing out-of-body experiences view images of their physical bodies from vantage points apparently outside their physical bodies. Even so, electrical stimulations of the brains of conscious people undergoing brain operations under local anaesthesia, reveal these two apparently different experiences to be no more than different manifestations of conscious, visual perceptions of personal mental body images.[4] The malfunctioning, or electrically stimulated brain is capable of generating all manner of sensations of position and movement, among which, perceptions of the personal mental body image from vantage points inside, or outside the body.[5] So out-of-body experiences are actually the same as autoscopic hallucinations, only the vantage point differs.

But if people undergoing out-of-body experiences are viewing internal mental images of their bodies within their minds, then a number of questions are immediately apparent. How can apparently unconscious and unresponsive people make detailed observations about what is happening to their bodies, and around their bodies during out-of-body experiences? Why do people undergoing out-of-body experiences feel a sense of displacement outside their bodies? Why is it nearly always impossible for people to arouse their bodies to speak, or to move during out-of-body experiences? Any explanation of how the body generates out-of-body experiences must also answer these questions.

To begin with, how can people undergoing out-of-body experiences make detailed observations about what is happening to their bodies, and around their bodies? After all, people usually lie unmoving, and apparently unconscious during out-of-body experiences. Paranormal sensory abilities do not exist, so people undergoing out-of-body experiences can only sense what is happening to their bodies, and around their bodies, with their normal physical senses. Even so, people who lie unmoving, and apparently unconscious, can make surprisingly detailed observations about what is happening to their bodies, and around their bodies. Each person can personally confirm this with a simple experiment:

> Lie on the floor, or lie on a bed. Close your eyes, and do not move your limbs, body, or head. Ask people to move around in the room, to speak, or to perform whatever actions arise in their minds. You will notice you can sense everything happening within your body and to your body, as well as just about everything happening around your body. You hear people moving and performing actions. From these sounds, together with your knowledge of what these sounds mean, you have a very good idea what is happening around you. If someone lifts one of your eyelids, you can see that person, their face, their clothing, as well as seeing what is happening around you through the corners of your opened eye. All this provides you with quite complete information about what is happening to your body, and around your body.

The reasons for the accuracy of such observations lies in the continuous stream of conscious, and unconscious observations each person makes of his own body and his surroundings. For example, before you lie still and start staring straight ahead, you know how your hair, your face, and your clothing appear. In fact, you always have a very good idea of the totality of your own appearance. You will also have seen how the room appears, and how everyone in the room appears. This means you also know the exact appearances, positions, and actions of yourself and others in the room at that time. So even if you do not see many things directly, you can still infer them from what you remember, from what you see through the corners of your eyes, from sounds, smells, vibrations, touch, and your other senses. Such use of the physical senses possessed by each person, enables people undergoing out-of-body experiences to learn what is happening within their bodies, to their bodies, and around their bodies.

In addition to such conscious perceptions, people undergoing out-of-body experiences also unconsciously perceive other sensations about what is happening within their bodies, to their bodies, and about their bodies. Some people undergo extremely violent or painful events during out-of-body experiences, but say they felt no touch, no movements, no blows, and no pain during these experiences. Such stories are examples of the fact that conditions such as extreme fear, terror, exultation, or sudden injury, can arouse a curious state of mind during which the brains of affected people register painful and violent sensations, but the minds of these people do not consciously perceive these sensations. This is called 'stress induced analgesia'. Typical examples of stress induced analgesia, are the reports of severely wounded soldiers who continue fighting heroically, only feeling the pain from their wounds when they are at rest. So people remembering painful and violent events occurring during their out-of-body experiences may well weave unconscious perceptions of these events into their reports of these experiences, even though they say they felt nothing at the time.

People perceive what is happening within their bodies, to their bodies, and around their bodies during out-of-body experiences. But this is not all they perceive. People also perceive themselves displaced outside their bodies, or actually flying, floating, and moving outside their bodies during out-of-body experiences. In fact, these sensations of displacement, flying, floating, or moving outside the body, are a fundamental aspect of out-of-body experiences. If these sensations of displacement, flying, floating, or moving outside the body did not occur, people would only see doubles of themselves, but not sense any displacement of their conscious minds outside the confines of their bodies. But how can the conscious mind perceive these sensations of displacement, flying, floating, or motion outside the body, when the body does none of these things?

This is explained by the way the mind senses body position, movement, and weight. Changes of body position, movement, and weight stimulate special sense organs. Stimulation of these sense organs generates nerve signals that are conducted along sensory nerves into the brain. The brain processes these sensory nerve signals in such a way that the conscious mind perceives sensations of position, movement, and weight. Such is the chain of sensation for sensations of position, movement, and weight. Abnormal functioning of the components in this chain of perception, such as the sense organs, the sensory nerves, or the brain, can also cause the mind to perceive hallucinations of position, movement, and weight. I will give some examples of such hallucinations.

The first is an example of a hallucination of movement caused by abnormal sense organ function. 'Semicircular canals' are sense organs sensing rotational movements. They are embedded within the skull next to the middle ear on each side of the head. The semicircular canals are so close to the middle ear that they cool down and malfunction when ice-cold water is squirted into the ear canals. When ice-cold water is squirted into an ear canal on one side of the head, the semicircular canals on that side of the head malfunction, and generate abnormal sense signals indicating rotation of the head. People to whom this is done, feel as if they are spinning violently, and may even fall down. This is an example of how abnormally functioning sense organs can cause the mind to sense abnormal movements.

The second is a hallucination of position caused by abnormal sensory nerve activity. A form of local anaesthesia of the arm called a 'brachial plexus block' provides a good example of a hallucination of position aroused by abnormal sensory nerve function. All the nerves going to an arm are bundled together just behind the middle of the collarbone. Injection of a local anaesthetic drug behind the collarbone at this point causes anaesthesia of the whole arm. This is because the local anaesthetic drug blocks conduction of nerve signals in all the nerves of the arm at this point, blocking conduction of nerve signals going from the brain to the muscles of the arm, as well as blocking conduction of sensory signals going from the arm to the brain. But not all the sensory nerve fibres conducting position information from the arm to the brain are anaesthetised at the same time. Before anaesthesia of all sensory nerve fibres is complete, some sensory nerve fibres are not anaesthetised. They continue to conduct sensory signals to the brain, while other sensory nerve fibres are anaesthetised, and conduct no signals to the brain. This means that the brain receives a very abnormal pattern of sensory signals from the arm at this time. The conscious mind often perceives such an abnormal pattern of sensory signals from a half-anaesthetised arm as a hallucination of position. People often say they feel their anaesthetised arm is lying in quite a different position than the real position, and are surprised when they see the real positions of their anaesthetised arms. This sensation of abnormal arm position is a hallucination of position aroused by abnormal function of the sensory nerves conducting position information from the arm to the brain.

The third is a hallucination of movement and position caused by abnormal nerve cell activity in the brain. For many decades, surgeons have studied the effects of administering small electrical shocks to the brains of fully conscious people undergoing brain operations under local anaesthesia. Small electrical shocks applied to parts of the temporal lobe in the area of the general association cortex (see figure 4), which is an area of the brain integrating sensations of body position and movement, can generate hallucinations of movement and position[6], and sometimes even arouse out-of-body experiences.[7] Such sensations were once aroused in the mind of a 33 year-old man who underwent a brain operation while conscious under local anaesthesia. Subjecting several parts of his brain to small electrical shocks produced the following effects:

> 'The stimulating current was shut off and the electro-corticogram showed that a slow wave 4 per second generalised rhythm had been set up as an after-discharge. While this was continuing the patient exclaimed: "Oh God! I am leaving my body". Dr. Karagulla, who was observing him, said he looked

terrified at the time of the exclamation and made gestures as though he sought help. When the electro-corticogram had returned to normal the patient seemed to be himself again. He was asked by the operator whether that had been like his habitual seizures. He replied, "A bit, Sir", then after a pause he added, "I had the fear feeling". Stimulations in the temporal lobe deep to point 11 produced vestibular sensations. Once he said he was spinning around. Once he felt as though he were "standing up".[8]

This man did not float above the operating table. Nor did anyone see his soul separating from his body. His body did not spin around, and he did not stand up. His sensations were not caused by real motion, changes of position, or separation of his soul from his body. His sensations of motion, changes of position, and feelings of disembodiment were hallucinations aroused by small electrical shocks generating abnormal nerve activity in various parts of his temporal lobe. Electric shocks are not the only way means by which abnormal electrical activity can be aroused in the temporal lobes. Brain diseases can also generate abnormal nerve activity in the temporal lobes. The case of an unfortunate woman suffering from a brain disease called 'multiple sclerosis' is a good example of out-of-body experiences generated by abnormal temporal lobe nerve activity:

'A female patient suffering from multiple sclerosis reported undergoing repeated out-of-body experiences. So her physicians performed a study of the nerve activity in different areas of her brain. This study revealed excessive nerve activity in both temporal lobes of her brain. She ceased undergoing out-of-body experiences after treatment with drugs which reduced the abnormal nerve activity in her brain.'[9]

These reports indicate that the temporal lobes of the brain are somehow involved in the generation, or maintenance, of the individual body image within the mind of each person, as well as the location of this body image. Nonetheless, these reports do not mean out-of-body experiences are only generated by abnormal temporal lobe function in the brain. After all, people can experience hallucinations of weight and motion, even when their brains, sensory nerves, and sense organs function perfectly normally. Such experiences are consequences of the functioning of the chain of perception for position, movement, and weight.

The body senses weight, movement, and position, with special nerve endings and organs that are sensitive to stretch. These special nerve endings and organs are called 'stretch receptors'. Movements and changes of position stretch the nerves in these stretch receptors, causing them to generate nerve impulses that are conducted along the sensory nerves into the brain.

The brain interprets these sensory nerve impulses to determine the weight, position, and movements of each body part.[10] Subsequently the brain combines this information with the current memory of the weight, position, and movements of each body part, to continuously refresh the mental image of the body. A thought experiment illustrates this process.

> Bend an elbow. The skin covering the outside of your elbow stretches and lengthens, while the skin covering the inside of your elbow shortens and folds. This means that the sensory nerve fibres in the skin covering the outside of your elbow are also stretched, and they generate nerve impulses in the sensory nerves. The faster you bend your elbow, the faster the sensory nerve fibres embedded in the skin covering the outside of your elbow are stretched, and the faster they generate nerve impulses. Sensory nerve fibres embedded in the skin covering the inside of your elbow are not stretched, so they generate no nerve impulses. Differences between nerve impulses transmitted into the brain from sensory nerves embedded in the skin covering both sides of your elbow, indicate your elbow is being bent, the speed with which your elbow is being bent, and the position of your elbow. But stretch receptors are not only found in the skin covering the elbow. They are also embedded in the tissues surrounding the elbow joint, in the muscles moving the elbow, and in the tendons of the muscles moving the elbow. The brain actually combines information contained in sensory nerve signals generated by stretch receptors located in all the tissues around the elbow, to determine the position, movement, and speed of movement of the elbow.

This is an example of how the body senses movement of the elbow. The same principles apply to all other sensations of body position, movement, and weight. 'Muscle spindles' are one of the many different types of stretch receptor. Muscle spindles are special types of muscle fibres embedded between the fibres of every voluntary muscle in the body. They are a special type of stretch receptor, because not only are they sense organs, but they are also muscle fibres. Muscle spindles contribute nothing to muscle strength, because muscle spindles comprise only about one in ten thousand, to one in one thousand of all the muscle fibres within each muscle.[11] When muscle spindles are stretched, they generate sensory nerve signals indicating position, movement, and weight. Muscle spindles are also muscle fibres, and when muscle spindles tense, they also generate sensory nerve signals indicating position, movement, and weight. Furthermore, the tension of muscle spindle fibres alters their sensitivity to the position of the body and its parts to movement, as well as to changes of weight of the body and its parts. Muscle spindles generate sensory nerve signals when body parts are moved, pushed, pulled, shaken, massaged, pummelled, vibrated, floated, or fall. Muscle spindles also generate sensory nerve signals when body parts move, thrash about, tremble, shudder, shake, or stiffen. The brain uses sensory nerve signals generated by muscle spindles to determine changes of position of the body and its parts, movements of the body and its parts, as well as the weight of the body and its parts. And even though there are relatively few muscle spindles in the body, sensory nerve signals generated by muscle spindles provide the brain with most information about sensations of body position, movement, and weight.[12]

Muscle spindles tense and relax under control of the brain, just like the muscle fibres between which they are embedded. Usually the brain controls muscle spindle tension unconsciously, so that muscle spindles, as well as the surrounding muscle fibres, tense and relax together to the same degree.[13] But conscious mental control, altered brain function, emotions, altered states of consciousness, exhaustion, and drugs, can cause muscle spindles to tense and relax to a different degree than the muscle fibres between which they are embedded.[14] Differences between the tensions of muscle spindle fibres, and the surrounding muscle fibres, changes the normal patterns of sensory nerve signals generated by muscle spindles in those body parts where this occurs. These changes in sensory nerve signal patterns generated by muscle spindles can induce hallucinations of position, movement, and weight. This is the mechanism by which changes in the functioning of muscle spindles can generate vivid hallucinations of position and movements, sensations of increased weight or lightness, as well as sensations of flying, floating, or falling.[15] This mechanism of differing tensions between muscle spindles, and their surrounding muscle fibres sounds rather abstract, but a simple exercise allows everyone to personally experience sensations of floating, as well as weightlessness induced by this mechanism.

> Stand in a narrow doorway. Keep your arms straight, move them away from your body, and forcefully press the backs of both hands against the doorframe for about a half-minute. Suddenly stop pressing against the doorframe. Let your arms relax and hang along the sides of your body, and you will experience something remarkable. You will feel your arms are weightless, or floating upwards, even though you know this is not true because your arms are hanging next to your body.

What is the explanation for this experience? Your arms hang next to your body, because the fibres of the muscles moving your arms away from your body are relaxed. But muscle spindles do not relax immediately after a short and intense muscular effort. Instead, they continue to tense for a short while after the muscle fibres between which they are embedded are totally relaxed.[16] The sensory nerve signals generated by these tensed muscle spindles indicate that the muscle fibres between which they are embedded, are tensed, and moving your arms away from your body, so deceiving your conscious mind into perceiving your arms as floating or weightless. This is just one example of how the mechanisms of the normally functioning body can generate sensations of changes of weight, generate sensations of movements, as well as generate sensations of floating or even flying.

Powerful low frequency[17] vibration of muscles specially stimulates sensory nerves in muscle spindles, generating sensory nerve signals indicating illusory movements, as well as changes of weight.[18] Perhaps this is why the beating of powerful drums, the low frequency beat of dance music played at deafening sound levels, the throbbing of powerful piston motors in motorcycles as well as racing cars, and the regular pounding and kneading of massage, exert such an attraction upon many people. The powerful, low-frequency vibrations, produced by all these things are felt throughout the body, and stimulate sensory nerves in muscle spindles to generate sensory nerve signals perceived by the conscious mind as pleasurable sensations of floating, or weightlessness.

Altered states of consciousness also affect the functioning of muscle spindles, and this changes the nature of the sensory information generated by muscle spindles.[19] Furthermore, the changes in brain function causing altered states of consciousness, can also modify conscious interpretation of sensations of position, movement, and weight generated by muscle spindles, as well as by other sense organs. This is why people sometimes perceive sensations of motion, floating, flying, and even out-of-body experiences during altered states of consciousness. This is why people sometimes undergo out-of-body experiences during the mental excitement aroused by extreme pain, violent events, terror, or sexual orgasm. This is also why people may undergo out-of-body experiences during the mental relaxation occurring during near-death situations, meditation, sleep, or general anaesthesia.

Out-of-body experiences occurring during general anaesthesia beautifully illustrate how the functioning of the body can generate out-of-body experiences. General anaesthesia is a curious condition. People are unconscious during general anaesthesia, but their brains still register sensations.[20] Their brains register the sensations of the operation being performed upon their bodies, the cutting, prodding, probing, stitching, drilling, and burning. Their brains register the sounds in the operating theatre, as well as the sounds of doctors and nurses speaking. Their brains register images, light, and darkness as their eyelids are opened or closed. Their brains register the tastes and smells of the anaesthetic drugs coursing through their bodies. Their brains register the smells of the warm wetness of their opened bodies, the odours of blood and intestines, the scent of pus, the stench of decaying body parts, and the acrid smoke from scorched flesh. Their brains register all these things. But their brains do not react to these things in a normal manner, because they are unconscious and feel no pain. So after awakening from anaesthesia they never remember anything of the sensations registered by their brains during their operations.[21] However, very rarely, some people may awaken during general anaesthesia and perceive all these sensations, even though they appear to be unconscious.[22]

Anaesthetic drugs cause the brain to function abnormally, regardless of whether the person is conscious or unconscious. Powerful painkilling drugs are administered during general anaesthesia, which is why people who awaken during an operation often feel no pain. Muscle paralysing drugs may be administered as part of the combination of anaesthetic drugs, which is why many people who awaken during anaesthesia cannot move, even though they may try to move. Muscle paralysing drugs paralyse normal muscle fibres, as well as muscle spindle fibres, although muscle spindle fibres are more sensitive to the effects of muscle paralysing drugs than are the surrounding muscle fibres.[23] Other general anaesthetic drugs also paralyse, and weaken muscle spindles to a greater degree than the muscle fibres between which they are embedded. Anaesthetic drugs such as suxamethonium activate muscle spindles, causing them to twitch and tense to a greater degree than the surrounding muscle fibres, so generating a flood of sensory nerve signals signifying changes of position, movement, and weight. Indeed, the enormous flood of sensory signals generated by suxamethonium is known to induce dreams in lightly anaesthetised people.[24]

There is an important practical aspect to operations performed under general anaesthesia. The patient must awaken on time, so that subsequent planned operations can occur within the time allotted to that operating session. Anaesthesiologists and nurse-anaesthetists know from experience the speed and style with which each surgeon performs each operation, the effects of the operation upon the body, and the sensitivity of each patient to the anaesthetic drugs used. This knowledge and experience enables them to appropriately adjust the dosages, as well as the concentrations of anaesthetic drugs, so that each patient is free of pain, and awakens within a few minutes after the operation finishes. But sometimes the dosages and concentrations of anaesthetic drugs are too low, and an occasional patient has insufficient anaesthesia for the pain of the operation. This is why some patients may make reflex movements in response to the pain of the operation, even though they are totally unconscious. This is why some patients may even awaken during general anaesthesia, even though they do not move and appear to be unconscious. And this is why some patients may awaken as well as move in response to the pain of the operation.

All movements are products of the tensing and relaxation of muscle fibres as well as muscle spindles. And the stretching, tensing, and relaxation of muscle spindles during all movements generates sensory nerve signals signalling changes of position, motion, as well as weight. The stretching, tensing, and relaxation of muscle spindles during reflex movements sometimes occurring during operations performed under general anaesthesia also generate sensory nerve signals signalling changes of position, motion, as well as the weight of the body and its parts.[25] Sensory nerve signals are also generated by the many different types of sensory receptors in the bodies of people undergoing operations under general anaesthesia. All these sensory nerve signals are combined, and interpreted within the unconscious brains of people under general anaesthesia. However, very rarely, some people may be partly conscious, although the anaesthetic drugs cause their brains to malfunction, which is why these people may interpret the totality of all perceived sensory signals as vivid dreams, or even out-of-body experiences.[26]

But this is not all. People undergoing operations under general anaesthesia cannot speak. So they can only report experiences they undergo during general anaesthesia after they awaken. And they can only report these experiences if they can remember these experiences. A young woman once told me of an out-of-body experience she underwent during a nose operation for which I administered general anaesthesia. Her experience demonstrates all these aspects of out-of-body experiences occurring during general anaesthesia.[27]

> She told me that she awoke during her nose operation. She saw her body as it lay upon the operating table, as if she was standing outside her body in a position at the right-hand side of her body. She realised it was she who lay upon the operating table, but felt no alarm or consternation upon realising that she was apparently standing outside her body. She saw the surgeon operating upon her nose, but felt neither the operation, nor any pain from the operation. She saw the assistant of the surgeon. She saw the anaesthetic assistant sitting next to the anaesthetic machine located at the left-hand side of her body. And she remarked that she could not see the faces of any of these people.

I was fascinated by this report, because I finally had an account of an out-of-body experience where I knew all the circumstances surrounding the reported observations. So what happened to this woman before, during, and after her operation? She was fully conscious when brought into the operating theatre. General anaesthesia was induced. Her blood pressure, blood oxygen content, heartbeat, as well as the concentrations of inhaled and exhaled oxygen, carbon dioxide, nitrous oxide, and other anaesthetic gases were continually measured. She was aroused from the general anaesthetic upon completion of the operation. We brought her to the recovery room only after she was fully conscious. And there she reported undergoing a short out-of-body experience during her operation.

Her blood pressure, blood oxygen concentration, and blood carbon dioxide concentration remained normal throughout the operation. No-one in the operating theatre observed anything unusual during the operation. No-one saw her soul standing next to the operating table. Her body remained upon the operating table during the operation. She could not move, breathe, or speak during the operation, because she had received a drug that almost totally paralysed all the muscles of her body, and was being mechanically ventilated through a tube placed between her vocal cords. But shortly before the end of the operation, when the effects of all the drugs she received were partly worn off, she made slight movements of her arms and legs. So, just in case she was awake, the anaesthetic assistant promptly administered extra doses of powerful sleep inducing and painkilling drugs. Otherwise there was no reason to think she was conscious at any time during the operation. She was only capable of speaking after she awoke from the general anaesthetic.

The observations she made during her out-of-body experience were correct, but her normal sensory functions explain all her observations. She was fully conscious when brought into, and out of the operating theatre, so she saw the people in the operating theatre, their clothing, the instruments, and the anaesthetic machine at the left-hand side of the operating table. She saw all these things before, and after her operation. She was apparently conscious for a short time at the moment when she moved slightly. But at that moment, her brain and the rest of her body were still affected by the anaesthetic drugs she had received. So she felt no pain from the operation she was undergoing, nor was she able to speak and tell people what was happening at that moment. In fact she did not even think of speaking during the experience. The effects of low concentrations of general anaesthetic and muscle paralysing drugs caused her muscle spindles to function abnormally. Her slight movements caused her abnormally functioning muscle spindles to generate a flood of sensory nerve signals about her body movements, weight, and position. Her brain malfunctioned due to general anaesthetic drugs, so she interpreted this flood of abnormal sensory nerve signals in such a way that she perceived herself as being outside her body, as well as generating an autoscopic hallucination. Finally, she was able to remember her experience after awakening. Her out-of-body experience was a product of abnormal muscle spindle and mental function occurring during reflex movements while under the influence of anaesthetic drugs.

Not everyone undergoes general anaesthesia, but nearly everyone experiences sensations of disembodiment, or even out-of-body experiences at some time. Sensations of disembodiment, or out-of-body experiences are actually very common. After all, nearly everyone has had a dream of flying, or a dream of falling. These are also out-of-body experiences.

Flying dreams are very common. Nearly everyone has had at least one dream during which they dreamed they were flying. During such dreams, people may dream of flying over known or unknown landscapes, and often these dreams are very vivid. These flying dreams are also out-of-body experiences, because the dreamer knows it is a dream, as well as perceiving themselves flying over known and unknown landscapes. I remember having just such a dream when I was a teenager. It was a vivid dream during which I dreamed I was flying and swooping over an unknown city landscape. It was such a vivid dream that I still remember it. But how can the sleeping body generate these dreams of flight?

Muscle spindles and muscle fibres are relaxed and weakened during sleep. Even so, it is quite normal for sleeping people to change their position every fifteen to twenty minutes, moving while changing from one level of sleep to another, moving slightly while dreaming, and moving during the eight to fifteen periods of awakening that occur quite normally during each period of sleep.[28] All muscle fibres are relaxed and weakened during sleep, but sleep relaxes and weakens muscle spindles to a greater degree than the surrounding muscle fibres.[29] These normal movements during sleep, cause the relaxed and weakened muscle spindles to generate sensory nerve signals indicating illusory movements, or illusory changes in body weight and position. Furthermore, sleep also changes the way the mind interprets sensory nerve signals. So the sleeping mind may interpret these sensory nerve signals as sensations of weightlessness, movement, and flying. And the sleeping mind may even clothe these sensations with dreams of flight over known, or unknown landscapes. This is the origin of flying dreams.

Sometimes, just before falling asleep, some people suddenly awaken with jerking movements of their limbs. These are called 'hypnic jerks'. More than nine in ten people have had at least one such experience.[30] Just before awakening in this manner, many people first feel as if they are floating above their bed. Then they suddenly feel themselves fall onto their bed with a jerking movement of their limbs. Sometimes a person notices a bed partner suddenly awakening with jerking limb movements. And their bed partner tells them that they felt their body floating and falling just before suddenly awakening with a jerk. These observations and experiences are as old as humanity. Some people say these experiences are caused by the soul suddenly and forcefully reuniting with the body. They say these hypnic jerks are proof of the reality of a soul. Yet no-one ever reports seeing the body of their bed partner, or the soul of their bed partner floating above the bed just before their bed partner awoke in this manner. So these feelings of floating and falling just before awakening apparently only occur in the mind of the person undergoing them. But how can the body generate these sensations?

Hypnic jerks are actually a product of altered sensations together with a dream. The causes of pleasurable floating sensations experienced just before falling asleep are the same as for flying dreams. That is, the slight movements occurring during normal sleep cause muscle spindles to generate sensory nerve signals interpreted by the half-sleeping mind as pleasurable floating sensations. Subsequently, a sudden random jerking movement of the limbs generates a flood of sensory nerve signals interpreted as falling onto the bed. This is how the body generates sensations of floating, followed by sensations of falling.

Vivid dreams often occur together with hypnic jerks. These vivid dreams are a type of dream that often occurs during light sleep, just as people fall asleep, or just before awakening. They are called 'hypnagogic hallucinations'.[31] Most people can remember having such bright and vivid dreams just before awakening. And most people also know these dreams often contain elements related to what they sense outside or inside their bodies during these dreams. A dream I had on Sunday morning on the 31st of October 1999 CE is a good example of just such a hypnagogic hallucination.

This Sunday morning, I was feeling lazy, and lay sleeping next to my wife who was reading a magazine and listening to the radio. While sleeping I had a vivid dream. I dreamed I was at the dentist for a regular check-up. He examined my teeth and explained that he also had to go to his dentist, but wanted to have his teeth examined before going there. I am not lazy, nor unwilling to help others, so I examined his teeth, as if this was a normal thing to do while at the dentist. While I examined his teeth, a female dental-assistant came into the consulting room and said that a woman in the waiting room wanted to speak with the dentist about a near-death experience she underwent while being treated by him. Surprisingly, this dental-assistant was a well-known faith healer, but I did not think this was surprising at the time. I also wanted to hear the story of this woman, so after leaving the consulting room of the dentist, I looked for her, and found her being interviewed in the middle of a busy waiting room by a psychologist. My interest in this woman's experience disappeared immediately, because I was not going to take part in this type of public 'near-death experience circus'. Accordingly, I left to go to my work in the adjacent hospital, where I was amazed to hear her interview being broadcast over the public announcement speakers throughout the whole hospital! My revulsion with this type of 'near-death experience spectacle' was complete, and was even sufficient to awaken me. I immediately told my wife about this dream. She laughed, and told me that she had listened to the radio as I lay sleeping next to her. And on the radio, she first heard an interview with a dentist, followed by an interview with this same well-known faith healer. Furthermore, this faith healer had also talked about holding a special 'healing session' for people who had undergone near-death experiences.

My dream contained several subjects discussed during this radio program. It was a wonderful example of the way signals from outside the body influence hypnagogic dream content. Hypnagogic dreams often occur in the same phase of sleep as hypnic jerks. So during hypnic jerks, some people clothe their sensations of floating or falling with vivid dreams whose content is related to these sensations of floating and falling. All these things explain the imagery and sensations of hypnic jerks.

Out-of-body experiences are usually chance events. But some people can voluntarily generate out-of-body experiences. These people say they really do experience a dissociation of their minds from their bodies. They claim their disembodied conscious minds really do float, fly, and move as directed by their minds. They claim the ability to direct their disembodied minds to travel from one place to another in their surroundings, to other parts of the world, to other planets, to other stellar systems, and even to other universes. They call this ability 'astral travel'. Some of these astral travellers have been studied under laboratory conditions while undergoing out-of-body experiences.[32] The scientists studying these astral travellers never saw the souls of these people departing from their bodies, nor did they see the bodies of these astral travellers float above their beds. None of these scientists ever managed to photograph or film the souls of these astral travellers departing from their bodies. But these studies did show that astral travellers were in a state of light sleep at the times they reported undergoing out-of-body experiences. And this is the same state of mind as that in which people experience hypnic jerks, or undergo out-of-body experiences during light general anaesthesia.

So out-of-body experiences reported by astral travellers are most likely experiences occurring only within their minds. Astral travellers are actually people who have trained themselves to enter a mental state similar to that between sleep and awakening. During this mental state they unconsciously make slight movements, as well as tense and relax their muscle spindles independently of the surrounding muscles fibres, so generating sensory nerve signals giving rise to sensations of disembodiment, of floating, and of movements. Their minds clothe these sensations of disembodiment, floating, and movements with autoscopic hallucinations, as well as visions of their surroundings so as to generate out-of-body experiences. But astral travellers are different to people reporting hypnic jerks, and flying dreams, because they are people who have trained themselves to arouse these experiences at will.

All these things explain how the body generates two key aspects of out-of-body experiences. The vision of the body is a result of displacement of the individual body image housed within the mind of each person, and the sense of displacement is a result of altered position sensation. But I have not yet explained why people undergoing out-of-body experiences are nearly always unable to consciously arouse their bodies to speak, or to move during these experiences. The preceding paragraphs have partly provided the answer to this question. Most reports of out-of-body experiences contain statements that the people felt serene and unconcerned at the time, and did not even think of trying to speak or to move. Accordingly, none of these people spoke or moved during their out-of-body experiences. However some people do try to speak, and do try to move during their out-of-body experiences, only to find they can neither speak nor move. This is not at all surprising in these situations, because these people are always in a condition in which they are physically unable to move: they are paralysed by sleep, paralysed by anaesthetic drugs, or paralysed by brain oxygen starvation due to any of a multitude of causes. This explains why people do not move during their out-of-body experiences.

Finally, all these things teach the circumstances during which the body can generate out-of-body experiences. These circumstances are:

- *Altered muscle spindle function.* A person may perceive sensations of abnormal body position, flight, and weightlessness when their muscle spindles tense or relax to a different degree than the surrounding muscle fibres.
- *Altered brain function.* Misinterpretation of sensory nerve signals from the body due to altered brain function may arouse autoscopic hallucinations, dreams of flying, as well as out-of-body experiences.
- *A combination of both.* Altered muscle spindle function, together with al-

tered brain function may also generate perceptions of out-of-body experiences.

Now I was able to explain all the properties of the out-of-body experience as defined in the chapter 'Disembodiment Defined'. So I made a list of these properties, together with the body mechanisms generating these properties, so as to show how changes in body and brain function can generate out-of-body experiences.

- *The out-of-body experience is a conscious experience.* This is true, because people must be conscious in order to undergo conscious experiences.
- *The disembodied mind is displaced outside the body.* The sensation of disembodiment is a hallucination generated by changes in the functioning of the brain, changes in sensory nerve signals generated by the body, or both. Either one, or both of these factors can generate hallucinations of disembodiment, floating, and flying, together with autoscopic hallucinations.
- *The disembodied mind is invisible.* This is true, because out-of-body experiences occur only within the minds of those undergoing these experiences, and no-one can see, or photograph the minds of people undergoing any sort of experience.
- *The disembodied mind is immaterial.* The mind is immaterial, and out-of-body experiences are hallucinations generated within the minds of those undergoing them. Hallucinations are no more than immaterial imaginings during which people are capable of doing anything imaginable.
- *The disembodied mind is the conscious mind of the person undergoing the out-of-body experience.* This is certainly true, because out-of-body experiences are experiences occurring within the conscious minds of those undergoing these experiences.
- *The disembodied mind cannot control the body.* This is true, because the functioning of the body during nearly all out-of-body experiences is such, that nearly all people undergoing these experiences lose all control over speech and movements.
- *The disembodied mind can accurately observe everything in the vicinity of the body.* This is also true, because immobile, paralysed, but conscious people can sense much of what occurs within their bodies, to their bodies, and around their bodies. These sensations enable the conscious minds of these people to generate surprisingly accurate imagery of all these things.
- *The out-of-body experience is a remembered experience.* People undergoing out-of-body experiences are nearly always incapable of controlling their bodies to move or to speak. They can only tell others about their out-of-

body experiences after recovering the ability to voluntarily move and to speak. This is why out-of-body experiences are always remembered experiences.

So the genesis of out-of-body experiences does not require the existence of an invisible and immaterial soul. The functioning of the mechanisms of the body can generate all aspects, and all manifestations of out-of-body experiences. These explanations are based upon measurable and provable aspects of human body function. The very fact that the functioning of the mechanisms of the body can generate out-of-body experiences, means these experiences are very likely no more than hallucinations generated by the functioning of the mechanisms of the body.

Nonetheless, even though it is very likely that the functioning of the body does generate out-of-body experiences, this explanation does not prove this is true for all out-of-body experiences. After all, is still possible that separation of a soul from the body also generates out-of-body experiences. I cannot prove this does not occur. So even though this explanation of the ways the body can generate out-of-body experiences is most likely to be the correct explanation for many, if not all out-of-body experiences, it is still no more than an alternative explanation of the genesis of out-of-body experiences. Accordingly, this explanation of how the body can generate out-of-body experiences neither proves, nor disproves the existence of the soul. This meant that my search for proof of the reality of the human soul was not yet at an end. I had to search further.

Chapter 13

Diabolical Dreams

Nightmares, nocturnal visitations by hags, incubi, succubi, and terrifying presences under the bed. Wild nocturnal flights over vast distances to attend orgiastic celebrations organised by diabolical entities. Nocturnal kidnap by little grey people from outer space. Such stories of nocturnal attacks, visitations, and experiences have been reported throughout all known history. People reporting such nocturnal experiences are not insane or hysterical fantasts, instead they are reporting what for them are wondrous, often terrifying, yet real experiences. But what is the nature of these experiences? Are they reports of real nocturnal experiences, visitations, and kidnap by real physical entities? Are they reports of nocturnal experiences caused by immaterial entities that are somehow able to make contact with, and influence the material world during the darkest hours of the night? Or are they events occurring only within the minds of those undergoing these experiences?

Such experiences are surprisingly common. One survey revealed that about one to eight out of every one hundred persons in the United States of America has undergone at least one such nocturnal experience.[1] The population of the world in the year 2001 CE was about six billion people. So if the world-wide chance of undergoing such an experience is about the same as in the United states of America, this means that about sixty, to four hundred and eighty million people now alive have undergone at least one such experience. A large number of people indeed! This also means that countless millions of people have undergone such experiences during past ages.

These experiences are quite common, so if people undergoing these experiences really are undergoing real physical experiences caused by real physical entities, then other people should be able to see, photograph, or film these entities as well as the experiences these people are undergoing. Yet despite the fact these nocturnal visitations are quite common, and despite the fact they have been reported for many thousands of years, no person has ever made a verifiable report of these entities visiting or attacking a sleeping person, nor have any verifiable reports been made of people being whisked away at night to attend orgiastic ceremonies organised by diabolical beings, nor have any verifiable reports of kidnapping by extraterrestrial beings ever been made. In addition, centuries of intensive observation, photographing, and filming of untold thousands of sleeping persons in sleep laboratories, hospitals, dungeons, prisons, police cells, and other institutions, have never yielded observations, photographs, or films of visitations by nocturnal entities, of people being whisked away at night to attend orgiastic ceremonies organised by diabolical beings, or of extraterrestrial entities kidnapping people.

Millennia of observation have failed to reveal that visitations by these nocturnal entities are visitations by real physical entities. These facts mean that only two other explanations for these visitations are possible: such visitations are hallucinations, or they are visitations by invisible and immaterial entities, because they cannot be seen, photographed, or filmed. If such invisible and immaterial entities really do exist, their existence is indirect evidence for the reality of other invisible and immaterial entities, such as the human soul. So I had to learn the true nature of these experiences of nocturnal attacks and visitations, because they were possible indirect evidence for the reality of the human soul.

My problem with determining the reality of immaterial nocturnal entities was similar to the problem of determining the reality of out-of-body experiences. No-one has ever managed to detect, sense, or photograph these nocturnal entities. This is not surprising, because such entities are supposedly invisible and immaterial. But this fact did mean I could not directly determine their reality. So I decided to examine whether the functioning of the mechanisms of the body could generate these experiences of nocturnal visitation, or experiences of nocturnal attack by invisible and immaterial entities. Here again, my reason for using this method was to provide an alternative explanation for these experiences. After all, if the functioning of the mechanisms of the body can generate experiences of nocturnal attack or visitation by invisible and immaterial entities, then these experiences are no longer proof of the reality of these entities, because the functioning of the mechanisms of the body can also generate these same experiences.

I began my study of nocturnal visitations and attacks by first examining the nightmare. Everyone has had at least one nightmare. Nightmares are terrifying dreams during which dreamers attempt to escape from horrible fates, or try to warn others of fearful and terrifying things. During such dreams, the dreamers try to escape, but discover their limbs feel extraordinarily heavy. They feel every movement requires enormous effort, as if they were walking through thick syrup or mud. Or they discover they cannot move at all, feeling as if they were pinned down to one place. They try to shout or scream, but little, or no sound issues from their mouths. Feelings of helpless despair and terror oppress and overwhelm them. The dreamers awaken, and remember the imagery of their dreams, as well as their emotions of overwhelming fear and helplessness. Such nightmares are as old as mankind. A Roman philosopher called Valentinus once described these same sensations more than eighteen hundred years ago in a Gnostic holy book called 'The Gospel of Truth'. He wrote:

> '... as if they were sunk in sleep and found themselves in disturbing dreams. Either there is a place to which they are fleeing, or without strength they come from having chased after others, or they are involved in striking blows, or they are receiving blows themselves, or they have fallen from high places, or they take off into the air though they do not even have wings. Again, sometimes it is as if people were murdering them, though there is no-one even pursuing them, or they themselves are killing their neighbours, for they have been stained with their blood. When those who are going through all these things wake up, they see nothing, they who were in the midst of all these disturbances, for they are nothing.' [2]

The functioning of the mechanisms of the human body during sleep explains all these sensations. Sleep is an unusual state of consciousness, because the body is partly paralysed during sleep. This is called 'sleep paralysis'. Sleep paralysis begins at the same time as sleep begins, is most extreme during a phase of sleep called 'rapid eye movement sleep', and ceases upon awakening. After falling asleep, people first develop paralysis of the eyelids, progressing to paralysis of the neck muscles, subsequently progressing to paralysis of nearly all body muscles during rapid eye movement sleep. The only muscles that are not paralysed during rapid eye movement sleep are the heart muscles, breathing muscles, muscles regulating intestinal function, muscles regulating urinary bladder function, and the eye muscles. Heart and breathing muscles are not paralysed during rapid eye movement sleep, otherwise everyone would die during sleep. Muscles controlling the functions of the intestines and the urinary bladder are not paralysed during rapid eye movement sleep, otherwise everyone would defecate and urinate during sleep. Muscles moving the eyes are also not paralysed during rapid eye movement sleep, because during rapid eye movement sleep the eyes move about actively, as if the sleeping are actively looking at the things of which they are dreaming.

The muscle weakness and paralysis occurring during sleep arouses the same sensations and emotions as muscle weakness and paralysis due to all causes. Muscle weakness and paralysis arouse very characteristic sensations and emotions, and these sensations and emotions explain what people experience during their nightmares, as well as the other experiences people sometimes undergo during sleep.

– Muscle weakness and paralysis cause people to feel helpless, because the body no longer responds normally to mental commands. Each attempt to move a weakened body part requires intense mental effort, while even intense mental effort fails to move totally paralysed body parts.[3]

- Muscle weakness and total paralysis arouse different sensations. Intense mental effort is needed to move weakened, or partially paralysed body parts, and these body parts feel as if they weigh much more than normal, as if they are 'made of lead', or 'weighed down by stones'. Even so, weakened body parts will move, albeit sluggishly and abnormally, and affected people say they feel as if they are trying to move though thick syrup or mud. But a totally paralysed body part will not move at all, even when intense mental effort is used to try to get the affected body part to move. Furthermore, totally paralysed body parts do not feel heavy at all.[4]

- Weakening and paralysis of speech muscles also affects speech. Weakening, or partial paralysis of the muscles generating speech means that intense mental effort is required to speak, shout, or scream, but very little sound issues from the mouth. Total paralysis of speech muscles means that even intense mental effort fails to generate sounds, and no sound issues from the mouth at all.

- Weakening, or partial paralysis of breathing muscles arouses feelings of anxiety, because people with weakened breathing muscles feel as if they are suffocating, or feel as if there is a 'tight band around their chest', or feel as if there is 'a great weight pressing upon their chest'.[5]

These are the sensations and emotions aroused by muscle weakness and muscle paralysis, and people whose muscles are weakened or paralysed sometimes translate these unpleasant and fearful sensations into experiences of fear, of terror, or of helpless despair. But this is only one aspect of the relationship between emotions and muscle strength, because emotions themselves can also affect muscle strength. Everyone knows the expressions 'paralysed by fear', 'weak with terror', or 'weak with laughter'. Everyone knows that powerful emotions sometimes cause people to become 'weak in the knees'. All these expressions are common sensations experienced by nearly everyone at some time. It is strange, but powerful negative emotions such as rage, anger, fear, terror, disgust, and loathing, as well as powerful positive emotions such as love, ecstasy, joy, and laughter may all cause muscle weakness. A rare disorder called 'cataplexy' is an extreme example of how emotions cause muscle weakening or actual muscle paralysis.[6] Cataplexy is a rare disorder during which people notice that even the mild emotions of daily life cause them to become weakened, or even paralysed and helpless. The case of a salesman was a classic example of this:

'A salesman, aged 45, married, who registered on May 17, 1927, for the previous three years had noticed an increasing desire to sleep. This had become worse in the past few months, and he would go to sleep whenever he sat down or when things were not particularly interesting. He had given up driving a car because of the frequent drowsiness. A few minutes' sleep was sufficient to refresh him. About the same time that the drowsiness started, he began to experience attacks of weakness. The first one occurred while he was dancing with his daughter; he became amused at some innocent remark and suddenly felt weak; his knees gave way, and he slowly settled to the floor, fully conscious but totally unable to help himself. Similar attacks of weakness had recurred frequently and were initiated by mirth or anger. The attacks were of a few seconds' duration and were usually associated with shaking and trembling of the extremities. The patient had an attack while in the clinic; he suddenly seemed agitated, the head slumped forward on the chest, the eyes closed, and he was unable to speak; he said afterward, however, that he was perfectly conscious of what was going on. He stated that he dreamed considerably at night and that these dreams were usually in the nature of a struggle or a fight with someone.'[7]

Emotions can cause muscle weakness or paralysis, and muscle weakness or paralysis can arouse fearful and unpleasant emotions. This relationship between emotions and muscle strength is something every person knows from personal experience. It is knowledge deeply rooted within the mind of each person, colouring all personal experiences of weakness and paralysis. And because the sensations of muscle weakness and paralysis are so unpleasant and frightening, most people associate muscle weakness and paralysis with emotions of despair, fear, loathing, horror, or terror. Sometimes the altered consciousness of a sleeping person senses the weakness or paralysis caused by sleep, and deep within the mind of each person is the knowledge that emotions of despair, fear, loathing, horror, or terror will render them helpless by weakening or paralysing their muscles. So the mind of the sleeping person perceives these normal sensations of weakness or paralysis, as well as the suffocating oppression caused by sleep paralysis, and clothes them with terrifying dreams of overwhelming despair and helplessness. People know deep within themselves what they fear and dread most of all, and they express these personal fears and terrors as dreams whose content is related to the sensations of weakness and paralysis they perceive during sleep. This is the nightmare; and people dread their nightmares, because their nightmares are dreams of overwhelming despair and helplessness in the face of their worst fears.

So if the greatest fear of some people is to see their loved ones being attacked, they may have a nightmare in which their loved ones are attacked.

And sleep paralysis will render them incapable of aiding their loved ones during their nightmare.

If the greatest fear of some people is to be kidnapped and mistreated by extraterrestrial beings, then they may have a nightmare during which they are kidnapped and mistreated by extraterrestrial beings. And sleep paralysis will render them incapable of resisting their extraterrestrial kidnappers during their nightmare.

If the greatest fear of some people is of rape or sexual attack, they may have a nightmare during which they are raped or sexually attacked. And sleep paralysis will render them incapable of resistance to rape or sexual attack during their nightmare.

Many more examples are possible. But all examples demonstrate that each individual determines the imagery he experiences in his personal dreams of terror. The imagery of individual nightmares originates within the deepest recesses of each person's mind, and reflects the innermost fears and desires of each person. Furthermore, the imagery of the nightmare provides an intuitively satisfying explanation for the sensations of weakness, paralysis, and helplessness perceived during these terrifying dreams.

But sleep paralysis does not always coincide with sleep. Sometimes sleep paralysis may start just before falling asleep, and sometimes sleep paralysis may continue after awakening. Affected persons suddenly discover they are paralysed and helpless just before they fall asleep, or paralysed and helpless just after they awaken. This is called 'conscious sleep paralysis'. Conscious sleep paralysis is quite common, because as many as three in twenty people have experienced at least one episode of conscious sleep paralysis.[8]

People with conscious sleep paralysis experience all the sensations and emotions aroused by muscle paralysis. Paralysis of limb muscles means they cannot move, and they feel their paralysed limbs to be heavier than normal, as if 'weighted by stones', or 'made of lead'. Paralysis of speech muscles means they cannot speak, and even though they may try to speak, they can utter no sound. Sometimes they also develop paralysis of chest wall muscles, causing them to experience sensations of crushing weight upon the chest, or feelings of suffocation.[9] Some people develop numbness and tingling of their limbs, hands and feet at the onset of sleep paralysis.[10] During episodes of sleep paralysis, some people even sense the presence of other persons or entities near to them, under their bed, or in the same room.[11] Most people are anxious, or even terrified the first time they experience conscious sleep paralysis, but this anxiety disappears with subsequent attacks of conscious sleep paralysis after they realise they are in no danger.

Vivid dreams known as hypnagogic hallucinations are common during the period between sleeping and awakening. The period between sleeping and awakening is also the period when sleep paralysis may be present, which is why some people have hypnagogic hallucinations during these periods of conscious sleep paralysis. Affected people combine their perceptions of the unpleasant sensations of helplessness, and suffocation aroused by sleep paralysis, with imagery arising from individual and collective fears into terrifying hypnagogic hallucinations. They may have hallucinations of horrid and fearful things, of beings that try to hurt, strangle, suffocate, kill, or even attempt sexual intercourse with them.[12] These sensations explain many of the legends of our ancestors. Our ancestors experienced their world as a wondrous, sometimes dark, and terrifying place. They believed their world to be dominated by forces of which they had no understanding, and over which they could exert no control. Their mental world was equally wondrous, dark, and terrifying. It was a world populated by malevolent, invisible, and immaterial entities forever trying to steal, and gain power over their minds and their souls. And because the sensations of paralysis are so unpleasant, our ancestors clothed their sensations of conscious sleep paralysis with dreams of nocturnal attacks and visitations by malevolent demonic beings. Such visitations were described in a passage written in 1834 CE, in which we read that:

> '... Imagination cannot conceive the horrors it (the Nightmare) frequently gives rise to, or language to describe them in adequate terms ...
> Everything horrible, disgusting or terrifying in the physical or moral world is brought before him in fearful array; he is hissed at by serpents, tortured by demons, stunned by the hollow voices and cold touch of apparitions ...
> At one moment he may have the consciousness of a malignant demon being at his side; then to shun the sight of so appalling an object, he will close his eyes, but still the fearful being makes its presence known; for its icy breath is felt diffusing itself over his visage, and he knows that he is face to face with a fiend. Then if he looks up, he beholds horrid eyes glaring upon him, and an aspect of hell grinning at him with even more hellish malice. Or he may have the idea of a monstrous hag squatted upon his breast mute, motionless and malignant.'[13]

People still report undergoing the same experiences, although they no longer express them in the same terms. So a woman who recently told of her experiences, wrote:

> 'Hi, I am a 27 year old female and have been suffering from what I think is "sleep paralysis" for the past 12 or so years. It started just being unable to move, like someone was on top of me, pinning me down. And although I

was trying with all my might to move or to scream, all I could do was barely wiggle my toes and faintly murmur. In the beginning it was very frightening and I would try with all my might to wake up. Upon waking I would be unable to resume sleep for at least a few hours. Now I have become somewhat used to them. Sometimes I even lie back and see how long I can take that awful, overpowering feeling. In the end, I always try to wake myself up. Over the years this " thing" (as I imagine it) has kind of metamorphosized into a dark being, something who is doing this deliberately to me for some reason. I guess this is something that I may have invented in my head to deal with it. I am not really sure. After I got used to it, I never really questioned it. It still occurs about every 2 months or so. Sometimes once a night, other times it can happen several times in one night.'[14]

These nocturnal beings sometimes make sounds, or speak, as one man who regularly experienced sleep paralysis wrote:

'I've had maybe 10-15 or so of these episodes over my 38 years so far – the majority or perhaps half of these when I was a kid, when they were very frightening, the more so for not knowing how to explain them. The most typical pattern these events take in my case is as follows: just after falling asleep – occasionally later – I'll "hear" a hissing sound which appears to "close in", coupled with the real and intense feeling that someone else (unseen) is very near in the room or who is approaching fast and who is certainly malevolent. Very occasionally this might be accompanied by undefined voices very near my head – (as a kid this may in fact have been the presence of brothers or sisters in the room). At this point my eyes are open, heartbeat very fast and I am aware that this is happening (again) and I that I am semi-conscious. I am totally unable to move – even eye movements and I know I am not asleep, my eyes are open and I'm looking at some part of the room. The panic and struggle lasts maybe 10-15 seconds then I "wake" fully. As a child this was a very intense and frightening experience, and remains slightly less so as an adult – ...'[15]

People with conscious sleep paralysis awaken to find they are unable to move, and they may clothe their unpleasant sensations of paralysis with visions of demonic attack. This is the origin of the stories of malignant entities or demons that attack people at night. But our ancestors believed in these stories. They believed in the reality of malevolent nocturnal entities, and even developed a demonology of the night based upon this belief.[16] They recognised several forms of nocturnal demonic attack, such as nocturnal attack by hags, nightmares, incubi, and succubi. These terms are worth defining, because their definition, together with knowledge of the known effects of sleep paralysis, reveals the nature of such demonic attacks. Hundreds of years ago, the nightmare was defined as 'a female monster supposed to settle upon people and animals in their sleep producing a feeling of suffocation'.[17] The nightmare was also known by other names, such as hag, incubus, or succubus. The meaning of the term nightmare has changed with time, and now a nightmare is defined as 'a feeling of suffocation or great distress felt during sleep, from which the sleeper vainly tries to free himself; a bad dream producing these or similar sensations'.[18] And many newer dictionaries simply define a nightmare as a frightening or terrifying dream.

A hag is 'an evil spirit, demon, or infernal being, in female form'.[19] A person tormented by a hag was said to be 'hag-ridden'. They were ridden and oppressed by a hag in the same way as by a nightmare.

A demon is defined as 'a being of a nature intermediate between gods and men; an inferior divinity spirit (including the souls of deceased persons)'. A demon is supposedly superhumanly evil and malevolent. A fiend is another name for a demon. [20]

A 'succubus' is defined as 'a demon in female form supposed to have carnal intercourse with men in their sleep'. [21] The experience of a succubus is the same as that of an incubus.

An incubus is 'a person, or thing that weighs upon and oppresses like a nightmare'.[22] An incubus is also defined as 'a feigned evil spirit or demon, supposed to descend upon persons in their sleep, and especially to seek carnal intercourse with women'.[23] The incubus is the male form of the succubus. Incubi may descend upon sleeping women in the forms of demons or strangers. Sometimes incubi appear to women in the form of men they love, desire, or know. Muscle paralysis renders women helpless in the presence of the incubus, and helpless to resist the sexual attentions of the incubus. Sexual intercourse between an incubus and a woman can even cause pregnancy. This last belief was extensively explained and propagated as official truth in an infamous book written in 1483 CE called the 'Malleus Maleficarum', which is Latin for 'The Hammer of Evil'. Indeed, at the time this book was written, it was even an offence punishable by death to believe otherwise. The Malleus Malifecarum clearly expounded the belief that a demon could have sexual intercourse with a man in the form of a succubus, somehow contain and transport the semen of that man, subsequently transform into an incubus, and inject this semen into the next woman with which it had sexual intercourse, so inseminating and rendering this woman pregnant.[24] People once wholeheartedly believed in these things. After all, the word of God as revealed to them in their main religious book, the Holy Bible, affirmed this belief.

'There were giants[25] on the earth in those days; and also after that, when the sons of God came in unto the daughters of men, and they bare children to them, the same became mighty men which were of old, men of renown.'[26]

Sleep paralysis generates all the sensations of weakness, crushing weight, helplessness, and suffocation attributed to these demonic visitors. People perceiving these sensations of muscle weakness and paralysis during sleep may clothe these sensations with terrifying imagery, and fantastical entities arising from their own innermost fears and terrors. But no person lives alone. The thinking and the thought patterns of each person is determined and modified by their upbringing, other influences from the society in which they live, as well as other matters that occupy their individual minds. These factors all determine the nature of the imagery contained in individual nightmares and dreams of demonic attack.

Yet these are not the only factors determining the imagery contained in nightmares and dreams of demonic attack. Random movements occurring during sleep also determine the imagery contained in these dreams. Everyone has seen sleeping people make slight movements, twitch slightly, make sounds, or sometimes even speak. Indeed, it is quite normal to move during sleep. People are continuously paralysed during sleep, but this is not a total paralysis, otherwise people would stop breathing and die during sleep. This is why it is possible for people to move and to speak during sleep. Most people awaken about eight to fifteen times each night, but they never remember these short awakenings. In addition, most sleeping people change their position every fifteen to twenty minutes, make movements while changing from one level of sleep to another, and make movements while dreaming.[27] So a sleeping person may not only experience sensations of paralysis and helplessness caused by sleep paralysis, but the sensory nerve signals generated by random movements occurring during sleep, may at times also arouse sensations of movements, of fighting and struggle, of walking and running, of wading though thick mud, of floating, and even of flying.[28] Such sensations may generate dreams where people sense they are moving, flying, or floating at one part of a dream, or paralysed and helpless during another part of the same dream. These sensations are universal, even though the visual, auditory, and emotional content of such dreams differs from one person to another, as well as from one culture to another.

Even now, in some less developed parts of the world, as well as among some people in more technologically developed parts of the world, there is a belief that some people, almost always women, possess supernatural powers as a result of some sort of unholy pact with demons.[29] In past ages this belief was widespread, even universal. These people were called 'witches', and were generally feared and loathed. A generally held attitude towards witches was once expressed in a book called 'The History of Witchcraft':

> *'In the following pages I have endeavoured to show the witch as she really was; an evil liver; a social pest and parasite; the devotee of a loathly and obscene creed; an adept at poisoning, blackmail, and other creeping crimes; a member of a powerful secret organisation inimical to Church and State; a blasphemer in word and deed; swaying the villagers by terror and superstition; a charlatan and a quack sometimes; a bawd; and abortionist; the dark counsellor of lewd court ladies and adulterous gallants; a minister to vice and inconceivable corruption; battening upon the filth and foulest passions of the age.'*[30]

Such attitudes towards witches were the origin of the official persecution, and witch hunts occurring in Western Europe from about 1233 CE until the last judicial execution of witches in 1792 CE.[31] About 100,000 accused witches were judicially executed during these centuries, mainly during the witch hunting mania in Western Europe between 1500 to 1650 CE. And of those executed, somewhat more than three quarters were women.[32] People also believed witches held unholy celebrations called a 'Sabbat', in mimicry of the normal accepted official worship of God on Sunday called the 'Sabbath'. The witches Sabbat is defined as 'a midnight meeting of demons, sorcerers, and witches, presided over by the devil'.[33] During the centuries of official witch hunting, local judicial authorities complied enormous amounts of witness, and personal descriptions of the properties, as well as the personal experience of the witches Sabbat.

A witches Sabbat was typically held in a remote location, sometimes near, and sometimes far from the homes of those attending. It always began after midnight, and would last until dawn. Those attending the Sabbat would walk to the location of the Sabbat, if it were held close to their homes. However, if the Sabbat was held at a location far from their homes, they would fly there on a broomstick, fly there on the back of a goat or other beasts, or were flown there by demons. Once congregated at the place of the Sabbat, they would perform rites of abasement, homage and sacrifice to the devil, dance wildly, drink copiously, gorge themselves upon the plentiful food and drink present, and perform sexual acts, including copulation with each other, as well as with the demons present at the Sabbat. Most of those reporting attendance at a Sabbat participated wholeheartedly in all aspects of the Sabbat. Yet this was not always so, because some people reported feeling themselves powerless to resist being transported to and from the Sabbat, as well as powerless to resist participation in the Sabbat. At the moment of daybreak, or upon the sound of crowing of a cock, all participants would return home the same way they came. Such experiences are nearly always only reported by the witches themselves, seldom, or never by others. No-one ever witnessed these things happening, except in those rare situations where people actually were physically present at such meetings. However, there are reports of women and men saying they were present at a Sabbat, at the same time as their bodies were witnessed to be lying still and motionless in bed, or in a prison cell.[34]

Except for those witnessed accounts where people physically walked to and from a Sabbat, actually physically attending a locally arranged Sabbat, these Sabbat-experiences are readily explained as products of the sensations generated by sleep paralysis in the minds of sleeping people, covered with a sheen of the then current socio-cultural belief systems. But societies and popular thought processes are ever changing. Most people no longer believe in succubi, incubi, demons, hags, nightmares, or the witches Sabbat. This ancient demonology of the night and the Sabbat, has now been replaced in some parts of the world with the demonology of abduction, and misuse by technologically advanced beings from distant planets. There are many reports of such extraterrestrial abductions and abuse, among which is the story of a young woman called 'Kathie D.':

> 'Under hypnosis, Kathie D. recalled seeing her first UFO[35] in the winter of 1977. The memory is disjointed, blurred and discontinuous but, briefly, she remembered being parked in a car with two friends, when she was assailed by feelings which would later become familiar – a scared, tingly sensation of dread and uncanniness. She found herself paralyzed. She could see nothing, but felt her legs being pulled away from her body, a feeling more unpleasant than painful. She then felt something hard being pushed into her uterus. At this point Hopkins[36] persuaded her to take a peek at her surroundings. She was surprised to find that she was not, as she thought, in the car, but in a curved lit room. She also saw the big-eyed grey alien who was by now familiar to her from other remembered abductions. (He was not always terrifying by any means; he often smiled, with his eyes rather than his mouth, and sometimes patted her reassuringly so that she felt happy and relaxed.)'[37]

The experience of this woman is a modern version of a visitation by an incubus, or of a witches' Sabbat. It is very likely that this woman suffered from a sleep disorder called 'narcolepsy'. This is a disorder causing people to suddenly fall asleep at random moments during the day. Narcolepsy caused her to fall asleep, and she experienced the effects of sleep paralysis as well as other sensations generated by the slight movements she made while partly paralysed. She also experienced hypnagogic hallucinations of that which she feared most, sexual attack, perceiving her assailants as small, grey, anonymous, man-like beings.

All other reports of abductions and sexual misuse by extraterrestrial beings contain similar recurring elements. For example, other than in the report of Kathie D., most extraterrestrial abductions occur at night, often during the early hours of the morning. Abducted persons are usually not asleep at the time of the abduction, but have often just woken. They find themselves paralysed, and are floated, or transported to a waiting spacecraft which brings them to a larger mother ship. Once in the mother ship they are brought to an examination room, where they find they are paralysed and unable to speak. They are subjected to a thorough bodily examination by their extraterrestrial abductors, during which most attention is directed at examining their genital and reproductive organs. During all these procedures, mental calm and physical immobility are enforced by telepathic contact with a 'mentor', or special mind-control machines. Instruments may be inserted into the vaginas of women to further examine their reproductive systems, to harvest eggs, or to introduce hybrid alien and human foetuses. Men may sometimes be induced to have sexual intercourse with extraterrestrial females, or machines may be attached to their penises to extract semen. Occasionally, men and women kidnapped at the same time are compelled to engage in sexual intercourse with each other. Finally, the victims are returned in the same way as they were abducted to the locations from which they were kidnapped. They soon forget their experiences, subsequently only remembering their abduction experiences while under hypnosis. No-one ever witnesses these abductions. Husbands and wives sleeping next to abducted persons are seemingly 'switched off', or sleep through the period of the abduction. The same occurs with others who are in close proximity to abducted persons during the period of the abduction. They also never notice aliens kidnapping the person near to them, because they are apparently 'frozen', acting as if 'time had stopped' for them.[38]

Stripping Sabbat and extraterrestrial abduction experiences of all the trappings, as well as the obsessions prevalent in the societies reporting these experiences, reveals both experiences contain the same elements. Superficial details certainly do differ, but both experiences are essentially identical. Normal changes in body function during sleep, or narcolepsy, explain the experiences undergone by Sabbat participants, as well as the experiences undergone by those reporting abduction by extraterrestrial entities.

Consider reports of experiences of extraterrestrial abduction. These experiences nearly always occur at night during the early hours of the morning. Everyone dreams about four to six times, and awakens about eight to fifteen times each night. But most people seldom remember all their dreams and awakenings. Early morning is when most of these dreams occur, and this is also the time when people are most likely to experience a period of conscious sleep paralysis. So abducted persons are most likely not asleep at the time of the abduction, but have just awoken to discover they are paralysed, and they experience sensations aroused by sleep paralysis. Slight movements, together with altered muscle spindle function, generate a flood of sensory nerve signals informing their minds that they are floating and moving, even though they are helpless. They explain these sensations with the illusion of being floated and transported by extraterrestrial beings to a spaceship. They arrive in the spaceship, and continued sleep paralysis ensures that they remain helpless and immobile. Continued sleep paralysis arouses sensations of other entities, of touch, of movements, sensations of body examinations and probing, as well as sensations of being operated upon. People explain their helplessness and calm acceptance of all these things with hallucinations of telepathic commands, or mind-controlling machines. Some people report being forced to engage in sexual acts during their experiences of extraterrestrial abduction. In fact, sexual arousal while dreaming is normal for both men and women. Men experience penile erection both during normal dreaming[39], as well as during narcoleptic dreams[40], and sometimes this is coupled with erotic dreams progressing to ejaculation. Similar changes also occur in the minds and genitalia of dreaming women.[41] These facts explain the sensations of sexual arousal reported by men and women during experiences of extraterrestrial abduction. People in the vicinity of those abducted by extraterrestrial beings appear to be 'frozen in time', because these illusions of extraterrestrial abduction are of very short duration, even though the person undergoing the illusion feels that the experience lasted longer than it really did. All these things mean that normal changes in body function during sleep or narcolepsy explain all aspects of experiences of extraterrestrial kidnap.

Sabbat experiences contain exactly the same sensory elements as extraterrestrial abduction experiences. The time period they occur is the same, because both experiences usually occur during the early hours of the morning. Sabbat participants are transported to the locations of their experiences by demons, fly there on broomsticks, or on the backs of goats or other beasts. The basic fact of flying to the location of the experience is also reported by those who say they were abducted by extraterrestrial beings, because these people fly to the destinations of their experiences in spaceships. Participants are powerless to resist participation in a Sabbat, because during the Sabbat they are under the mental control of devils or demons. People reporting kidnap by extraterrestrial beings also report being under a form of forced mental control, only they say this is a form of telepathic control exerted by their extraterrestrial kidnappers, or by extraterrestrial mind-control machines.

Sabbat participants undergo sexual experiences in the form of orgies, or forced sexual contact with demons. This is similar to experiences reported by those who said they were abducted by extraterrestrial beings, because these people also report undergoing forced sexual experiences while subject to mental control exerted by extraterrestrial beings. People observing those undergoing Sabbat experiences, report that the persons undergoing such experiences lie still and unmoving during the period they report attending a Sabbat, exactly the same as is reported for those abducted by extraterrestrial abductions. In other words, the sensory elements of Sabbat attendance and experiences of extraterrestrial abduction are the same.[42]

All these things indicate that experiences of visitations by such invisible and immaterial entities are most likely visions arising only in the minds of those undergoing these experiences. Indeed, the functioning of the mechanisms of body can generate all aspects of these experiences of nocturnal demonic attack, experiences of the witches Sabbat, as well as all aspects of experiences of kidnap by extraterrestrial beings. Furthermore, the functioning of the mechanisms of the body explains all aspects of these experiences with provable and measurable phenomena. In my opinion, this is the explanation of all these truly wondrous experiences.

Yet, no matter how convincing this explanation appears, it can only be regarded as an alternative explanation for these experiences, because even though the functioning of the mechanisms of the body can generate all aspects of these experiences, this is not absolute proof that there are no immaterial aspects to the universe. After all, these experiences of nocturnal demonic visitation may be real visitations by immaterial entities, and experiences of a witches Sabbat may be real experiences of attendance at some unholy celebration held by immaterial entities, just as experiences of kidnap by extraterrestrial beings may be real experiences of kidnap by extraterrestrial beings. All I have done in this chapter is to provide provable alternative explanations for these experiences. Yet the very fact that all aspects of these experiences can be generated by the functioning of the mechanisms of the body, means these experiences can neither be regarded as proof of the reality of immaterial entities, nor as indirect proof of the reality of the human soul.

This study of the experiences of nocturnal attack and visitation completed my analyses of all direct and indirect proofs of the reality of the soul. I knew of no other indications of the possible reality of an invisible and immaterial human soul. So I decided to review all the studies I had made up till this point.

Chapter 14

Body, Mind & Soul

Individual consciousness, intellect, thoughts, memories, personality and emotions are properties of the mind, and occur within the mind. Many people believe deep within themselves that their minds are somehow different and separate from their bodies. Furthermore, many people also believe each person has a soul, and that the soul is the vehicle of the mind. But is the soul the vehicle of the mind? Does each person have a soul? Are mind and body different?

These questions are not new. Untold numbers of theologians, scientists, and philosophers have attempted to answer these questions during the course of many millennia. So I searched for these answers in the works of philosophers and scientists. But to me, the rarefied thinking of many philosophers and scientists appeared bogged in a wondrously incomprehensible mire of verbal sophistry, without any regard for physiological reality. Others only concerned themselves with questions about the nature of the mind and consciousness, while altogether disregarding the possibility of an immaterial soul. On the other hand, a problem with many theologians, and believers in the reality of immaterial aspects to the universe, was that they assumed that invisible and immaterial aspects of the universe, such as the soul, really do exist, dismissing all other physical interpretations. My systematic studies of the various phenomena apparently proving the reality of an immaterial soul yielded no definite answers to my questions. I eventually realised that the only way I could answer my questions was to examine the totality of all the evidence collected in this book. So I made a list of each of the individual direct and indirect apparent evidences for the reality of the human soul.

- Many people believe the immaterial soul interacts with the body to animate the body. A careful study of the consequences of this belief revealed that the soul does not animate the body.
- Many people believe paranormal sensory abilities are indirect evidence for the existence of the soul. Yet decades of careful scientific research, as well as observation of the world in which we all live, reveals that paranormal sensory abilities do not exist.
- Many people believe there is an aura of light surrounding the human body, and that this aura is a manifestation of the soul, or of other im-

material properties of the body and world. Some people really are able to see such an aura of light surrounding each person. But this ability to see this aura is nothing wondrous or mysterious. Instead, the ability to see an aura of light surrounding each person is a consequence of the physical properties of the optical system of the human eye. So the aura is not indirect evidence of the existence of immaterial aspects of the world or the body.

- Many people believe the soul to be the vehicle of the mind. They believe the soul controls the body, controlling every movement, every word, and every deed. But if the soul controls the body, then the soul can only control movements, speech, and deeds through the mechanisms of the body. Furthermore, every aspect of mental function, such as memories, emotions, intellect, and personality, can only manifest, and can only be expressed, as well as controlled through the mechanisms of the body. These are facts. And these facts indicate that the brain, and not the soul, is most likely to be the generator and the vehicle of the mind, controlling all aspects of mental function. Nonetheless, this is only an alternative explanation, because the soul may, in some as yet incomprehensible way, exert some control over the body.

- Many people believe out-of-body experiences prove the reality of the soul. But the functioning of the mechanisms of the body explains all aspects, and all properties of out-of-body experiences. This means these experiences are not proof of the reality of the soul.

- Many people believe experiences of nocturnal attack and visitation by immaterial entities are possible indirect evidence for the reality of the soul. But the functioning of the mechanisms of the body explains all aspects, and all properties of nocturnal attack and visitation by immaterial entities. This means these experiences are also no indirect proof of the reality of the soul.

Careful analysis of each of these phenomena and beliefs yields no evidence for the reality of the soul. In fact, these analyses show that natural phenomena, as well as the functioning of the mechanisms of the body, explain all these apparent direct and indirect evidences for the reality of the soul. Some people might argue these are no more than alternative explanations for very real spiritual phenomena. These same people may even say that the soul, or immaterial and spiritual aspects of the universe, provide an elegant unifying explanation for all these phenomena, and that these multiple, alternative physical explanations prove nothing. Now this would be a very reasonable argument, if only some aspects of these direct and indirect evidences for the soul could be explained with physical phenomena, and the functioning of the mechanisms of the body. But every aspect of each of these apparently spiritual, and immaterial aspects of the body and the world, can be explained by the functioning of the mechanisms of the body, or by physical phenomena. Furthermore, the functioning of the mechanisms of the body and physical phenomena, explain these things with measurable, provable phenomena, with which it is possible to predict, as well as explain other so-called immaterial phenomena. These facts make any explanation based upon intangible and immeasurable wonders so untenable, that only one conclusion is possible; there is no indirect, or direct evidence for the existence of a human soul. The totality of all these explanations based upon physical phenomena, and the functioning of the mechanisms of the body proves there is no soul.

Even so, to believe in an invisible, immaterial, and immortal human soul is enormously appealing. It offers freedom from the terror of transient life and certain doom. It gives the believer eternal life, and a purpose in existence as part of some grand supernatural plan. Yet, no matter how appealing such a belief, it is only based upon millennia of uncritical interpretation of relatively common sensations and experiences. And after so many millennia, this intense belief in the soul has become so ingrained within the human psyche, that this belief has itself become the proof for the reality of the soul. More than fifteen hundred years ago, one of the founding fathers of Christendom, Saint Augustine, wrote about this aspect of faith and belief, saying:

> 'Faith is to believe what you do not yet see; the reward for this faith is to see what you believe.'[1]

Saint Augustine was correct. But faith and belief in the reality of something is not proof of the reality of that belief. This is also true even when everybody shares the same belief. It is only possible to say that something exists when physical evidence and independent observers verify that belief. Physical phenomena, as well as the functioning of the mechanisms of the body explain all aspects of the sensations and experiences said to be proof of the reality of the soul. Accordingly, it is impossible to believe in a soul whose reality is based only upon uncritical belief unsupported by any proofs whatsoever. All these things proved to me there is no soul. The soul is no more than an ancient delusion nestling within the human psyche. Nonetheless, a nagging doubt remained to gnaw at my mind. After all, just about everyone feels deep within themselves that their mind is somehow different and separate from their body. So I asked myself whether there is any proof that the mind is somehow different and separate from the body. I examined this belief carefully, and found it to have the same consequences, as well as the same proofs, as belief in the existence of the soul. An immaterial and immortal mind which is separate and different to the body is the soul. The relationship of the mind to the body proves this. The mind only senses what is happening within the body, to the body, and in the world around the body through the mechanisms of the body. The mind cannot sense any of these things except through the mechanisms of the body. The mind requires a functioning brain to perceive what is happening within the body, to the body, and in the world around the body. Consciousness, will, thoughts, personality, emotions, speech, and behaviour are all expressions of the properties of the mind. And these properties of the mind can only be expressed through the mechanisms of the brain and the body. If the mind is different and separate from the brain, then changes in the functioning of the mechanisms of the brain should not affect the properties of the mind. But disease, bodily malfunction, as well as changes in normal body function all change the functioning of the mechanisms of the brain, and change the properties of the mind as expressed by consciousness, will, thoughts, personality, emotions, speech, and behaviour. I can only draw one conclusion from these facts. The functioning of the brain generates the properties of the mind, as well as determining and modifying the perception of sensations by the mind. Mind is a product of the functioning of the brain, and the functioning of the brain generates the properties of the mind. Mind and brain function are one; mind and body are one.

The body houses the functioning brain, and the functioning brain is the mind. The mind of each person interacts with the world in which that person lives by reacting to sensations from within the body, as well as to sensations from the world outside the body. Reactions of sense organs to events within the body and outside the body generate sensory nerve signals. The brain processes these sensory nerve signals, and the mind interprets these processed sensory nerve signals as perceptions of the sensations generating these sensory nerve signals. The very fact of survival, means that each person interprets sensations from their body, and from the world around their body according to the physical reality of the world in which they live. A person may modify this interpretation somewhat according to individual beliefs and upbringing, but the very fact of survival dictates that physical reality is never ignored.

Nonetheless, some people consider the physical reality they observe and experience to be no more than an interpretation determined by their belief system. Their belief system is the reality for these people. Yet this is not always correct, because even though an interpretation provided by a belief system may be very satisfying, it does not mean that the belief system bears any relation to physical reality. Some things can be interpreted according to a belief system, but physical reality remains the same regardless of belief system. I will give two extreme examples illustrating the consequences of differences between belief system and physical reality.

For example, a man believes he can fly without the aid of any machines. He jumps from a high building, and while falling, he thinks he is flying. He really does experience his fall as flight, because as he falls, he feels himself flying through the air. His sensations of flight prove the truth of his belief to him. But observers see something quite different. Observers see a man who leaps from a high building to fall to the ground below. Observers are neutral, while the man who believes he is flying really does experience his fall as flight. The belief system of this man does not correspond with physical reality, because the reality is that the man jumps and falls to the ground below, no matter how fervently he believes he is flying. His flight lasts as long as his fall. This is physical reality, and his belief system is a delusion.

Another extreme example is that of a man who in all seriousness, says that this world is illusion, saying that all he sees, experiences, and senses is mere illusion. So he wanders around taking no heed of the illusory traffic on the streets, taking no heed of illusory obstacles, ignoring illusory holes in the ground, does not eat any illusory food, nor drink any illusory water. Everyone knows this man will rapidly die of thirst, starvation, or an accident. This is physical reality, and the belief system of this man is a delusion.

These are examples of extreme belief systems whose consequences threaten the survival of the believer, because these belief systems take no account of physical reality. But there are many differences between belief systems and physical reality that do not threaten the functioning, well-being, or survival of the believers.

An example of such a difference between belief system and physical reality is that of two friends who telephone each other at the same time. Many people have experienced this. For example, a person decides to telephone a friend. Just at that moment, the telephone rings, they pick up the telephone, and hear the voice of the friend they were about to call. Such situations do not happen often, which is why they arouse a sense of surprise and wonder. There are two possible explanations for such an event. The rationalist would say that these two people are friends, which means they have reasonably regular contact with each other. So it is only to be expected that they will decide to make contact with each other, and occasionally they may both decide to do so at the same time. The chance is not large that they will try to make contact with each other at about the same time, but it will occur occasionally. Another person may explain these synchronous telephone calls quite differently. They may say these two friends made unconscious telepathic contact with each other. Both reacted to this contact by telephoning the other person, only one was quicker than the other. A belief in unconscious telepathic contact is an example of a harmless difference between belief system and physical reality. It is a belief that does not correspond with physical reality, because paranormal sensory abilities do not exist. Nonetheless, such a belief system has no consequences for the functioning, well-being, survival, or actions of the believer.

All these things illustrate that some things are physical reality, while others are simply belief systems used to explain observed reality. A belief system used to interpret sensations from within, and without the body must correspond reasonably well with reality. Only then can an individual function normally and survive. This is the interaction between the mind and the body, as well as between the mind, and the world in which the body lives. Knowledge of all these things finally enabled me to summarise the relationship between the body and the mind. Sensory nerves transmit information from within, and outside the body into the brain. The brain processes this sensory information, and the mind perceives these sensations. The brain is the generator and the vehicle of the mind, generating all aspects of mind such as consciousness, intellect, thoughts, emotions, personality, perceptions, speech, and behaviour. The body is the vehicle of the brain, providing the brain with protection and nutrients, as well as being consciously and unconsciously directed by the brain to ensure personal and genetic survival. This is the relationship between body and mind.

Finally, the totality of all these provable physical explanations for all direct and indirect evidence for the reality of the immaterial human soul proved to me that I have no soul. This means there is no immaterial part or aspect of my body, which means my mind will die together with my body. So I had learned answers to two of the three questions I asked myself in the beginning of this book. I had learned the true nature of death, and I had learned there is no life after death. But my third question remained unanswered. I still had not learned what all people, including myself, will experience while dying.

Chapter 15

Dying

I know I will eventually die. I know my consciousness will cease upon my death. I know the nature of death. But I must first die before I am dead. So what is dying? Why do people die? When do people begin to die? Answers to these questions made it possible for me to learn what dying people experience, and even to predict what the dying may experience.

To begin with, a person is dead when all brainstem functions cease forever. But brainstem functions must first fail before they cease forever at death. This is the process of dying, and this means that dying is the process of failure of body functions ultimately ending in the irreversible failure of all brainstem functions that defines death. A person starts to die at the beginning of a series of events ending in death, unless those processes causing the person to die are halted or reversed. For example, a person with severe tuberculosis of the lungs is dying, and effective treatment of the tuberculosis will halt, or even reverse the dying process.

This understanding of the meaning of the term 'dying' made it possible to define the meanings of other terms describing conditions leading to death, such as 'life-threatening experience', 'near-to-death', and 'nearly dead'. A 'life-threatening experience' is any experience endangering life, or potentially causing death. Such an experience may be the result of being threatened with weapons, being condemned to death, undergoing an accident, or suffering from a potentially lethal disease. And a person is 'near-to-death', or 'nearly-dead', during the period they are dying.

These terms describe conditions a person may experience while dying, but they reveal nothing about the dying process. I approached the problem of describing the process of dying with some temerity. There are so many ways to die. I thought for some time about this problem. Finally I realised that the first step in learning the nature of the process of dying was to learn the most common causes of death. Causes of death are to be found in the population registries of just about every country in the world, and these population registries reveal the total numbers of deaths world-wide, as well as the causes of these deaths. Information from these registries revealed that about 50,467,000 people died world-wide during the year 1990 CE.[1] And of these people:

- 14,327,000 died of heart and blood vessel diseases,

- 9,329,000 died of infectious and parasitic diseases,
- 7,315,000 died of lung infections and diseases,
- 6,130,000 died of cancers of all types,
- 5,084,000 died of unintentional and intentional injuries,
- 2,443,000 died of infant disorders,
- 1,851,000 died of digestive disorders.

These were the seven most common causes of death world-wide during the year 1990 CE, and they caused 46,479,000 people to die during that year.[2] As a physician, I know that the process of dying due to these seven most common causes of death all affect the chain of oxygen supply. These seven most common causes of death ultimately cause people to lose consciousness due to oxygen starvation induced brainstem malfunction, and subsequently to die of irreversible brainstem failure due to oxygen starvation. Accordingly, these statistics mean that about 92% of all deaths in the world during the year 1990 CE were due to oxygen starvation. Furthermore, comparison of the causes of death in different countries reveals that while the disorders causing death may differ between different countries, the relative proportion of deaths due to oxygen starvation does not really differ much from one country to another, or from one year to another. All this means that more than nine in ten people world-wide dies of oxygen starvation.

So what is this chain of oxygen supply? Oxygen is in the air. Oxygen enters the body through the lungs where it chemically combines with blood flowing through lung blood vessels to the heart. The heart pumps oxygen-enriched blood through other blood vessels to all parts of the body. Oxygen diffuses out of blood vessels into the cells of the body. Oxygen is an essential ingredient in vital chemical reactions occurring inside cells. These vital chemical reactions generate the energy-rich substances powering all the cells of the body. This is the chain of oxygen supply.

Failure of any single link in this chain of oxygen supply causes death of the cells forming the body. When the cells forming the body are subjected to sufficiently severe oxygen starvation, insufficient quantities of energy-rich substances are produced to sustain normal cell function, and the oxygen-starved cells malfunction. Total oxygen starvation means these energy-rich substances are no longer generated at all. After a few minutes of total oxygen starvation, the few remaining molecules of these energy-rich substances are consumed, and the internal structures of oxygen-starved cells fail and begin to break down, a process causing irreversible damage, and death of oxygen-starved cells.

Likewise, when the cells forming the structures of the brainstem are subjected to sufficiently severe oxygen starvation, insufficient quantities of vital energy-rich substances are produced to sustain normal brainstem cell function. This results in brainstem malfunction which initially manifests as altered consciousness, or loss of consciousness. If oxygen starvation causes an even greater degree of brainstem malfunction, breathing also stops, resulting in total oxygen starvation of all body and brainstem cells, and failure of all brainstem functions. Total oxygen starvation means that no energy-rich substances are generated within the brainstem cells to sustain the internal structures of these cells. After several minutes of such total oxygen starvation, the internal structures of the cells forming the brainstem break down irreversibly, so resulting in the irreversible failure of all brainstem functions that defines death. This is why oxygen starvation causes death. In order to further clarify my thinking, I decided to describe how each of the seven common causes of death causes failure of the chain of oxygen supply.

Oxygen is in the air we all breathe. Air is a mixture of gases, of which about 21% is oxygen. Normal atmospheric pressure at sea level is 1013 millibars, so the pressure of oxygen in air at sea level is about 210 millibars (see Appendix 5). The lower the pressure of oxygen in the air, the less oxygen is able to enter the blood. And when the oxygen pressure in air is less than 110 millibars, oxygen starvation is severe enough to affect mental function. When the oxygen pressure in air is less than 66 millibars, oxygen starvation causes a degree of brainstem malfunction sufficient to result in loss of consciousness. Lower oxygen pressures cause such severe oxygen starvation that brainstem functions fail totally, resulting in loss of consciousness, cessation of breathing, and death (see Appendices 6 and 7). The pressure of oxygen in air decreases with altitude. This is why people develop oxygen starvation while flying at high altitudes, or while climbing high mountains. At an altitude of 5,000 meters, oxygen pressure in the air is low enough to affect mental function. At an altitude of 9,000 meters, oxygen pressure in air is so low, that nearly all people lose consciousness due to brainstem malfunction caused by oxygen starvation. At even higher altitudes, oxygen starvation is extreme, and always causes loss of consciousness, cessation of breathing, and death (see Appendix 7). People can develop some resistance to the effects of oxygen starvation by regularly exposing themselves to increasing degrees of oxygen starvation. This is why people can tolerate slow exposure to oxygen starvation developing over a period of several hours to days, better than they can tolerate sudden exposure to oxygen starvation. This is also why some mountaineers can climb to the peak of Mount Everest at a height of 8,848 meters above sea level without breathing any supplemental oxygen. These hardy mountaineers actually function at the limit of what is possible for the human body (see Appendix 7).

Very few people ever develop oxygen starvation due to breathing oxygen deficient air. Lung diseases are a much more common cause of oxygen starvation. Lungs are the organs through which oxygen enters the body. People inhale fresh air into their lungs, and exhale to remove oxygen depleted air from their lungs. Inhaled air enters the millions of small cavities in the lungs, out of which oxygen diffuses into, and chemically combines with oxygen-depleted blood flowing though small capillary blood vessels in the walls of these small cavities. The function of the lungs is to expose oxygen-depleted blood flowing through blood vessels in the lungs to oxygen in the fresh air contained within the lungs. The speed with which oxygen diffuses from the lung cavities into the oxygen-depleted blood flowing through the lungs, depends upon the volume of normally functioning lung tissue. The larger the volume of normal lung tissue through which oxygen can diffuse into blood vessels, the faster the oxygen in the lung cavities can diffuse out of the lungs into the blood flowing through the lungs. Lung diseases and lung injuries reduce uptake of oxygen by blood flowing through the lungs, either by reducing the volume of normally functioning lung tissue, by destroying lung tissue, or by both of these things. These effects of lung diseases and lung injuries may reduce oxygen uptake by the lungs to such a degree that oxygen starvation occurs. Oxygen starvation caused by lung damage or disease may be severe enough to cause failure of brainstem functions, resulting in loss of consciousness, cessation of breathing, and death. For example, lung infections such as pneumonia cause many of the myriad small air cavities in the lungs to fill with pus and fluid, so reducing the volume of normally functioning lung tissue out of which oxygen can diffuse into blood. Oxygen starvation occurs when the volume of lung tissue out of which oxygen can diffuse into blood is too small to provide the body with sufficient oxygen.

Lung diseases such as emphysema, lung cancer, and lung tuberculosis all cause destruction of lung tissue, so reducing the volume of normally functioning lung tissue out of which oxygen can diffuse into blood. Oxygen starvation occurs when the volume of lung tissue out of which oxygen can diffuse into blood is too small to provide the body with sufficient oxygen. Lung diseases such as asthma, bronchitis, and allergic reactions narrow the air passages within the lungs, so hindering movement of air into, and out of the lungs. This means that the air within the lungs is not effectively refreshed. Extreme narrowing of the lung air passages may reduce the movement of air into, and out of the lungs to such a degree that air within the lungs is almost not refreshed at all. The oxygen concentration within this stale air may decrease to such a degree that oxygen starvation occurs. Water fills the lungs of drowning people, filling the lung cavities, so reducing the volume of normally functioning lung tissue out of which oxygen can diffuse into blood. Oxygen starvation occurs when the volume of lung tissue out of which oxygen can diffuse into blood is too small to provide the body with sufficient oxygen.

War gases, such as mustard gas, chlorine, and phosgene, all cause extreme lung tissue irritation and damage. Damaged and irritated lung tissues produce enormous amounts of fluid and mucus inside the lungs, filling the lung cavities with fluid and mucus. Fluid and mucus filling the lung cavities reduces the volume of normally functioning lung tissue out of which oxygen can diffuse into blood. Oxygen starvation occurs when the volume of lung tissue out of which oxygen can diffuse into blood is too small to provide the body with sufficient oxygen. These war gases literally cause people to drown in their own lung secretions.

There are many nerve toxins: curare, (also known as 'deadly South American Indian arrow poison'), war gases such as 'Tabin' and 'Sarin', and snake venom's like that of the African 'green mamba' snake. All these substances paralyse breathing muscles, as well as all the other muscles of the body. People affected by these substances cannot breathe, so no oxygen enters their lungs, and they die of oxygen starvation.

Oxygen enters the body through the lungs. Oxygen-enriched blood in the lungs must be pumped from the lungs into the tissues and organs of the body, otherwise no oxygen will enter the cells of which all tissues and organs of the body are made. This is the function of the heart. The heart is no more than a pump, pumping oxygen-enriched blood through the blood vessels permeating all body tissues and organs, so supplying all the cells forming these tissues and organs with oxygen. Reduced pump function of the heart due to disease or injury reduces the flow of blood to the body, and this means a reduction of the supply of oxygen to all the cells of the body. Most importantly, reduced pump function of the heart reduces the flow of blood through the brain. A reduction of blood flow through the brain below eighty percent of normal always causes brain oxygen starvation, even when blood is filled to maximum capacity with oxygen (see Appendix 8). When the flow of oxygen-enriched blood through the brain is sufficiently reduced, brainstem malfunction due to oxygen starvation causes loss of consciousness. Even more extreme reduction of the flow of blood to the brain causes such a degree of brainstem oxygen starvation that failure of all brainstem functions occurs, resulting in loss of consciousness, cessation of breathing, and death.

The heart is a pump whose function is to pump blood around the body. There are four valves within the heart to direct the flow of blood. These valves may malfunction due to diseases or birth abnormalities. Malfunctioning heart valves either leak, or are too narrow to permit a normal flow of blood through the heart. But, regardless of the cause of heart valve malfunction, the effect of all types of heart valve malfunction is always the same; the heart is unable to pump normal volumes of oxygen-enriched blood into the body. This is why severe heart valve malfunction causes oxygen starvation.

The heart is a pump made of muscle. Sometimes the muscles forming the heart are so weakened by disease, that the heart is unable to pump normal volumes of blood into the body. This is called 'heart failure'. Severe heart failure causes oxygen starvation, because the heart can no longer pump normal volumes of oxygen-enriched blood into the body.

The beating of the heart is a manifestation of the pumping of the heart. But sometimes the rhythm of the heartbeat is abnormal, which reduces the pumping efficiency of the heart, so reducing the volume of blood pumped by the heart into the body. Sometimes the rhythm of the heartbeat is so abnormal that the heart pumps no blood into the body at all. And sometimes the heart stops beating, which also means that no blood is pumped into the body. Reduction of the volume of oxygen-enriched blood pumped into the body in all these situations causes oxygen starvation. Experiments have been carried out on human volunteers in which the flow of blood to the head was temporarily stopped by efficient strangulation[3], or by temporarily stopping the heartbeat.[4] These experiments clearly showed that abrupt cessation of blood flow to the head does not cause immediate unconsciousness and death. This observation is readily explained. Abrupt cessation of blood flow to the head does cause sudden cessation of the supply of oxygen to the head, but a small amount of oxygen remains in the tissues of the head, and this remaining oxygen sustains brain function and consciousness for a short time. This is why after sudden cessation of the flow of blood to the head, it takes four to nineteen seconds before oxygen starvation alters mental function and induces muscle paralysis, and five to twenty seconds before oxygen starvation causes loss of consciousness.[5] Many physicians, including myself, have observed this. We observe that some people remain conscious for several seconds after their hearts suddenly stop beating. These people sometimes even complain bitterly about the painful procedures necessary to restore their heartbeat, if these procedures are started before they lose consciousness. The same is also true for people who die as a result of violent events abruptly stopping the flow of blood to their heads. For example, shooting and stabbing in the heart cause the heart to stop beating as a result of which no blood is pumped into the head of a person who is shot or stabbed in the heart. This is the same situation as is caused by strangling, hanging, cutting the throat, or beheading. In all these situations, the flow of blood to the head abruptly stops, and if the brainstem is undamaged, a person may remain conscious for several seconds after such lethal events.

The heart pumps blood to all tissues and organs of the body through blood vessels. Blood vessels are the tubing through which blood flows to, and from each tissue and organ of the body. The blood vessels through which blood is pumped from the heart to all tissues and organs are called 'arteries', and the blood vessels through which blood returns from the tissues and organs back to the heart are called 'veins'. Blood flowing through the arteries contains the oxygen and the nutrients that all cells of the body require for life and function. Arteries divide within each tissue and organ into countless microscopically small blood vessels called capillaries. Oxygen and nutrients diffuse out of these capillaries into each living cell. At the same time, waste products such as carbon dioxide, acids, ammonia, as well as many other products produced by each cell diffuse into these capillaries. Further downstream, these myriad capillaries within each organ and tissue of the body coalesce to form the veins in which blood depleted of oxygen and nutrients flows back to the heart. Blood vessel diseases are a common cause of death in most parts of the world.[6] Blood vessel diseases nearly always affect the arteries, causing affected arteries to become narrower, to be blocked, or to bleed. If an artery becomes narrower, is blocked, or bleeds, then those body tissues supplied by the diseased artery no longer receive sufficient blood to supply them with the amounts of oxygen, and nutrients required for normal function. Body tissues require many different substances to function normally, and the supply of all these substances usually vastly exceeds tissue requirements, except for one substance, oxygen. The supply of oxygen to most tissues usually only slightly exceeds the requirements of each tissue. This is why all blood vessel diseases cause tissue damage by causing oxygen starvation, and this is why blood vessel diseases cause people to die of oxygen starvation. I will give a few examples.

The arteries supplying the brain with blood may be diseased. A diseased artery may be blocked by a blood clot, or burst open and bleed. Those parts of the brain receiving their blood supply through a blocked, or bleeding artery, become starved of oxygen, cease to function, and die. Cessation of the functioning of some parts of the brain causes affected people to suddenly become paralysed, to develop speech difficulties, or to develop personality changes. These effects of bleeding or blockage of a blood vessel in the brain are called a 'stroke'. The same events can happen within the brainstem. If the arteries supplying the brainstem with blood are suddenly blocked by a blood clot, burst open and bleed, or are clamped shut by swelling in the brainstem, all brainstem functions cease, and affected persons suddenly lose consciousness, stop breathing, and die. These are the effects of a stroke in the brainstem.

The heart is a pump made of muscle. Heart muscle tissue requires a lot of oxygen, because the muscles of the heart work continually to pump blood around the body. Heart muscles receive blood through arteries embedded within the muscles of the heart. Disease of the arteries supplying heart muscles with blood almost always causes these arteries to narrow, or become blocked. When an artery supplying part of the heart muscles suddenly becomes blocked, the region of heart muscle receiving blood from that artery becomes oxygen starved and dies. This is called a 'heart attack' or a 'myocardial infarction'. If a heart attack causes a sufficiently large amount of heart muscle to be suddenly deprived of blood, then the heart can no longer pump sufficient quantities of blood around the body to sustain normal activities and function. This is heart failure. If an even larger amount of heart muscle is suddenly deprived of blood, the heart stops beating altogether, and the affected person dies of brain oxygen starvation because no blood is pumped to the brain.

I speak of the flow of blood, because the flow of blood is crucial in the chain of oxygen supply. Blood is the fluid transporting oxygen to all parts of the body. Blood is contained within blood vessels. The heart pumps and circulates blood through all the blood vessels of the body, and blood must be present within, and flowing through the capillaries if any oxygen is to reach the cells forming the tissues and organs of the body. An average adult human body contains about five litres of blood. The bodies of large people contain more blood than do the bodies of small people. Internal or external bleeding reduces the volume of blood within the blood vessels of the body, and if a sufficiently large volume of blood is lost, insufficient blood remains within the blood vessels to fill all the capillaries within each tissue, and organ of the body with oxygen-enriched blood. No oxygen enters the cells of tissues whose capillaries are not filled with blood, and this is why oxygen starvation occurs when the volume of blood within the body is less than normal. Human studies show that rapid loss of more than one fifth of the blood contained within the body, by internal or external bleeding, is the point at which tissue oxygen starvation begins to occur in most people.[7] Loss of even greater volumes of blood causes an even greater degree of tissue oxygen starvation, and massive blood loss causes lethal tissue oxygen starvation.

Blood transports oxygen to all parts of the body. But very little oxygen is actually dissolved in blood. Instead, almost all the oxygen in blood is chemically bound to a protein called 'haemoglobin' present within the red blood cells that comprise 35-45% of the blood volume. It is this haemoglobin within red blood cells that gives blood its characteristic red colour. Anaemia is present when the percentage volume of red blood cells falls below 30% of the blood volume. Skin, lip, and tongue colour are largely determined by the red colour of haemoglobin. So when a person is anaemic, their skin, lips, and tongue appear pale or grey instead of being a healthy reddish colour. Anaemia reduces the amount of oxygen able to be carried within a given volume of blood. The body can compensate to some degree for the effects of anaemia, but anaemia causes symptoms of oxygen starvation when the volume of red blood cells falls below 25-30% of blood volume (haematocrit less than 25-30%), and anaemia may cause lethal oxygen starvation when the volume of red cells is less than 10% of the blood volume (haematocrit less than 10%).[8] Anaemia is usually a longstanding condition caused by chronic malnutrition, limited food variation, starvation, or vitamin deficiencies. Anaemia may also be a product of long lasting infestations with parasites, bacteria or viruses. Anaemia may also be a product of slow blood loss due to excessive menstruation or parasitic infestations. And anaemia may be a product of long lasting liver, kidney, or intestinal diseases. But regardless of the cause, the effect of anaemia is the same in all situations; anaemia reduces the amount of oxygen that a given volume of blood can transport. This is why anaemia aggravates the effects of oxygen starvation due to all causes. This is why severe degrees of anaemia cause oxygen starvation. And this is why extreme degrees of anaemia may actually cause lethal oxygen starvation.

Injuries are a common cause of death world-wide. There are two types of injuries, intentional, and unintentional. Unintentional injuries are those caused by accidents such as drowning, road traffic accidents, falls, and so on. Intentional injuries are those resulting from suicide, or any conceivable form of purposeful violence inflicted during times of peace or war. Injuries usually do not affect a single point in the chain of oxygen supply. Instead, injuries usually affect more than one link in the chain of oxygen supply, because they are often a combination of damage to many tissues and organs, as well as blood loss. But regardless of the cause of the injury, death nearly always results from oxygen starvation.

Starvation also causes people to ultimately lose consciousness and die due to oxygen starvation. A starving person ingests no food, or far too little food for the energy requirements of his body. So the body of a starving person consumes the fats and proteins forming the tissues of their body to generate the energy-rich chemical compounds required to sustain life. Sustaining life by consuming the substances forming body tissues is like keeping a house warm by burning its framework; eventually the house collapses. The same goes for the human body. Consumption of the substances forming the tissues and organs of the body finally affects the functioning of the body to such a degree that the functioning of vital organs eventually fails. This is why starvation finally causes the heart to fail, causes anaemia, or permits massive infections due to immune system failure. All these things ultimately cause death due to oxygen starvation. People dying of cancer also ultimately lose consciousness and die of oxygen starvation. Cancers generate a substance called 'tissue necrosis factor' which causes body tissues to break down. This tissue breakdown is unstoppable, and even eating huge amounts of food fails to reverse this massive tissue loss. This is why people dying of cancer lose a lot of weight, appearing skeletal shortly before dying. The effect of such massive loss of body tissue is the same as the effects of starvation: lethal heart failure, anaemia, immune system failure, and death due to oxygen starvation. Cancer may also spread to the lungs, reducing lung function to such a degree that lethal oxygen starvation occurs. Occasionally, spread of cancer to the brain may destroy or distort the brainstem, causing loss of consciousness and death due to brainstem failure.

There are many lethal poisons. Some of these poisons cause people to lose consciousness, and die of oxygen starvation. Strychnine is just such a poison. It causes death due to protracted epileptic convulsions. The brain requires such large amounts of oxygen during epileptic convulsions, that brain oxygen consumption always outstrips brain oxygen supply during epileptic convulsions, regardless of how efficiently the heart pumps blood though the brain. Breathing muscles also twitch and contract in an uncontrolled and uncoordinated fashion during epileptic convulsions, reducing the efficiency of breathing, so worsening the degree of oxygen starvation. This is why epileptic convulsions always cause brain oxygen starvation. Severe, protracted epileptic convulsions cause brain damage and death due to oxygen starvation. Cyanide is another example of a poison causing people to die of oxygen starvation. Cyanide administered as tablets, powder, liquid, or gas, poisons the cells of the body in such a way, that the cells are unable to use oxygen to generate the energy-rich substances needed to sustain normal cell function. So even if sufficient oxygen arrives in the cells of the body of a person poisoned with cyanide, the cells of the body cannot use this oxygen to generate vital energy-rich substances, and death occurs due to oxygen starvation.

Intestinal diseases and infections causing uncontrollable diarrhoea are a common cause of death world-wide. Diseases causing diarrhoea caused more than 2,900,000 people to die during the year 1990 CE.[9] Diarrhoea is excessive loss of water contained in faeces. A person with diarrhoea must drink water to replace water lost in diarrhoea. The body dries out when the rate of water loss in diarrhoea is greater than the rate of water replacement by drinking. This is 'dehydration'. Vomiting, together with diarrhoea, aggravates this water loss, as well as making it almost impossible to replace lost water, because anything the person drinks is vomited out. Blood is eighty five percent water, which is why dehydration also reduces the volume of blood within the body. This is why the effects of losing more than one fifth of the water contained within the body are similar to those of massive blood loss. The reduced volume of blood within the body causes oxygen starvation. Further loss of water may reduce the blood volume to such a degree that oxygen starvation is severe enough to cause loss of consciousness, cessation of breathing, and death.

Cholera is an example of a serious diarrhoeal disease. It is caused by the Vibrio cholerae bacteria. Toxins produced by the Vibrio cholerae bacteria cause the cells of the small intestine to secrete enormous amounts of fluid and body salts into the small intestine, which then come rushing out of the anus as the massive and uncontrollable diarrhoea of cholera. Loss of enormous amounts of fluid from the body decreases the amount of blood circulating around the body, so that the person is in a state similar to that caused by massive blood loss. Lethal dehydration occurs when an adult rapidly loses more than eight litres of water and body salts. Cholera is one of the most terrifyingly rapid of the lethal infectious diseases, because cholera can kill an average healthy adult within three, to twelve hours after diarrhoea starts.

Other infectious and parasitic diseases are also major world-wide causes of death. For example, tuberculosis killed about 1,960,000 people, measles killed 1,058,000 people, malaria killed 856,000 people, whooping cough killed 347,000 people, and Acquired Immune Deficiency Syndrome (AIDS) killed 312,000 people during the year 1990 CE. The effects of the multitude of different parasites, viruses, and bacteria infecting the human body are diverse, but death caused by infections of all sorts is nearly always due to lethal oxygen starvation. For example, Ebola virus infections, as well as malaria parasite infections may cause uncontrollable bleeding resulting in lethal oxygen starvation. The toxins produced by some bacteria can affect heart, lung, and blood vessel function to such a degree that lethal oxygen starvation occurs. Some viruses, bacteria, and parasites can affect brain function by causing convulsions, so causing brain oxygen starvation. Encephalitis and meningitis due to bacteria or viruses may cause brainstem malfunction resulting in loss of consciousness, and cessation of breathing.

Measles is an example of a common and sometimes lethal infectious disease. Many people believe measles is a relatively harmless childhood disease. But this is not true. As I already mentioned, measles killed 1,058,000 people world-wide during the year 1990 CE, about one fiftieth of all deaths world-wide during that year! One in ten thousand persons infected with measles dies, because the measles virus causes a massive infection of the brain substance resulting in convulsions, loss of consciousness, cessation of breathing, and death. About one in twenty persons infected with measles develops a severe lung infection. Indeed, severe lung infection progressing to pneumonia is the cause of six in ten of all deaths caused by measles. Measles is a relatively harmless disease in healthy people living in wealthy, technologically advanced countries. However, poor and malnourished people with existing anaemia are much more likely to die of measles, because they are less able to resist the effects of infections. Disorders causing children up to five years of age to die are often considered separately from disorders causing adults to die. This is because children up to five years of age are very vulnerable, being totally dependent upon adults. The causes of death in such young children differ from one country to another. For example, in technologically developed countries, children dying in this age range nearly always die of birth abnormalities, cancers, accidents, violence, heart abnormalities or heart diseases, inherited Acquired Immune Deficiency Syndrome, and severe lung infections.[10] The situation is different in undeveloped and poor countries. Young children in these countries usually die of lung infections, diarrhoea, measles, malaria, tetanus, malnutrition, starvation, and anaemia due to many causes.[11] But regardless of the specific disorder, all these disorders ultimately cause loss of consciousness, cessation of breathing, and death due to oxygen starvation.

More than nine in ten people die of these seven common causes of death. The multitude of different disorders represented by these seven common causes of death all interrupt the chain of oxygen supply, causing affected people to ultimately lose consciousness due to brainstem malfunction caused by oxygen starvation, and then to die of oxygen starvation induced failure of all remaining brainstem functions. Oxygen starvation is the primary cause of failure of brainstem functions in these people.

Somewhat less than one in ten people die of disorders where oxygen starvation is not the primary cause of failure of their brainstem functions. These people suffer from disorders initially causing such a degree of brainstem malfunction that loss of consciousness occurs. Further progression of the severity of these disorders causes an even greater degree of brainstem malfunction, eventually resulting in failure of breathing, after which total oxygen starvation develops, causing the irreversible brainstem failure of death. I will give a few examples.

To begin with, sudden destruction of the brainstem may occur during road traffic accidents, explosions, falling upon the head, a savage blow to the back of the head, or being shot in the back of the head. Brainstem destruction causes loss of consciousness as well as cessation of breathing in all these situations, after which the body dies of oxygen starvation.

Many drugs cause loss of consciousness by inducing brainstem malfunction. Examples of some of these drugs are sleeping pills, sedative drugs, alcohol, drugs used to treat epilepsy, and anaesthetic drugs. Low doses of these drugs cause abnormal brain function manifesting as altered mental function. Higher doses of these drugs cause failure of some brainstem functions, manifesting as loss of consciousness. Even higher doses of these drugs cause more extensive failure of brainstem functions, manifesting as loss of consciousness, as well as cessation of breathing, after which the body may die of oxygen starvation.

The kidneys and the liver remove waste products from the body. Severe disease of these organs means that these waste products are no longer removed from the body, and so they accumulate in the body. Loss of consciousness occurs when a sufficiently high concentration of these waste products causes failure of some brainstem functions. Even higher concentrations of these waste products in the brainstem cause more extensive degrees of brainstem malfunction. Such degrees of brainstem malfunction manifest as loss of consciousness and cessation of breathing, after which the body dies of oxygen starvation.

Diabetes is a disease affecting the regulation of glucose concentration in blood. Failure of brainstem functions occurs if the concentration of glucose in blood is too high, or too low. Extremely high, as well as extremely low blood glucose concentrations cause brainstem malfunction manifesting as loss of consciousness. Even higher or lower extremes of blood glucose concentrations cause more extensive degrees of brainstem malfunction. This manifests as loss of consciousness and cessation of breathing, after which the body dies of oxygen starvation.

There are many more possible examples, but they all illustrate the same things. Slightly more than nine in ten people lose consciousness and die of oxygen starvation, while less than one in ten people lose consciousness due to other disorders, after which they die of oxygen starvation. Furthermore, regardless of the cause of death, the ultimate cause of death in all people is failure of brainstem functions. It is failure of brainstem functions that causes the eternal loss of consciousness of death. And it is failure of all brainstem functions that causes breathing to stop, resulting in total brainstem oxygen starvation, so causing the irreversible failure of all brainstem functions that is death. Accordingly, dying is a process of progressive failure of brainstem functions terminating in the irreversible failure of all brainstem functions, which is death. These insights into the fundamental causes of dying and death finally made it possible for me to learn about, as well as to understand the experience of dying.

Chapter 16

Oxygen Starvation

Oxygen starvation profoundly affects the functioning of the body, especially the brain and the sense organs. More than nine in ten persons die of disorders where the eternal loss of consciousness of death is ultimately caused by oxygen starvation. This means that the effects of oxygen starvation modify, and determine, the last conscious experiences of more than nine in ten dying people. So to understand the effects of oxygen starvation upon the brain, and the sense organs, is to understand the dying experiences of more than nine in ten people.

There is a vast body of knowledge about the effects of oxygen starvation on the body. Knowledge of these effects of oxygen starvation comes from many sources: from studies of the effects of oxygen starvation upon healthy people, from studies of the effects of oxygen starvation experienced by people during near-death states, and from studies of the effects of oxygen starvation undergone by the dying. All these studies show some organs and tissues are more sensitive to the effects of oxygen starvation than others. Of all the organs and tissues in the body, the brain, and the eyes, are the organs most sensitive to oxygen starvation. But the brain and the eyes have many parts, and some parts of the brain and the eyes need more oxygen to function normally than do other parts. Those parts of the brain and eyes consuming most oxygen, are more sensitive to the effects of oxygen starvation, than are those parts of the brain and eyes consuming least oxygen. So increasingly severe oxygen starvation first causes malfunction, and failure, of those parts of the brain and eyes consuming more oxygen, before causing malfunction and failure of those parts of the brain and eyes consuming less oxygen. Changes in the functioning of the brain and the eyes caused by increasingly severe oxygen starvation are the same for each person, because each person has the same basic body structure and function, regardless of race, sex, culture, religion, or psyche. Furthermore, each degree of degree of oxygen starvation affects more than one part of the brain, as well as more than one part of the eyes, and worsening degrees of oxygen starvation cause increasingly more parts of the brain and the eyes to malfunction. So at each degree of oxygen starvation, mental and perceptual function is a product of the functioning of the abnormally functioning parts of the brain and the eyes, together with the functioning of the remaining normally functioning parts of the brain and the eyes. This means that each degree of oxygen starvation causes a specific cluster of mental and perceptual manifestations. Studies of oxygen starvation show it is possible to divide the effects of oxygen starvation into four distinct degrees: mild, moderate, severe, and extreme oxygen starvation (see Appendix 3). A detailed study of the effects of these four degrees of oxygen starvation reveals many aspects of the experience of dying.

Mild oxygen starvation is the mildest degree of oxygen starvation. Mild oxygen starvation does not affect the functioning of the brain or the senses. Nonetheless, some people are more sensitive to the effects of oxygen starvation than others, and may develop changes in the functioning of the brain, and the senses at mild degrees of oxygen starvation.

Moderate oxygen starvation is a more severe degree of oxygen starvation. Moderate oxygen starvation does not cause loss of consciousness, nor does moderate oxygen starvation affect breathing. But moderate oxygen starvation does affect the functioning of the brain and the senses.[1]

For example, moderate oxygen starvation always causes malfunction of a part of the brain surface called the 'prefrontal cortex'.[2] The prefrontal cortex is that part of the frontal cortex lying behind the forehead and above the eye cavities (see figures 1 and 4). Prefrontal cortex malfunction alters mental processes, causing forgetfulness, causing difficulty concentrating and planning, causing difficulty with mathematical calculations, and always induces an attitude of serene unconcern, of calm and tranquil indifference to everything, including pain.[3] In the words of one writer, prefrontal cortex malfunction caused by moderate oxygen starvation nearly always causes people to experience:

'... *a reduction of self criticism, together with a loss of sense of judgement. However, we feel that our mind is quite clear, but also that our mental processes are also unusually keen. We develop a fixity of purpose and continue to do what we were doing at the time that we were first affected by oxygen deficiency.*'[4]

Prefrontal cortex malfunction induced by oxygen starvation explains why the dying, and nearly dead are so serene and composed, apparently indifferent to their fate, sometimes even happy and joyful. A man who once underwent a near-death experience during a well-documented cardiac arrest, and resuscitation, reported experiencing all these effects of prefrontal cortex malfunction:

'*He had an out-of-body experience during which he saw the physicians and nurses resuscitating him. He was subjected to a variety of painful medical procedures during his resuscitation. There were two unsuccessful attempts at inserting a large needle under his collarbone.[5] He underwent heart massage, a forceful and uncomfortable procedure that is sometimes so violent that ribs are fractured. He was administered five or six electrical shocks through his chest, each shock powerful enough to cause his whole body to jump. These procedures were necessary to maintain circulation, inject drugs and fluids, and to restore normal heartbeat. This man reported viewing all these events as if from a point above his own body. He realised at the time that it was his body to which all these things were happening. He also understood that he was in an abnormal, life-threatening situation. Nonetheless, even though he realised the gravity of his situation, he felt calm and peaceful, even indifferent.'[6]*

The feelings of indifference and serenity reported by this man are typical of prefrontal cortex malfunction. But these changes in mental function caused by oxygen starvation do not immediately return to normal after restoration of normal body function. Indeed, it may take several months, and sometimes even longer than one year before the functioning of the prefrontal cortex returns to normal after a period of severe oxygen starvation.[7] This is why many people notice personality changes after recovering from oxygen starvation severe enough to affect the functioning of their brains. Many people even report becoming calmer, more tolerant, more caring, and even more sociable after a period of oxygen starvation. One man reported just such personality changes after resuscitation from a cardiac arrest. He wrote:

'When I "came back", (from being "dead"), no-one quite know what to make of me. When I had my heart attack, I had been a very driven and angry type A personality (aggressive, impatient and selfish). If things didn't go right for me, I was impossible to live with. That was at home as well as work. If my wife wasn't dressed on time when we had some place to go, I would blow up and make the rest of the evening miserable for her. Why she put up with it, I don't know. I guess she grew accustomed to it over the years, though, because after my near-death experience she could hardly cope with my mellowness. I didn't yell at her any more. I didn't push her to do things, or anyone else for that matter. I became the easiest person to live with and the change was almost more than she could bear. It took a lot of patience on my part – which is something I had never possessed before – to keep our marriage together. She kept saying, "You are so different since your heart attack". I think she really wanted to say, "You've gone crazy."'[8]

The personality changes reported by this man were a product of residual prefrontal cortex malfunction, caused by the episode of severe oxygen starvation that occurred during his cardiac arrest. These residual changes in prefrontal cortex function caused him to become calmer, and somewhat indifferent, as well as to react less irritably and aggressively. As a result of these changes, he had apparently become more sociable.

The mental effects of prefrontal cortex malfunction induced by oxygen starvation may even be one of the reasons why holy people seek high, and lonely places to meditate and undergo religious experiences. After climbing high in the mountains, prefrontal cortex malfunction induced by oxygen starvation alters the functioning of their brains. They become unconcerned and indifferent to cold, weariness, and hunger. Wonderful feelings of calm exultation arise, and their mental processes seem unusually keen and sharp. Isolation and fixity of purpose ensure that their feelings of mystical exultation and rapt concentration continue without thought of rest or food for a considerable time. After several weeks, their bodies adapt to the low oxygen pressure in the air they breathe, and their bodies become less oxygen starved. Their feelings of religious exultation fade along with their indifference to hunger and discomfort, and they decide to return to the lowlands. It takes three months to one year before the functioning of the prefrontal cortex returns to normal after several days exposure to moderate oxygen starvation at high altitudes.[9] So these holy people develop long-lasting changes in the functioning of the prefrontal cortex during their sojourn in the mountains. Upon their return to the lowlands, their followers observe the changes caused by their stay in the mountains. They interpret the indifference caused by prefrontal malfunction as a renewed inner calm and transcendence of the world about them. And all are happy, because meditation high in the mountains has indeed wrought wondrous changes.

Moderate oxygen starvation also causes malfunction of that part of the brain surface controlling voluntary movements called the 'primary motor cortex' (see figure 4). Malfunction of the primary motor cortex causes muscle weakness. So people experiencing moderate oxygen starvation feel their limbs and body weigh more than normal, and that each movement requires enormous effort. A few people are very sensitive to the effects of moderate oxygen starvation, and these people may develop total failure of their primary motor cortex functions, resulting in paralysis of all voluntary movements. These people cannot speak, and they cannot move their bodies, arms, or legs, no matter how hard they may try to do these things. A man once described the sensations he felt in the half of his body which was intermittently paralysed, due to disease of the blood vessels supplying his primary motor cortex with oxygen and nutrients:

'I can only describe my condition during the period of complete paralysis by saying that when I formed the intention of moving my limbs I felt no effort,

but that it was absolutely impossible for me to bring my will to the point of executing the movement. On the other hand, during the phases of imperfect paralysis, and during the period of convalescence, my arm and leg seemed to me enormous burdens which I could only lift with the greatest effort. The paralysed limbs retained their sensibility completely and thus I was enabled to be aware of their position and of their passive movements.'[10]

People subjected to moderate oxygen starvation experience the same sensations. These same sensations were once described as they happened to a scientist who exposed himself to oxygen starvation by simulating high altitudes in a low-pressure chamber. He became unwell during one experimental session, and was removed from the low-pressure chamber. A colleague described his condition and movements:

'When his respiration failed and artificial respiration became necessary, no concern was expressed, although he was quite aware of its significance. His motor responses were slow, and activity required a great deal of effort; still greater effort was needed for initiation of effort. There were no delusional or hallucinatory experiences.'[11]

The effects described above are those of moderate oxygen starvation. Worsening of the degree of oxygen starvation causes moderate to severe oxygen starvation, and the effects of these levels of oxygen starvation were well illustrated by an experiment reported in 1942 CE. The group of scientists reporting this experiment studied the effects of increasingly severe brain oxygen starvation caused by suddenly, but temporarily stopping the flow of blood to the heads of 126 normal healthy men, eleven schizophrenic patients, as well as themselves. This caused sudden oxygen starvation of the head progressing rapidly from mild, to moderate, to severe, and finally to extreme oxygen starvation. They used a special inflatable cuff placed around the lower one third of the neck, and inflated it within one eighth of a second to a pressure high enough to clamp all blood vessels going to, and from the head shut.[12] This inflatable cuff was specially designed not to stop breathing, so when the cuff was suddenly inflated around the necks of these men, they continued to breathe normally, and their hearts continued to pump oxygen-enriched blood around the rest of their bodies. The only effect of sudden inflation of this special cuff was to suddenly stop all blood flow to and from the head. In other words, inflation of this specially designed cuff around the neck, allowed the rest of the body under the neck to function normally, while subjecting the head to sudden, total oxygen starvation. During each experiment, each man held a finger on a valve, so he could release the pressure in the cuff whenever he wished. Sudden inflation of the cuff caused all the men taking part in the experiment to rapidly lose consciousness within five to twenty seconds, after which the pressure in the cuff was released, and all the men rapidly regained consciousness. This experiment rapidly induced an extreme degree of oxygen starvation in the heads of a large number of highly motivated volunteers. The scientists conducting the experiment reported:

> 'The observers noted that the men taking part in the experiment developed a fixed stare of their eyes, the eyes of some men turned upwards, and voluntary eye movements stopped four to ten seconds after inflation of the cuff. All the men were unconscious one second after eye movements ceased. Many of the men taking part in the experiment could not remember what had happened to them after they regained consciousness. Those that could remember their experiences reported first feeling tingling in their arms and legs. Shortly after the cuff was inflated, some men noted that they could not move their eyes, and one man even said that he tried to move his eyes but could not. At the same time as their eye movements froze, they were also unable to move their arms or legs. Each man had a finger on a valve so that the pressure in the cuff could be released, but none of the men participating in the experiment released the pressure in the cuff around their necks; this always had to be done by the experimenter. When asked afterwards why they did not release the cuff pressure the following was discovered: Most subjects stated that they did not realise that they were holding onto the jet (the valve). Some stated that they did not feel like bothering to release the pressure. Others stated that they tried to remove the finger from the jet but were incapable of the movement.'[13]

Such were the experiences and perceptions undergone by these brave men during their exposure to potentially lethal degrees of oxygen starvation. This experiment temporarily induced a situation similar to stopping the heartbeat, shooting or stabbing in the heart, strangling, throat-cutting, or beheading. The experiences of these men, as well as the experiences of other people, teach that moderate and severe oxygen starvation has several effects. Both moderate and severe oxygen starvation induce an emotion of calm indifference. Moderate oxygen starvation usually only causes muscle weakness, while severe oxygen starvation often causes paralysis of all voluntary movements, including eye movements. Muscle weakness and paralysis of the limbs and the body is due to malfunction of the primary motor cortex caused by oxygen starvation, while eye muscle paralysis is due to malfunction of a region of the frontal cortex, called the 'frontal eye fields' (see figure 4).

Moderate and severe oxygen starvation also induce malfunction of those parts of the brain enabling the conscious mind to perceive sensations of pain, touch, movement, and body position. Malfunction of these regions of the brain, such as the primary somatosensory cortex, the secondary somatosensory cortex, the prefrontal cortex, and the parietal cortex, induce a large variety of sensations in the mind (see figure 4). This is why people undergoing moderate or severe oxygen starvation may perceive sensations of touch, movement, changes of position[14], have sensations of floating, or even undergo out-of-body experiences.[15] Severe oxygen starvation eventually causes these regions of the brain to cease functioning altogether. So people who are conscious, and in whom the primary somatosensory cortex, the secondary somatosensory cortex, the prefrontal cortex, and the parietal cortex no longer function, are incapable of perceiving sensations of pain, touch, movement, body position, or body image, and may even ignore or forget their bodies altogether.[16] Such blurring, or total loss of the sense of body image and body position, may even result in a disintegration of all sense of space and self, causing affected people to feel a sense of being 'one with the universe'.[17]

Moderate and severe oxygen starvation also induces abnormal nervous activity in a part of the brain called the 'temporal lobe'[18] (see figure 3), especially in a part of the temporal lobe called the 'hippocampus'[19], a part of the brain concerned with the formation and recall of memories. Abnormal nervous activity within the structures of the temporal lobes can arouse recall of people and past events, together with the associated sounds, smells, and emotions perceived at that time. Abnormal nervous activity within the structures of the temporal lobes can cause emotions of déjà vu, strange and indescribable emotions, or even emotions such as fear, sadness, or anger. Abnormal nervous activity within the structures of the temporal lobes can induce tingling feelings all over the body, sensations of movement, or feelings of heat or cold. Abnormal nervous activity within the structures of the temporal lobes can arouse visual hallucinations of blinking or flashing lights, of strangers, of friends, and of relatives. Abnormal nervous activity within the structures of the temporal lobes can also arouse auditory hallucinations, such as of music, roaring, clicking, pinging, or buzzing sounds.[20] And abnormal nervous activity within the structures of the temporal lobes can also arouse a powerful sense of the presence of 'something', or actual hallucinations of entities, of people, or even of gods.[21]

Many of these sensations were experienced by a woman who had a near-death experience induced by oxygen starvation resulting from an allergic reaction to penicillin. She reported her experiences to her physician, who wrote:

'She had never before suffered from any allergic manifestations, nor was there a family history of allergy. Being a nurse, she was aware, however, of the occurrence of penicillin allergy, and when she took the tablet, the thought had crossed her mind that she might be allergic to penicillin. In the car, when her breathing began to become difficult, she realised what was happening and she experienced frantic fear, which, however, soon passed. (She would never fear dying again, she said.) ... She had then witnessed, in rapid succession, a great many scenes from her life. They seemed in retrospect to start from about the age of five. She remembered the impression of vivid colour. She had seen a beloved doll that she had had and was struck by how bright blue the glass eyes were. There was also a picture of herself on her bright red bicycle on the equally bright green lawn. She was confident that her whole life was not pictorially represented, only some scenes from her childhood and she emphasised that it was all ecstatically happy. Her next memory was of a state of "bliss" and of "ecstasy". There was a picture of the Taj Mahal[22] in which she was deeply idyllically engrossed. It was a picture she must have seen on several occasions – the usual one taken from the lily pond in front. It was coloured, the pond and lily pads blue and green, the minarets and the dome a very lovely gold and cream.'[23]

This woman had visions of the important episodes in her life, as well as a vision of a transcendental world in which she saw the Taj Mahal. But she had no visions of religious figures, nor did she have visions of deceased friends or relatives. Perhaps this was because her near-death experience was so unexpected. People undergoing unexpected life-threatening events have quite different types of near-death experiences than people who expect, and know they will undergo a life-threatening event. People who unexpectedly undergo life-threatening experiences seldom see gods, saints, religious figures, or deceased family members during near-death experiences. This is quite different from near-death experiences undergone by people who expect to die, or know they are dying. These people are more likely to have visions of gods, of saints, of supernatural beings, or of deceased friends and relatives shortly before they die.[24] This difference is difficult to explain by changes in the functioning of the brain. But it is possible that many people believe deep within themselves, that deceased friends and relatives will come to guide them in their passage from the world of the living into the world of the dead. There are many examples of such visions. For example, a woman once told of her experiences while maintaining a 'death-watch'[25] by the bed of a dying man who had just such visions of family members and friends:

'On Sunday, April 13th, I went to Hillside to sit with a Mr. Williams, who was dying of consumption[26] so that those belonging to him might have a little rest. He was in a state of great physical distress, and unable to lie down, and could only breathe with the greatest difficulty, with his head leaning down to within a few inches of the mattress.

He suddenly raised himself and stretched out his hands, and said very clearly, as though speaking to someone present and whom he was glad to see, "Edmund!! My dear brother Edmund!!" I was alone with him at the time, but when the family returned to the room later I at once related to them what he had said, and then learnt from them that his brother Edmund was dead.

During the time that I was with him – from 3.15 to 9.15 – although breathing very heavily all the time, he appeared to be quite conscious when he spoke, and called for the different members of his family. He knew me quite well, and kissed my hand and called me by my name. He also asked to have water at intervals, and asked for hot tea. In spite of his great bodily distress, his trust in God remained quite unshaken, and it was very moving to hear him say at intervals, "Dear Lord, let me go!"

I was told that before I arrived he had exclaimed, "Mrs. Hooper!" She had been a great friend of his, and had died here about 18 months or two years ago. He died about ten hours after I had left.'[27]

This man was dying of oxygen starvation resulting from extensive lung destruction and malfunction caused by tuberculosis. He was exhausted after many hours of the deep and rapid breathing necessary to get sufficient oxygen into his body for life and consciousness. Tuberculosis had also ravaged his body, wasting and weakening his muscles. In fact, the exhaustion and the havoc wreaked upon his body by tuberculosis, had weakened his breathing muscles to such a degree, that the small reduction of lung function due to lying flat in bed, caused him even more discomfort, because of the resulting slight increase in work required to breathe. So he remained sitting, because his breathing required less effort than when lying down. These typical manifestations of failing lung function, prove he was starved of oxygen. So it is likely that his socio-cultural expectations of the nature of death, together with the effects of oxygen starvation, generated the visions of his deceased brother and friend. But not everyone seeing visions induced by oxygen starvation has the same types of visions. Comparison of the near-death visions of people living in different countries and societies shows that personal, social, and cultural factors determine the content of these visions. Most differences occur in the religious content of these visions. These differences prove that religious visions are not confirmation of the truth of any particular religion. Instead, these visions

prove that personal beliefs, as well as the social and cultural forces mould-
ing each person's life, determine the nature of the religious figures and
gods seen during religious visions. A person raised in total ignorance of
Christian beliefs, the Christian pantheon, and Christian philosophy, does
not have Christian visions, because they know nothing of these things.
Their religious visions are of the pantheon and philosophy with which
they are familiar, and in which they believe. So a Hindu has Hindu religious visions, a Christian has Christian religious visions, a Buddhist has
Buddhist religious visions, a Moslem has Moslem religious visions, and a
Zoroastrian has Zoroastrian religious visions. A report of the near-death vision experienced by a practising Hindu illustrates this:

> 'A Hindu farmer in his fortieth year was suffering from liver disease. He told
> he felt himself flying through the air and into another world where he saw
> gods sitting and calling him. He thought that he was going to meet those
> gods; he wanted to be there, saying to those around him: "Let me go". Re-
> latives tried to talk him out of it. He would be OK, he should not go. But
> the patient was very happy to see those gods and he was ready to die. He
> went into a deep coma a short time later, and died in two days. He was
> clear and coherent while describing what he saw.'[28]

This man saw figures from the Hindu pantheon. However, a Christian
would have had visions of God, Jesus, or other figures from the Christian
pantheon. For example, a man whose heart suddenly stopped beating once
reported undergoing a near-death experience with a visionary content determined by his Christian religious beliefs. He reported that while his heartbeat was being restored, he actually went to the Christian heaven, where
he met his deceased parents who took him to see Jesus. He reported that:

> 'As we walked along together to find Jesus, I noticed that there was one
> building larger than all of the others. It looked like a football stadium with
> an open end to the building where a blinding light radiated from it. I tried
> to look up at the light but I couldn't. It was too brilliant. Many people
> seemed to be bowed in front of this building in adoration and prayer. I said
> to my parents, "What is that?" They said, "In there is God." I will never
> forget it. I have never seen anything like it. We walked on as they were tak-
> ing me to see Jesus and we passed many people. All of them were happy. I
> have never felt such a sense of well being. As we approached the place
> where Jesus was located, I suddenly felt this tremendous surge of electricity
> through my body as if someone had hit me in the chest. My body arched
> upward as they were defibrillating my heart. I had been restored to my for-
> mer life! But I was not too happy to come back. However, I knew that I

had been sent back to tell others about this experience. I plan to dedicate the rest of my life to telling anyone who will listen!'[29]

This man experienced God, and was on his way to visit Jesus during a Christian religious vision induced by oxygen starvation. But this is not all he experienced while in heaven. His experience also provided him with a reason for returning to life, as well as a new purpose in life. Other people who report near-death experiences also give reasons for returning to life after apparently dying. These reasons always reveal their personal, social, and cultural experiences. The near-death experience reported by an Indian man illustrates this point. This man had a Hindu near-death vision in which he saw the god Yamraj, lord over the realm of the dead[30], who gave him quite a different reason for returning to life. He told of his experience:

> 'Four black messengers came and held me. I asked, "Where are you taking me?" They took me and seated me near the god. My body had become small. There was an old lady sitting there. She had a pen in her hand, and the clerks had a heap of books in front of them. I was summoned ... One of the clerks said, "We don't need Chhajju Bania. We had asked for Chhajju Kumhar. Push him back and bring the other man. He (meaning Chhajju Bania) has some life remaining." I asked the clerks to give me some work to do, but not to send me back. Yamraj was there sitting on a high chair with a white beard and wearing yellow clothes. He asked me, "What do you want?" I told him that I wanted to stay there. He asked me to extend my hand. I don't remember whether he gave me something or not. Then I was pushed down (and revived).'[31]

This man apparently died, but was returned to life because of an administrative error made by the messengers of God. A Christian would never even think of giving such a reason for returning to life, because the all-knowing Christian God makes no mistakes. So Christians usually receive reasons such as, 'it is not yet time to die', or the person has 'work to do', such as raising a family, caring for others, 'spreading the word of God', and many other similar reasons. The reasons for returning to life may differ from one person to another, but one thing is certain, the reasons for returning to life during near-death-experiences are not so much religious, as they are insights into the effects of religion, culture, and individual psychology upon the content of visions aroused by abnormal brain function. The effects described above are those of moderate to severe oxygen starvation. But what happens during severe oxygen starvation? Severe oxygen starvation always induces extensive brain malfunction[32], yet does not affect brainstem functions, so people do remain conscious and continue breathing. But severe oxygen starvation does cause failure of all primary motor cortex functions[33], so resulting in total paralysis of all voluntary muscle movements. This means that people affected by severe oxygen starvation cannot speak, and cannot move their eyes, bodies, arms, or legs, no matter how hard they may try to do these things.[34] All this means that people affected by severe oxygen starvation may be conscious, but appear to be unconscious because they can neither move nor speak. This state of 'apparent unconsciousness' is typical of severe oxygen starvation.

Apparent unconsciousness may seem strange to those unfamiliar with the idea of conscious paralysis, but it does occur. For example, volunteers taking part in experiments where sudden onset of rapid and extreme oxygen starvation of their heads was induced by fainting[35] and by strangulation[36] reported experiencing just such apparent unconsciousness. Scientists observing volunteers taking part in such experiments, only observed that the eyes of these brave volunteers suddenly became fixed, staring straight ahead, at the same time as they suddenly became unresponsive and appeared unconscious. But some of these volunteers remembered the sensations, and perceptions they experienced just before they lost consciousness. They found they were totally paralysed, unable to move their eyes, unable to speak, and unable to move any muscles just before losing consciousness. They were conscious during this period, but only appeared to be unconscious to the observers, because they could neither move nor speak. Such apparent unconsciousness is a normal consequence of severe oxygen starvation, and descriptions of the effects of severe oxygen starvation often mention this effect.

> 'Another dramatic instance of muscular paralysis due to oxygen want is the experience of Tissandier, sole survivor of the three-man ascent in the balloon 'Zenith'. At great heights he realised that he needed oxygen but could not husband the strength to raise the mouthpiece of the oxygen container to his lips.
>
> Finally, it may be mentioned that individuals suffering from carbon monoxide poisoning[37] often become paralysed, so that although they are conscious and wish to leave the zone of danger, they are physically unable to do so.'[38]

The same paralysis also occurs during near-death experiences aroused by conditions causing oxygen starvation. The experience of a woman who underwent a period of severe oxygen starvation caused by nearly lethal lung disease is a good example of this. She reported:

'I saw them resuscitating me. It was really strange. I wasn't very high; it was almost like I was on a pedestal, but not above them to any great extent, just maybe looking over them. I tried talking to them but nobody could hear me, nobody would listen to me.'[39]

No-one heard her speak, even though she tried to speak. Failure of her primary motor cortex functions caused by severe oxygen starvation paralysed her, so she could not speak, no matter how hard she tried to speak. This report is unusual, because severe oxygen starvation usually causes failure of the supplementary motor cortex, as well as failure of the adjacent primary motor cortex. The supplementary motor cortex is a region of the brain surface next to the primary motor cortex, and is responsible for planning and initiating voluntary movements. People affected by failure of their supplementary motor cortex functions no longer even think of speaking or moving, because thoughts of speaking or moving simply do not arise in their minds.[40] So people who are still conscious after failure of the functioning of the primary and supplementary motor cortex only appear unconscious, because they cannot move or speak, and usually do not even think of moving or speaking. A man reported undergoing just such an experience during oxygen starvation caused by massive blood loss. He said:

'I lost so much blood that I was becoming unconscious. I felt my body separate. I was lying beside my own body. I looked over and watched the nurses and doctors working on my dead body. I myself felt very content and peaceful. I was free of pain and had a very happy feeling. I thought, if this was death it is beautiful. The thought of my family helped me to hang on to life, although I felt all my troubles were gone at the time. I couldn't feel a thing except peace and ease and quietness.'[41]

This man was conscious, but appeared unconscious to those resuscitating him. Severe oxygen starvation caused several changes in the functioning of his brain, all of which resulted in the experiences he described. Prefrontal cortex malfunction caused this man to be calm, indifferent, and happy, despite his realisation of his desperate situation. Supplementary motor cortex failure caused a lack of any desire to speak, or move, even though he realised the grave nature of his situation, and even though he was subjected to painful resuscitative measures. Other mental and perceptual functions were affected by malfunction of other regions of his brain, as is illustrated by his lack of conscious perception of touch and pain. Finally, the shaking and movements of his body caused by those resuscitating him, together with abnormal muscle spindle function in association with brain malfunction, caused him to undergo an out-of-body experience.

The effects described above are those of severe oxygen starvation. Progression of the severity of oxygen starvation finally results in extreme oxygen starvation. Extreme oxygen starvation is the most severe degree of oxygen starvation. The brainstem is a part of the brain most resistant to the effects of oxygen starvation, and only malfunctions and fails at degrees of oxygen starvation causing failure of the rest of the brain.[42] Extreme oxygen starvation causes failure of all cerebral cortex functions, as well as brainstem malfunction. Extreme oxygen starvation initially causes loss of consciousness, together with abnormal breathing. Even more extreme oxygen starvation causes failure of all brainstem functions, causing loss of consciousness and cessation of breathing, so resulting in total oxygen starvation, and the subsequent irreversible brainstem damage of death.

These are the effects of the four degrees of oxygen starvation experienced by people during the terminal phases of dying of oxygen starvation. I summarised the effects of these different degrees of oxygen starvation.

- *Mild oxygen starvation* does not affect the functioning of the brain.
- *Moderate oxygen starvation* affects the functioning of the brain and the senses, removes sensations of pain or discomfort, causes people to feel calm, sometimes even joyful, as well as arousing feelings of serene unconcern or indifference. Supplementary motor cortex malfunction results in a lack of desire to move, so people usually do not move. A degree of primary motor cortex malfunction causes muscle weakness, so that when some people do try to move, they discover that voluntary movement is difficult and requires intense effort. More severe degrees of moderate oxygen starvation may also induce life-review, or out-of-body experiences.
- *Severe oxygen starvation* induces all the effects of moderate oxygen starvation, except that the degree of brain malfunction is more extreme. Supplementary and primary motor cortex malfunction are such that people do not even think of moving, and when a few people do try to move, they discover they are totally paralysed. And because severely oxygen starved people do not move, they appear unconscious even though they are often still conscious.
- *Extreme oxygen starvation* causes failure of all brain and brainstem functions, causing loss of consciousness, abnormal, or actual cessation of breathing, and ultimately death.

These are not the only effects of oxygen starvation. Oxygen starvation also affects memory. The reason for this is that a part of the brain called the hippocampus, which transforms short-term memories into long-term memories, is very sensitive to the effects of oxygen starvation. This is why

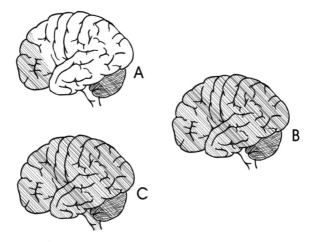

Figure 5 **Areas of the brain affected by differing degrees of oxygen starvation**
A - mild to moderate oxygen starvation mainly affects the cerebellum and the prefrontal cortex.
B - moderate to severe oxygen starvation affects increasingly more of the cerebral cortex.
C - extreme oxygen starvation affects all the cerebral cortex, as well as causing brainstem mal-
function, so causing loss of consciousness, and ultimately causing breathing to stop.

people recovering from oxygen starvation cannot always remember every-thing they experienced while starved of oxygen. The effects of oxygen star-vation upon the memories of experiences people undergo while starved of oxygen depend upon the degree of oxygen starvation. People can nearly al-ways remember what they experienced during mild to moderate oxygen starvation, can sometimes remember what they experienced during moder-ate and severe oxygen starvation, but can never remember what they ex-perienced during extreme oxygen starvation.[43] This is why most people never remember the thoughts and perceptions they experienced during near-to-death states. This is also why it is unusual for people to remember every group of mental, and perceptual changes characteristic of each of the differing degrees of oxygen starvation they experienced while near-to-death. These are the sensations, states of mind, emotions, and experiences caused by oxygen starvation, and people whose conscious mental function is final-ly terminated by oxygen starvation will experience some or all of them. This knowledge teaches me the changes of mental state, the perceptions, and the sensations I may undergo if I die of oxygen starvation. Furher-more, this knowledge also gives me understanding of the experiences of others I may see dying of oxygen starvation.

Chapter 17

Dying Eyes

Dying people sometimes say they see 'celestial landscapes', 'angels', 'bright figures of light', 'bright light that does not hurt the eyes', 'tunnels', and 'darkness'. Indeed, many people believe that because dying people are so close to the world of the dead, they are able to glimpse the world they will soon inhabit for the rest of eternity. But people have no souls, so there is no supernatural world inhabited by the dead. Nonetheless, some dying people really do see such visions of the eternity they believe awaits them. These dying people are neither mad nor hysterical; they are simply reporting their visual sensations in a clear and honest manner. But how is it possible for these people to see these things when they do not exist? I wanted to know answers to this question.

So I studied how the process of dying affects the functioning of the eyes, as well as the way the dying mind interprets visual sensations. And I found that the visions reported by the dying are actually products of changes in the functioning of the eyes, as well as the ways the dying mind interprets visual sensations.

The pupils of dying persons are often wide open shortly before death. There are several reasons why pupils may widen before death. Pupils may widen due to emotions, disease, fever, medicines, or oxygen starvation.[1] Widening of the pupils affects the functioning of the eyes in two ways. Widened pupils allow more light to enter the eyes, as well as reducing the focal depth of the optical system of the eyes. These two effects are evident in the reports of visions related by the dying.

People see because light enters their eyes, and light only enters the eyes through the pupils. Pupils have a circular shape, and the diameter of the human pupil may be as small as one millimetre, or as large as ten millimetres. This means that extreme widening of the pupils can allow as much as one hundred times more light to enter the eyes, than when the pupils are as small as they can be.[2] More light enters the eyes of a person with wide-open pupils than enters the eyes of a person with narrow pupils, which is why a person with wide-open pupils perceives their surroundings as brighter, or even bathed in light.[3] Consider the situation where several people are in a room where the lighting does not change. If the pupils of one of these people widens due to any one of many causes, that person will say that the lighting in the room has become 'brighter', or that the room is 'bathed in bright light that does not hurt the eyes'. But if the pupils of the other people in the same room do not widen, these people will notice no change in the lighting of the room. They may even say the person who claims the room has become brighter is mad. Yet the person saying that the lighting in the room has become 'brighter', or even 'bathed in bright light that does not hurt the eyes' is quite correct. More light does enter that person's eyes, causing that person to perceive the room as being brighter.

This is the same situation sometimes described during deathbed visions. Several people cluster around the bed of a dying person. The pupils of the dying person widen as their condition worsens. And as the pupils of the dying person widen, they notice that the lighting in the room becomes brighter, or even that the room is bathed in bright light. No-one else notices that the lighting in the room has changed, only the dying person, because only the pupils of the dying person widen. This is why dying people may say they see 'bright light', 'bright light that does not hurt the eyes', or even 'bright landscapes'.

Widening of the pupils has another effect. Widening of the pupils reduces the focal depth of the eyes. The pupil in each eye has the same function as the diaphragm in a camera. When the diaphragm in a camera is narrow, both near and far objects are in focus. But when the diaphragm of a camera is wide open, only the object upon which the camera is focussed is clear, everything else appears blurred and out of focus.[4] You can see the effects of different diaphragm openings on photographs. When you look at a photograph taken through a small diaphragm opening, you see that everything on the photograph, both in the foreground as well as in the background is clear and sharp. But when you look at a photograph taken through a wide-open diaphragm, you see that everything is blurred and out of focus, except for the object or person upon which the camera was focussed.

The same is true for the eyes. Many people say that a person with narrowed pupils appears hard and critical, or has a penetrating gaze.[5] This is true, a person with narrow pupils is able to clearly see near and far people and objects, so their gaze is penetrating, hard, and critical. But a person whose pupils are wide open has a shallow focal depth, and can only clearly see people upon which they focus their eyes. So people say a person with wide open pupils is warm and friendly, is interested in them, or has warm and friendly eyes. The reduced focal depth of the eyes of a person with wide open pupils, means they see all people, and objects upon which they do not focus their eyes, as vague and blurred forms. Furthermore, more light enters the eyes of a person with wide open pupils, so they perceive people upon which their eyes are not focussed as vague and blurred 'bright figures', or even as 'beings of light'. The mental function of the dying and nearly-dead is abnormal, so they may interpret these bright forms and figures as being supernatural, ethereal, other-worldly beings of light, or even as personages and gods from their religion. Brain malfunction during this period may also generate visual hallucinations of other surroundings, persons, or gods.

All the above effects are caused by widening of the pupils, but the functioning of other parts of the eyes also changes during the process of dying. Images seen with the eyes are focussed upon a membrane made of light-sensitive nerve tissue in the back of each eye called the 'retina'. Light falling upon the retina is converted by the nerve cells in the retina into sensory nerve signals that are conducted along sensory nerves into the brain. Nerve cells in the retina need a lot of energy to function normally. In fact, the cells of the retina need so much energy, that they consume oxygen at a higher rate than do nerve cells in the brain.[6] This is why oxygen starvation affects the functioning of the retina before affecting the functioning of the brain.[7] Malfunctioning parts of the retina generate no sensory nerve signals in response to light. So an affected person sees nothing, only 'greyness', or only 'darkness' in those parts of their visual fields served by the malfunctioning parts of their retina's. Furthermore, the sensitivity of the retina to oxygen starvation is not the same for all regions of the retina. The central retina has the richest blood supply, as well as a structure more resistant to oxygen starvation than the rest of the retina. Blood flow within the retina decreases with increasing distance from the central retina[8], even though outer regions of the retina consume just as much oxygen as the central retina. Accordingly, outer regions of the retina are more sensitive to oxygen starvation than the central retina.[9] This explains the effects of oxygen starvation on the functioning of the retina.

To begin with, moderate oxygen starvation first causes malfunction of the outer regions of the retina. This is why people suffering moderate oxygen starvation first notice failure of their peripheral vision. A young man once reported his experience of moderate oxygen starvation during an experiment in which he cycled as hard as he could while breathing air containing only 10% oxygen. A concentration of 10% oxygen in air at sea-level causes moderate oxygen starvation (see Appendix 6), and this oxygen starvation was further worsened by the increased body oxygen consumption resulting from cycling. This young man cycled until he nearly collapsed, and reported:

> '*I peter out at a measly 200 watts, utterly fatigued, sucking at the thin air, my peripheral vision fading out.*'[10]

His report is a clear description of muscle weakness, together with malfunction of the outer regions of the retina caused by moderate oxygen starvation. Increasingly severe oxygen starvation causes ever more extensive malfunction of the outer regions of the retina, so that eventually only the central retina functions normally. This means that those affected by moderate to severe oxygen starvation can only see a central spot of light surrounded by darkness: a situation similar to looking through a tunnel. This is 'tunnel vision', and this is the cause of the 'tunnel' seen by those undergoing near-death experiences caused by oxygen starvation.

Even more severe oxygen starvation causes even more extensive malfunction of the retina. For example, many reports of the last words of the dying, and the nearly dead, often include statements such as: 'it is getting darker', 'everything is becoming grey', or that these people report seeing only 'darkness' and 'blackness'. Nerve cells in the retina consume oxygen at a higher rate than nerve cells in the brain, so oxygen starvation affects the functioning of the retina before affecting the functioning of the brain. Furthermore, the brainstem is a part of the brain more resistant to the effects of oxygen starvation than the rest of the brain[11], which explains why people undergoing increasingly severe oxygen starvation notice that their vision fails before they lose consciousness. Such failure of vision occurring before failure of consciousness is a common observation, often included in reports of the sensory experiences of people who fainted.

Most people have fainted at least once. Fainting is an abrupt loss of conscious caused by sudden severe oxygen starvation of the head due to any of a large number of causes. People reporting memories of their perceptions while fainting nearly always say that 'everything went dark', 'everything went grey', or 'everything went black' just before they lost consciousness. These experiences are called a 'grey-out' or a 'black-out', and they are caused by a generalised malfunctioning of the retina. The very fact that people say they saw only 'grey' or 'blackness', means they were conscious at the time, otherwise they could not consciously perceive 'grey' or 'blackness'. So people reporting that everything went 'grey' or 'black' just before they lost consciousness due to fainting, are actually reporting that oxygen starvation of their heads first caused loss of vision due to retina malfunction, before causing loss of consciousness due to brainstem malfunction.

These same effects of moderate to extreme oxygen starvation on the retina were reported by many of the volunteers taking part in an experiment during which the flow of blood to their heads was stopped until they lost consciousness. The experimenters described the visual perceptions of the people taking part in this experiment as follows:

'Before loss of consciousness, many subjects experienced rapid narrowing of

the field of vision (tunnel vision), blurring of vision, with the field of vision becoming grey, and finally complete loss of vision. A number of subjects stated that they were unable to see but could still hear and were conscious.'[12]

These effects of different degrees of oxygen starvation upon the retina explain the experience of the 'tunnel', as well as the perception of 'light at the end of the tunnel', while total failure of vision due to oxygen starvation explains the 'darkness' reported by the dying and the nearly dead. A woman who almost bled to death during a caesarean section reported a typical tunnel-darkness experience. She reported that:

'I saw myself, or what was left of me lying there (on the operating table), and how busy the doctors and nurses were with me. You could say that I had left my body like leaving a coat. The worst part of it all was that at this point I lost all connection with my body, something which bothered me for quite some time afterwards. After I had floated close to the ceiling for a short time, I was sucked into a tunnel ... It was black and dark around me, somewhat frightening, but this did not last long: at the end of the tunnel I saw a clear light towards which I travelled.'[13]

This woman first experienced a degree of oxygen starvation causing the functioning of her retina's to fail, which is why she first experienced only 'darkness'. Subsequent improvement in the supply of oxygen to her eyes restored some function to the central parts of her retina's, and this caused her to pass from darkness into a 'tunnel'. Oxygen starvation also caused her brain to malfunction, so she combined her sensation of tunnel vision with other sensory effects of oxygen starvation to generate the experience of being sucked into a tunnel through which she travelled towards 'a clear light at the end of the tunnel'. Oxygen starvation also caused her pupils to widen, so more light poured into her eyes, which is why she perceived a 'clear light at the end of the tunnel'. Some people even describe passing through a tunnel to enter a region of bright light. A man who underwent a near-death experience caused by an accident once described just such perceptions:

'During the night I started to feel as if I was falling down and down a well, which was going round and round. At the end of this deep well I could see a wonderful blue light which was coming up and enveloping me. It was alive, like a living light.'[14]

Such experiences, and many experiments, all show that oxygen starvation causes blindness due to retina malfunction at lower levels of oxygen starvation than cause loss of consciousness. This is why the dying sometimes say that 'it is getting darker', or 'everything is dark'. This is also the experience of 'everything is going grey', of 'darkness', or of being 'engulfed by blackness' sometimes reported by the dying or people who nearly died.

Up till now I have only talked about failure of retina function caused by oxygen starvation. But other things also cause retina malfunction. The retina is formed of nerve cells that are more sensitive to the effects of some poisons and drugs than are the nerve cells of the brain. This is why many poisons and drugs first cause failure of the retina before they cause failure of brain functions. For example, everyone has heard the expression 'blind drunk'. A 'blind drunk' person has imbibed so much alcohol, that the concentration of alcohol in the blood is high enough to cause blindness due to retina malfunction, but is not high enough to cause loss of consciousness due to brainstem malfunction. The same is true of many other sleep-inducing drugs, such as anaesthetic drugs.

But the experience of darkness due to drugs, poisons, and alcohol, is quite different to the darkness caused by oxygen starvation. Drugs, poisons, and alcohol never cause tunnel experiences. Only oxygen starvation causes tunnel experiences. The blood supply of the retina explains why this is so. The central part of the retina has the richest blood supply, while the flow of blood to other parts of the retina decreases with increasing distance from the centre of the retina. Accordingly, the concentration of poisons and drugs in the nerve tissue of the retina is initially much higher in central parts of the retina than in the outer parts of the retina. This is why high doses of poisons and drugs first cause failure of central parts of the retina, before causing failure of the entire retina, while lower doses of poisons or drugs only cause failure of the central parts of the retina. People affected by such poisons and drugs describe these effects as 'seeing a central black spot surrounded by light'. Higher doses of these same poisons and drugs cause failure of the entire retina, and affected people see only darkness or blackness. This is the opposite of what happens with oxygen starvation, and this is why tunnel experiences are only caused by oxygen starvation. The effects of anaesthetic drugs illustrate these effects.

Thiopentone is one of several commonly used general anaesthetic drugs. People lose consciousness within twenty to forty seconds after Thiopentone is injected into a vein in their hand or elbow. A few people tell of seeing 'darkness' just before losing consciousness due to such anaesthetic doses of Thiopentone. Only a few people ever tell of seeing this darkness, because they must remember this observation in order to be able to relate it to other people after they awaken, and Thiopentone administered in anaesthetic doses usually blocks the formation of memories. So reports of this observation are rare, which is why I remember what one woman once told me of her experiences of several anaesthetics with injections of Thiopentone. She said: 'It felt like falling into a black hole.'

Her experiences were typical of many of those who undergo anaesthesia with these drugs. First the central parts of her retinas failed, causing her to see a central black area surrounded by light. This was the 'black hole' she saw. The concentration of Thiopentone in her retinas increased still further, causing her retinas to malfunction totally, causing her sight to fail totally. This was the darkness of the 'black hole' into which she fell. At the same time, Thiopentone also caused her brain to malfunction, as well as causing relaxation of her muscle spindles, so that she suddenly felt very heavy. After administration of Thiopentone, people often make slight irregular movements just before losing consciousness. These movements caused this woman's muscle spindles to generate sensory nerve signals interpreted by her malfunctioning brain as movements and falling. The combination of seeing a dark hole followed by blackness, together with abrupt onset of sensations of heaviness, falling, and movements, aroused the perception of falling into a black hole in her malfunctioning, but still conscious mind. After experiencing these sensations, she lost consciousness when the concentration of Thiopentone in her brainstem was sufficient to cause her brainstem to malfunction. Thiopentone is but one of many poisons and drugs causing such experiences of 'darkness', or of 'being engulfed by blackness'.

Knowing these things meant I could now explain all aspects of the visual experiences reported by the dying. So I studied one such report in detail. Between 1977 and 1978 CE, I was an anaesthetic resident in Hackney Hospital. Hackney Hospital was located in the then socially deprived district of Hackney in London (England), and was affiliated with a nearby maternity hospital called the 'Mother's Hospital'. The Mother's Hospital was a small, dilapidated maternity hospital located in Clapton, an adjacent, equally deprived district of London. As an anaesthetic resident in the Hackney Hospital, I was regularly rostered to work in the Mother's Hospital, and this is what drew my attention to the following story. Somewhat more than fifty years before I worked there, a woman died after giving birth in the Mother's Hospital. This was not so unusual at this time, because until the early years of the twentieth century, death as a result of pregnancy and childbirth was a relatively common cause of death in young women. This woman died of heart failure after a difficult delivery, and she experienced nearly all the visual effects reported by dying people. Her physician, Lady Florence Barrett, reported the perceptions and visions of this unfortunate woman:

'When I (Lady Barrett) entered the ward Mrs B. (the dying woman) held

out her hands to me and said, "Thank you for what you have done for me
– for bringing the baby. Is it a boy or a girl?" Then holding my hand tightly,
she said, "Don't leave me, don't go away, will you?" And after a few min-
utes while the House Surgeon carried out some restorative measures, she lay
looking up towards the open part of the room, which was brightly lighted,
and said, "Oh, don't let it get dark – it's getting so dark ... darker and dar-
ker." Her husband and mother were sent for. Suddenly she looked eagerly
towards one part of the room, a radiant smile illuminating her whole coun-
tenance. "Oh, lovely, lovely", she said. I (Lady Barrett) asked, "What is
lovely?" "What I see," she replied in low intense tones. "What do you see?"
"Lovely brightness – wonderful beings." It is difficult to describe the sense of
reality conveyed by her intense absorption in the vision. Then – seeming to
focus her attention more intently one place for a moment – she exclaimed,
almost with a kind of joyous cry, "Why, it's Father! Oh, he's so glad I'm
coming; he is so glad. It would be perfect if only W. (her husband) could
come too." Her baby was brought for her to see. She looked at it with inter-
est, and then said. "Do you think I ought to stay for baby's sake?" Then
turning towards the vision again, she said, "I can't – I can't stay; if you
could see what I do, you would know I can't stay." But she turned to her
husband, who had come in and said, "You won't let the baby go to anyone
who won't love him, will you?" Then she gently pushed him to one side,
saying, "Let me see the lovely brightness." I (Lady Barrett) left shortly after,
and the Matron took my place by the bedside. She lived for another hour,
and appeared to have maintained to the last the double consciousness of
the bright forms she saw, and also of those tending her at the bedside, e.g.
she arranged with the Matron that her premature baby should remain in
hospital till it was strong enough to be cared for in an ordinary household.[15]

This woman had several visual experiences. She experienced darkness, because her heart failure was so severe that her heart no longer pumped enough blood to her head to sustain normal retina function. So everything
became darker and darker as her sight progressively failed due to increasingly severe retinal oxygen starvation. Shortly after her sight failed, a temporary improvement in her heart function increased the flow of blood to
her head to a level sufficient to restore her retinal function. The massive
sympathetic nervous system activity sustaining her failing heart caused her
pupils to widen. So more light entered her eyes, and she saw a 'lovely
brightness'. No-one else in the room saw the 'bright light' perceived by the
dying woman, only the dying woman saw the 'lovely brightness'. Her act
of pushing her husband aside proves that widening of her pupils caused
her to see bright light. She pushed her husband aside, because the presence of his body in front of her eyes reduced the amount of light entering

her eyes so much that she could no longer see the 'lovely brightness'. Her pupils were widened, so she could only clearly see those people and things upon which she focussed her eyes. Accordingly, the other people in the room were seen as vague, unfocussed figures bathed in light, and she called them 'wonderful beings'. She knew she was dying, and subconsciously she also knew of the prior deaths of her father and sister. So she had a vision of these two family members, because they were two people she expected to act as guides in her transition from the world of the living into the realm of the dead. Abnormal brain function caused by oxygen starvation almost certainly contributed to activation of these memories of her father and sister, and may have also induced visions of other supernatural figures. The sensory and visionary experiences of this woman were not supernatural. They were products of oxygen starvation resulting from lethal heart failure, as well as her socio-cultural expectations of the experience of dying.

Nonetheless, to this dying woman as well as to her relatives, these visions and experiences were real. They were proof of the beliefs held by her and her family about the nature of the universe, as well as proof of the reality of a world inhabited by the souls of the dead. So even though her visions had a biological and socio-cultural origin, they transformed her death from a mere biological event, to an event with a profound spiritual meaning for her, for her family, as well as for those who attended her deathbed.

Dying people sometimes describe visions and experiences of 'tunnels', 'darkness', 'beings of light', and 'bright light that does not hurt the eyes'. These are all experiences caused by changes in the functioning of the eyes. Widening of the pupils causes the visions of 'landscapes bathed in light', of 'bright light that does not hurt the eyes', 'bright light at the end of the tunnel', and of 'beings of light'. Malfunction of the edges of the retina causes visions of being in a tunnel, of tunnel vision, or of 'light at the end of the tunnel', while malfunction of the entire retina causes the experiences of 'darkness' and of 'being engulfed by blackness'.

Now I understood the visual experiences reported by the dying. This understanding finally made it possible for me to describe, and explain the last conscious experiences undergone by the dying.

Chapter 18

The Experience of Dying

Everyone must first die before they are dead. So dying is an important moment in the life of each person, because dying is the last conscious experience each person undergoes. But what do people experience while dying? How do the disorders causing people to die affect their thinking, emotions, and perceptions? I also wanted to learn what I may eventually experience when I die.

I initially approached this problem with some temerity. After all, how could I learn about the thoughts, perceptions, and emotions occurring within the minds of the dying? But then I realised some facts already extensively discussed in this book: true death is brainstem death, a deceased person is unconscious, and all conscious experience ceases when brainstem functions fail forever. This means that the experience of dying is a conscious experience, continuing only as long as the brainstem sustains consciousness. So the experience of dying is actually the totality of the last thoughts, perceptions, and emotions occurring within the minds of the dying before irreversible failure of brainstem functions terminates all consciousness forever. Accordingly, this means that the fundamental causes of the terminal failure of brainstem functions that defines death will determine the experiences of the dying. All the studies of the basic causes of dying and death in the previous chapters show that people either die of disorders causing failure of brainstem functions due to oxygen starvation, or they die of disorders causing failure of brainstem functions due to other causes. So this means that the structure and functioning of the human body is such that there are only three fundamental ways people can develop the irreversible failure of brainstem functions that defines death.

1. *Sudden brainstem destruction.* This is sudden death.
2. *Progressive failure of brainstem functions.* Progressive failure of brainstem functions resulting from a multitude of causes eventually causes loss of consciousness. Further progression of failure of brainstem functions eventually causes breathing to falter and stop. The resulting extreme oxygen starvation causes the irreversible brainstem failure of death.
3. *Progressively severe oxygen starvation.* Progressive failure of brainstem functions caused by increasingly severe oxygen starvation eventually causes loss of consciousness. Further progression of oxygen starvation

causes failure of even more brainstem functions, eventually causing breathing to falter and stop. The resulting extreme oxygen starvation causes the irreversible brainstem failure of death.

Each living person will eventually develop the eternal loss of consciousness of death in one of these three ways. A worldwide study of causes of death revealed that few people die of sudden brainstem destruction, that fewer than one in ten persons dies of progressive failure of brainstem functions, while more than nine in ten people die of progressively severe oxygen starvation.[1] This definition of three basic mechanisms of death enabled me to learn what people may think, feel, and perceive while dying. So what are the experiences generated by these three fundamental mechanisms of death?

Sudden brainstem destruction is the first of the three fundamental mechanisms of death. Very few people die of sudden brainstem destruction, because there are only relatively few disorders causing sudden brainstem destruction. For example, there are diseases causing sudden massive bleeding within the substance of the brainstem, so destroying brainstem structures. Brain cancers may cause sudden distortion of brainstem structures, so causing sudden brainstem destruction. Accidents, falls, blows, explosions, beheading, or shooting may cause sudden brainstem destruction. All these things cause sudden death by causing sudden brainstem destruction, which means sudden irreversible failure of all brainstem functions, such as consciousness and breathing.

What do people experience while dying of sudden brainstem destruction? People first experience the effects of the conditions leading up their deaths. So before dying they may be in pain or feel comfortable, feel unhappy or happy, be anxious or calm, be terrified or serene. Sudden failure of all brainstem functions causes sudden loss of consciousness, and the dying pass abruptly from a state where they are fully conscious and able to experience all about them, to a state of unconsciousness in which they experience nothing. And because the sudden failure of all their brainstem functions is due to brainstem destruction, they never have any more conscious experiences. They are dead.

Progressive failure of brainstem functions is the second of the three mechanisms of death. Fewer than one in ten people die of progressive failure of brainstem functions. There are many disorders causing progressive failure of brainstem functions. Examples of such disorders are severe kidney and liver diseases, unregulated diabetes mellitus, thyroid gland diseases, and extremely high or low body temperatures. Furthermore, sufficiently high doses of alcohol, sedatives, sleeping pills, and anaesthetic drugs, also cause failure of brainstem functions. Dying of progressive brainstem failure may take only a few seconds or last many days. So what do people feel? What do people perceive? And what do people experience while dying of progressive failure of brainstem functions?

All these disorders and intoxications first cause abnormal mental function before causing failure of any brainstem functions, because the functioning of the brainstem is less affected by these disorders and drugs than is the functioning of the rest of the brain. Increasingly abnormal brain function first manifests as uncoordinated movements, together with changes in mental state such as loss of memory, errors in judgement, difficulty with complex thoughts, as well as mood changes such as euphoria or depression. Further progression of brain malfunction causes affected people to become confused, incoherent, and drowsy. They may have delusory interpretations of their sensations, delusory thoughts, or even hallucinations.

These are the perceptions of observers, but those experiencing progressive failure of brainstem functions often perceive things quite differently. They typically lose all insight into their condition, feeling that nothing is wrong with the functioning of their minds, feeling that their bodily functions and perceptions are normal, or even better than normal. They may interpret sensory perceptions in an abnormal manner, perceiving what they sense with indifference, as laughable, or threatening. And these people still have no insight into their condition, even when their mental function has deteriorated such that they feel that movement, walking, and eating are unnecessary.

An article in a medical journal related an experience illustrating all these effects of brain malfunction. A 72 year old 'literary gentleman' was admitted to hospital for treatment of extensive cancer. At one point during his hospital admission, this man suddenly lost consciousness due to a combination of medicines for treatment of pain and his cancer. After reviving, he was confused and struggled wildly in an attempt to escape from the doctors and nurses treating him, quite evidently undergoing terrifying delusional experiences and hallucinations during which malignant tormentors tried changing his body shape. Eventually, he regained normal consciousness and wrote a clear report of his experiences.

> ' I am lying on a bed, looking up into the eyes of the two beings who have been and are still 'manipulating' me. The scene has changed, moving from the sandy outdoor landscape with its great rock to this small room with its curtained door through which there are agitated comings and goings. How have I arrived here? I have dim impressions of being carried by my captors through overhanging trees to this hut in the forest. The figures too are becoming clear to me, and the use of instruments, and voices. In particular the insertion of a tube into my right wrist is something that I must resist

with all my strength. The dreadful conflict continues, through mounting le-
vels of intensity. Once, perhaps twice, there is a reversal, and for a moment
I taste the bliss of my authentic being, only to be returned to the rack. The
figures of my captors are becoming more distinct, and I too am putting on
a body. They are succeeding in their dreadful purpose. Yet, even at this late
hour, I am hoping against all hope to escape to return to my world and be
free. Nothing these monsters have done to me can efface that wonderful ple-
nitude of being. Kind eyes, yes; understanding eyes, yes; but are they perhaps
a little too small? The eyes smile too; and what lies behind that smile? it
would be impossible to be more convinced that I am in the hands of mon-
sters.'[2]

The delusions and hallucinations reported by this man are typical of what
may be experienced during the altered mental states induced by all conditions causing brain malfunction. His imagery and experiences were based
upon real sensations, but his malfunctioning brain interpreted them abnormally, clothing them with delusions and hallucinations. His malfunctioning brain first generated a hallucination of a sandy desert together with delusions of malignant attackers against whom he frantically struggled in an
unsuccessful attempt to escape capture and torture. The subsequent struggle, pulling, and tugging by hospital staff necessary to restrain his wildly
struggling body was interpreted by his brain as capture, as well as an attempt to change his body form. And chief among his tormentors were
monsters in the guises of doctors and nurses who also inserted an intrave-
nous needle into his arm to administer medicines. His hallucination of
being transported from a sandy desert to a hut in a forest was quite evidently the way his abnormally functioning brain interpreted transportation
from one room to another by the hospital staff. All these things explain
his terrifying experience.

Now it is possible to summarise what people experience while dying of
progressive failure of brainstem functions. First, these people experience
the sensory and mental effects of the disorders causing their deaths. Different disorders causing death induce widely different sensations and states
of mind. So before dying they may be in pain or feel comfortable, feel unhappy or happy, be anxious or calm, be terrified or serene. Further progression of these disorders causes progressively severe brain malfunction, during which they may be euphoric, depressed, hallucinate, feel fear, or experience other sensations and emotions. Progressive failure of brain functions
eventually causes such a degree of brainstem malfunction that loss of consciousness occurs. This is the point at which individual conscious existence
ceases. Further progression of failure of brainstem functions eventually
causes breathing to falter, ultimately to stop altogether, so resulting in ex-

treme oxygen starvation and the subsequent irreversible failure of brain-stem functions of death.

Progressively severe oxygen starvation is the third of the three fundamental mechanisms of death. More than nine in ten people die of disorders ultimately causing death due to oxygen starvation. Progressively severe oxygen starvation eventually causes brain and brainstem malfunction, ultimately causes irreversible failure of all brainstem functions, after which death is present. The time taken to die of progressively severe oxygen starvation may be as short as several seconds or as long as many days, depending upon the cause of death.

The causes and effects of oxygen starvation are extensively discussed in earlier chapters. Nonetheless, there is another aspect to oxygen starvation. This is the degree of oxygen starvation at which death becomes inevitable, unless medical treatment is administered. The body is a biological mechanism developed by aeons of merciless evolution to survive all manner of diseases and injuries. So the body is capable of compensating to some degree for disorders causing oxygen starvation. But there is a degree of oxygen starvation at which these mechanisms begin to fail in the diseased or injured bodies of the dying. Careful observation, and study, reveals that moderate oxygen starvation is the degree of oxygen starvation at which these aeons-old survival mechanisms begin to fail in the bodies of the dying.

There are a number of reasons why moderate oxygen starvation is a turning point in the dying process. Moderate oxygen starvation weakens muscles, rendering breathing less efficient, so worsening any oxygen starvation. Moderate oxygen starvation diminishes the will to move, so oxygen starved people remain still, moving only in response to discomfort or necessity. Moderate oxygen starvation diminishes hunger and thirst, so oxygen starved people no longer want to eat or drink. Moderate oxygen starvation induces a sense of calm indifference, even of serene acceptance of death. Moderate oxygen starvation typically causes loss of insight, and most oxygen starved people do not even realise they are oxygen starved. Moderate oxygen starvation is also the point at which people lose the desire and the ability to care for their bodily needs. All of these things mean that moderate oxygen starvation is the starting point of a vicious circle of body malfunction causing even more body malfunction. This is why moderate oxygen starvation is the turning point after which death becomes inevitable, unless active measures are taken to reverse the dying process.

Moderate oxygen starvation is not just the turning point in the dying process signalling the inevitability of death, but it is also the point at which the sufferings experienced by the dying diminish and their mood changes. Indeed, moderate oxygen starvation changes the mood of many dying people to a calm and serene indifference, sometimes inducing a mood of joy,

sometimes even inducing visions and hallucinations. These things were often remarked upon by priests who were called to the bedsides of the dying
to administer the comforts of their religion. Their reports of the last moments of dying people are often descriptions of the effects of moderate to
severe oxygen starvation upon the mental state of the dying. For example:

> 'The priest, by virtue of his office, is often present at a deathbed, and knows
> that many people die a beautiful death. He knows of situations where the
> dying are fully conscious at the moment of death, and with eyes open wide
> with amazement, stare ecstatically at something that only their dying eyes
> can see. Often the expression of the dying radiates a supernatural rest and
> peace, and their last breath is a sigh of release and happiness.'[3]

This description reveals that many of the dying people visited by the priest
had already developed moderate oxygen starvation. This is evident, because
many of the dying were free of any discomfort or pain, as well as being
serene and calm. Some people even had visions and ecstatic experiences.
Yet, before reaching this point, people may suffer horribly from the disorders causing their deaths. This means the experience of dying of progressive oxygen starvation can be separated into two phases. People first experience the sensations, perceptions, and emotions aroused by the cause of
death. Finally, when moderate oxygen starvation eventually develops, all
discomfort, pain and distress disappear, and dying people experience a serene and accepting calm. This sequence of events is true, because the experiences of the dying reveal this. A typical report of such a death is that
of a man who died of cancer. His physician reported:

> 'A male patient in his seventies had been suffering from advanced cancer.
> He had been in great pain, sleepless and restless. One day after he had
> managed to get a little sleep, he woke up smiling, seemed suddenly free
> from all physical pain and agony, detached, calm, and peaceful. For the last
> six hours the patient had only received a very moderate dose of Phenobarbi-
> tal, a relatively weak sedative. He bade all goodbye, one by one, which he
> had not done before, and told us that he was going to die. He was fully
> alert for some 10 minutes. Then he fell into a coma and died peacefully a
> few minutes later.'[4]

This man first suffered considerable pain caused by the cancer causing his
death. This is not unusual, because about six in ten people with cancer
suffer pain caused by their cancer. Progressive worsening of his bodily
functions finally caused him to develop moderate oxygen starvation. From
this point onwards, his sufferings diminished, and his mood changed to

calm and peaceful detachment. Further progression of oxygen starvation eventually caused failure of his brainstem functions, so he lost consciousness. Ultimately, he stopped breathing, and died. People who survive lethal degrees of oxygen starvation often report undergoing a similar sequence of experiences. Indeed, a man whose heart stopped beating as a result of a heart attack reported just such a sequence of experiences to his physician:

> 'Suddenly I felt relief from my terrible chest pains. Now I felt exhilaration. I can't fully express it. I was floating into an area that looked like heaven. It was wonderfully bright with streets of gold and I saw a figure with long hair in a brilliant white robe. A light radiated all about him. I didn't talk to him. I am sure that it was Jesus. As he took hold of my hand, the next thing I remember was a jerking on my body. You [5] were shaking me and then the pain came back. But I was back on earth again!'[6]

This man first felt severe chest pain due to a heart attack. Then he rapidly developed oxygen starvation because his heart had stopped beating and no longer pumped sufficient blood containing oxygen around his body to sustain consciousness and life. Moderate to severe oxygen starvation removed his perception of pain, caused him to feel blissful and exhilarated, and he underwent an out-of-body experience. Successful restoration of his heartbeat restored normal oxygen supplies to the tissues of his body, restoring normal brain function, at which point his chest pain also returned. The changes of mental function experienced by the people in these examples are typical of the mental changes nearly all people undergo while dying of oxygen starvation.

All these things explain what each person can observe in someone dying of progressive oxygen starvation, as well as what people will experience while dying of progressive oxygen starvation. People must first endure the sufferings and discomforts of the disorders causing them to die, and during this period they may be in pain or feel comfortable, feel unhappy or happy, be anxious or calm, be terrified or serene. Oxygen starvation develops as the process of dying continues, eventually developing into moderate oxygen starvation, at which point suffering diminishes, and changes in mood as well as perceptions occur. Further progression of oxygen starvation to severe oxygen starvation causes apparent unconsciousness. Development of extreme oxygen starvation causes loss of consciousness. Ultimately oxygen starvation causes such extreme failure of brainstem functions that breathing falters and stops, causing irreversible brainstem damage and death.

Finally, I was able to explain the experiences and perceptions of the dying. I divided these experiences and perceptions into three stages.

1. The dying person first experiences the discomforts and indignities of the cause of death. So they may be in pain or feel comfortable, feel sick or healthy, feel terrified or calm, feel sad or happy.
2. The cause of death eventually affects the functioning of the brain. A person dying of sudden brainstem destruction suddenly loses consciousness and experiences nothing more. A person dying of progressive brainstem failure develops increasingly abnormal mental function due to the cause of progressive brainstem failure. And a person dying of progressively severe oxygen starvation develops increasingly abnormal mental function due to increasingly severe oxygen starvation.
3. Progressive worsening of brain functions finally causes loss of consciousness due to failure of some brainstem functions. Conscious existence ceases at this point. Finally, more brainstem functions fail, causing breathing to falter and stop, after which extreme oxygen starvation causes the irreversible failure of all brainstem functions that is death.

All these things answered the third question I asked myself in the beginning of this book, 'What will I experience as I die?' I now understood the appearances, emotions, behaviour, and sensations of the dying. I had also learned how my dying will affect my thoughts, emotions, and perceptions. If I can remember this knowledge as I die, then I will understand what I am undergoing while dying. Such knowledge may well enable me to undergo my own last moments with an equanimity based upon understanding of what I am undergoing.

I speak of equanimity, but this is something easily said now while I am not dying. After all, even though I have learned much about the process of dying and death, I still harbour an ingrained fear of dying. I pondered how I could approach this problem of the natural fear that I, and nearly all other people have of dying, and even worse, of a possible terrible death. Many great thinkers have written of this problem. All implicitly state that some mental preparation will give fortitude, possibly even mitigate the trials of any degradation, distress, or torment experienced before brain malfunction, and unconsciousness finally put a stop to all suffering. Of all these writings, the words of Saint Augustine are surely the most appropriate. More than fifteen hundred years ago he wrote:

> *'Of this at least I am certain, that no one has ever died who was not destined to die some time. Now the end of life puts the longest life on a par with the shortest. For of two things which have alike ceased to be, the one is not better, the other worse - the one greater, the other less. And of what consequence is it what kind of death puts an end to life, since he who has died once is not forced to go through the same ordeal a second time? And*

as in the daily casualties of life every man is, as it were, threatened with numberless deaths, so long as it remains uncertain which of them is his fate, I would ask whether it is not better to suffer one and die, than to live in fear of all? I am not unaware of the poor-spirited fear which prompts us to choose rather to live long in fear of so many deaths, than to die once and so escape them all; but the weak and cowardly shrinking of the flesh is one thing, and the well-considered and reasonable persuasion of the soul quite another.'[7]

This is practical advice indeed. To view dying and death in this way is to live a life without fear, in full knowledge, understanding, and acceptance of individual and collective mortality. It is a way to accept the certainty of death with courage and dignity.

Chapter 19

A Vision of Eternity

I had learned the true nature of death. I had learned what I will experience as I die. I had learned I have no soul. My mind is a product of the functioning of my body, so my mind will die with my body, and I will not live for eternity in a life after death. I had learned answers to all my questions. But I did not feel triumphant after learning answers to my questions. Instead, I was oppressed by thoughts of my transience and imminent mortality. I even felt a strange sense of betrayal, though I did not know by whom, or by what. After all, the knowledge and analysis presented in this book finally does away with all the hope, and all the comfort afforded by uncertainty about the possibility of a life after death, as well as finally demolishing many ancient belief systems forming my upbringing. True, this hopeful uncertainty, and these belief systems were based upon incorrect interpretations of sensations, as well as vain longings, fantasies, and imaginings. Yet they were comforting. They meant that perhaps my existence was part of some grand plan, and that perhaps my existence had some purpose, while the knowledge in this book appears to offer only the darkness of ultimate futility. I read and I thought further. I eventually realised that the knowledge contained within this book offered me more than just the bleak futility of ultimate extinction. It gave me a provable, physical foundation for the way I have come to regard my personal mortality. So I wrote this chapter as a summary of the way I have come to regard the certainty of my mortality.

At first, I also found it difficult to fully comprehend, as well as to accept the absolute extinction, and eternal dissolution of my mind upon the death of my body. Eternal dissolution of my mind upon my death seemed to imply that all my conscious endeavours, struggling, suffering, joy, love, and hopes are ultimately futile. Ultimate futility is a disconcerting and repellent concept. Many people share these same emotions, and these same thoughts. Indeed, many people feel this concept of ultimate futility to be so hideous, that it is a force driving a desperate hope, or actual belief, in the reality of an eternal life after death. But when carefully examined, this almost universal longing for an eternal life after death is very strange, because many of those who long for an eternal life after death are people for whom death is a welcome ending to the boredom of their lives. Suzan Ertz once expressed this last idea in a single pithy sentence:

'Millions long for immortality who don't know what to do with themselves on a rainy Sunday afternoon.'[1]

Nonetheless, this is not true of everyone. Some of those longing for eternal life after death have grand designs, ambitions, and plans, or they feel their lives are far too short for all they wish to do and experience. There are also those who long for eternal life after death who have no grand designs, or perform no important functions in society. They are simply people who enjoy the pleasurable sensations of being alive, the company of others, the tastes and smells of what they eat and what they drink, the warmth of the sun upon their bodies, and countless other human pleasures.

I share these same emotions. I pondered the various ideas and beliefs regarding the nature of life after death, and I asked myself whether eternal life after death is something I would want. Eventually, I realised a basic principle underlying all ideas, and beliefs regarding individual intelligence and personality in a life after death. All these ideas and beliefs explicitly state, or clearly imply, that there is no change in individual intelligence, or personality, in a life after death. This is a very logical belief. After all, if people would become more intelligent, or develop another personality in a life after death, they would no longer be the same as when they were alive. This would make a mockery of the idea of just punishment of the evil, and just reward of the virtuous in a life after death. I will explain this last idea with an example:

Imagine a man drinking heavily at a bar. This man eventually becomes very drunk. Normally, he condemns drunken driving, knowing it to be dangerous. Yet, despite being drunk, this man still decides to drive home in his car. While driving in this drunken state, he runs down and kills a group of children crossing the road.

According to many religions, such a man would merit eternal torment in an afterlife for this deed. Many people believe the soul manifests its natural superhuman intelligence and insight in an afterlife. So in an afterlife this man would know, and fully understand, things he was too stupid to realise while alive. But if this man had such superhuman intelligence and insight while alive, he would never have even thought of driving while drunk. He would not even have become drunk. Eternal punishment of the soul of this man in an afterlife under such circumstances would be bitter and unjust indeed. It would make a mockery of any idea of divine justice, and God is supposed to be just.

Even if this belief in justice in a life after death is only a fantasy, one fact about an eternal life after death is implied by the name. An eternal life after death is just that, eternal. Eternity is not just one hundred years, nor a thousand years, nor a million years, nor even a billion years.[2] Eternity is forever, an uncountable number of years until the universe itself dies. During an eternal life after death, each person will eventually have thought every possible thought, done everything possible, and experienced everything possible within the limits set by their individual intelligence and personality. They will remember all these things as they endlessly repeat them, again, again, and again. This is the true horror of eternal life: the memory of all thoughts, deeds, and experiences, together with the endless repetition of these same things throughout all eternity. All people will eventually experience eternal life after death as an unrelenting torment of everlasting monotony. A drear and horrid prospect.

This is why I am glad my mind will die with my body. This is why I will welcome the eternal nothingness of death when I eventually die. But does the termination of my mind after my death mean my existence has no more worth than the dust, stones, plants, and animals with which I share this world? This question is answered by Zarathustra, the main character in a work of philosophical fiction written by Friedrich Nietzsche in 1885 CE, called 'Thus Spoke Zarathustra'.[3] Zarathustra is a prophet. In the beginning of the book he speaks to a crowd gathered in a market square at the same time as a tightrope walker commences his performance above them on a rope stretched between two towers. This tightrope walker is so surprised by the sudden appearance of another tightrope walker on the same rope that he loses his balance and falls to the square below. The people in the square scatter away from the place where the tightrope walker was going to fall:

> 'But Zarathustra remained still and the body fell quite close to him, badly injured and broken but not yet dead. After a while, consciousness returned to the shattered man[4] and he saw Zarathustra kneeling beside him. 'What are you doing?' he asked at length. "I've known for a long time that the Devil would trip me up. Now he's dragging me to Hell: are you trying to prevent him?"
>
> "On my honour, friend", answered Zarathustra, "All you have spoken of does not exist: there is no Devil and no Hell. Your soul will be dead even before your body: therefore fear nothing any more!"
>
> The man looked up mistrustfully. "If you are speaking the truth," he said then, "I leave nothing when I leave life. I am not much more than an animal which has been taught to dance by blows and starvation."
>
> "Not so," said Zarathustra. "You have made danger your calling, there is nothing in that to despise. Now you perish through your calling: so I will bury you with my own hands."[5]

Zarathustra spoke the truth when he told the dying man that soul and body are one and the same. After all, the brainstem is the generator of consciousness, the functioning of the brainstem is what makes conscious mental activity possible, and the brainstem always fails before the rest of the body dies. So in a sense, the soul of the tightrope walker did indeed die before his body died. But a person is not just a soulless animal driven by biological imperatives developed during aeons of evolution, because unlike an animal, each person is aware. Each person is aware of the immediacy of their mortality, aware of their individual fate, aware of the fates of the societies in which they live, and aware of their relationship to the universe. And unlike animals, plants, and lifeless objects, each person has sufficient intelligence to alter their individual effects upon their societies and their world. So even though each person is mortal, even though the mind of each person dies with their body, and even though each person has no immaterial soul coupled to their body, each person does have a form of immortality. Indeed, the nature of each individual, the nature of the society in which each individual lives, and the nature of the universe in which each person lives gives each person a form of immortality. I will explain why this is so.

To begin with, a person exists, and the very fact of their existence is imprinted forever upon the fabric of the universe. Everyone is familiar with the concept that something occurs at a certain place and time. The location of any place is defined by a set of co-ordinates called spatial co-ordinates. But an event also occurs at a certain time. This is the time, or temporal co-ordinate of that event. Past, present, future, here and there, are all co-ordinates within the four dimensional universe in which we live. Indeed, people speak of deceased persons in terms of just such a four-dimensional co-ordinate system. This is also the same way people think and speak of historical persons. The biography of Confucius is an example of this way of looking at the life each person.

> *Confucius, also known as Kung Fu-tze, is the name of a venerated Chinese philosopher who lived from 551 to 479 BCE. He was born and buried in the city of Chufoo. He never travelled outside China. He worked as a public administrator from about 532 to 517 BCE, after which he devoted the rest of his life to studying Chinese literature and philosophy.[6]*

This small biographical sketch of Confucius provides the temporal, and spatial co-ordinates defining the life of Confucius. The temporal co-ordinates defining the period he lived are from 551 to 479 BCE. The spatial co-ordinates where he lived are on the planet Earth, in the country now called China. The temporal and spatial co-ordinates of his every deed, and his

every movement, can be precisely defined. The temporal and spatial co-ordinates at which each of his thoughts occurred, and during which his every
spoken word was uttered, can also be precisely defined. Confucius lives forever within this set of temporal and spatial co-ordinates.

The same reasoning applies to each person. Each person is born, and will
eventually die. Each individual life occurs within a series of temporal and
spatial co-ordinates. Individual thoughts, words, and deeds at any time and
place exist unchanging for all eternity at the temporal and spatial co-ordinates at which they occurred. This does not mean that conscious existence
will somehow continue throughout eternity. After all, people experience
time as something with a direction, from young to old, from then to now,
and from now to the future. This perception of time is immutable. It is
forced upon everyone by the natural laws of the universe. This immutable
nature of time means that death is the end of time for each person, because this is the point at which consciousness ceases. Even so, each person
does exist forever within the continuum of temporal and spatial co-ordinates in which they lived.[7]

Each person exists, and memories of this existence survive individual
death. This means that memory is also a form of survival after death.
Nonetheless, survival of memory is a very transient form of survival after
death for most people. After all, who remembers the meek and unassuming, the anonymous bulk of humanity who never aspire to greatness or
public recognition. If their memories only reside in the minds of equally
unassuming and anonymous friends, relatives, and acquaintances, then the
post-mortem survival of their memories is short-lived indeed. This con-
trasts starkly with the enduring post-mortem survival of memories of those
who caused enormous suffering and death in their own times: people such
as Alexander the Great, Cleopatra of Egypt, Czar Peter of Russia, Napoleon
Bonaparte, Adolf Hitler, or Genghis Khan. The memories of these people
are as enduring as the memories of great philosophers and holy people
such as Moses, Aristotle, Confucius, Buddha, Jesus of Nazareth, Mohammed, or Albert Einstein. Memories of these persons have endured
long after their deaths, because their works and deeds profoundly affected
the lives of many people, both during and after their lifetimes. Even so,
the memories of these great and famous people endure only a short time
in relation to the eternity of death, because all people, all civilisations, all
philosophies, and all memories are transient. In 1818 CE, the English poet
Percy Bysshe Shelley[8] once expressed this same thought in a sonnet
called 'Ozymandias':

> '*I met traveller from an antique land*
> *Who said: Two vast and trunkless legs of stone*

Stand in the desert ... Near them, on the sand,
Half sunk, a shattered visage lies, whose frown,
And wrinkled lip, and sneer of cold command,
Tell that its sculptor well those passions read
Which yet survive, stamped on these lifeless things,
The hand that mocked them, and the heart that fed:
And on the pedestal these words appear:
"My name is Ozymandias, king of kings:
Look on my works, ye Mighty, and despair!"
Nothing beside remains. Round the decay
Of that colossal wreck, boundless and bare
The lone and level sands stretch far away.'

This sonnet is a bleak and powerful evocation of the ultimate transience and futility of all human endeavours, as well as the certain oblivion awaiting the memories of each person. Yet, even though the cruelty of ultimate oblivion is truth, even though a person may be powerful or insignificant, and even though a person may live a short or a long life, these evanescent memories of the existence of each person carried in the minds of the living are still a form of individual immortality.

But existence and memory are only two aspects of individual immortality. The mere fact of existing, and being alive implies that each person affects his fellows and the world. This is another aspect of individual immortality. There are countless examples illustrating this, and I will mention a few of them.

People must eat to live. Food is grown, caught, slaughtered, collected, processed, and sold to each person by others. These people are supported by the services and products produced by those who buy the food. So the individual and collective consumption of food by each person affects others, as well as the world in which each person lives.

People wear clothing and shoes. Many people produce the clothing and shoes worn by each person. These people are supported by the services and products produced by those who buy clothing and shoes. So the individual and collective consumption of clothing and shoes affects others, as well as the world in which each person lives.

People live and work in houses and other buildings. These buildings are constructed and built by people. Those people producing the building materials, and constructing these buildings, are supported by the services and products produced by those who buy and use these houses and buildings. So the individual and collective requirement for housing and buildings affects others, as well as the world in which each person lives.

People produce foul water by washing themselves, their clothing, and their eating utensils. People urinate and defecate. People produce waste products from food, as well as producing waste and rubbish during work, and other activities. Waste products affect the environment, as well as the world in which each person lives. And each person's production of waste contributes to this.

People speak and act. The words and actions of each person affect the thoughts, speech, and behaviour of others. Mean and vicious actions affect people differently than do kind and generous deeds. A blow has a different effect than a tender caress. Insults and harsh words have different effects than do thoughtful and gentle speech. So the speech and deeds of each individual affect others, as well as the world in which each person lives.

The meeting and coupling of man and woman, the resulting pregnancy and birth of a baby; this is the way each person comes into being. All these aspects of the way each person comes into being affects the mother and the father of each person, the immediate surroundings of the mother and the father, as well as the world in which they live. Babies are born out of such unions. Babies are vulnerable, requiring a long period of feeding and nurturing if they are to survive. The feeding, nurturing, and upbringing of babies and children is only possible because of co-operation within groups of individuals. This affects the people of the societies into which these babies are born, their immediate surroundings, as well as their world. Children also speak, act, and have the same requirements for food, clothing, and housing as their parents. Furthermore, children usually survive the deaths of their parents, so transmitting their parental genetic material and thoughts into the future. This means that the having of children profoundly affects the world in which we live.

Ancestors, environment, and societies form each person's body, and mould each person's thoughts. So the form and functioning of each person's body is a product of genetic material inherited from their ancestors, their environment, the food they eat, and their upbringing. Each person's thoughts, and the way they think, are products of their genetic constitution, the functioning of their bodies, their diet, their upbringing, as well as the prevailing patterns of thought in the societies in which they live. Buddha once expressed these same thoughts thousands of years ago:

> 'Is not this individuality of mine a combination, material as well as mental?
> Is it not made up of qualities that sprang into being by a gradual evolution?
> The five roots of sense perception in this organism[9] have come from ancestors who performed these functions. The ideas which I think, came to me partly from others who thought them, and partly they rise from combinations of the ideas in my own mind. Those who have used the same sense-organs, and have thought the same ideas before I was composed into this indi-

viduality of mine are my previous existence's; they are my ancestors as much as the I of yesterday is the father of the I of to-day, and the karma[10] of my past deeds conditions the fate of my present existence.'[11]

So the legacy each individual leaves after death is a product of his interactions with his fellows, his children, and the consequences of his consumption. All these things affect others, as well as the world in which each person lives. These effects are transmitted into the future to affect future generations. So this world, the future of this world, and the life of each person are products of the past and the present. The sum of all these things forms the triad of individual immortality:

1   A person exists, and the fact of his existence is eternally imprinted upon the fabric of the universe;
2   the existence of each person affects other people and the world during his life and after his death;
3   a person is remembered after death.

This triad of individual immortality gives me a way of viewing my existence, and my relation to the world about me. My brain will die with my body, after which my mind, my personality, my emotions, my thoughts, and all that makes me a unique conscious being will revert to nothingness. I have no immaterial soul, so I had no existence before my birth, nor will I exist after my death. I have no immortality in the sense that my mind will continue to consciously think and possess personality throughout eternity. Nonetheless, I do possess a form of immortality. My immortality lies in the fact of my existence, the effects of my existence upon my fellows and the world, and the memories of my existence carried in the minds of the living. These things are forever imprinted upon the fabric of the universe.

This triad of individual immortality also has implications for the way I interact with all about me. What I think, what I speak, and what I do: all these things determine what happens to me, to those around me, to my descendants, and to my world. These effects are my responsibility. So I must think, speak, and act in a worthy manner. I must cherish learning and reasoned argument. I must have an active interest in, and a thirst for knowledge of all about me. The opposites of these things are blind faith, ignorance, and a lack of desire to learn. These things make me a brutish slave of my emotions, lusts, and passions, as well as a thrall of those with an insatiable and conscienceless thirst for power, prestige, and the gratification of their personal desires.

I was born, and I will die. My life occurs between these two points. There is no more than this. This life is all I have. There is no second chance. My existence, the memories I leave after my death, and the influence I had on the world about me are my eternal imprint upon the universe. During my life I may commit mean and spiteful deeds, I may hurt others, and I may even cause others to suffer and die. At other moments during my life, I may love, I may make others happy, and I may aid my fellows. My life is the sum of all these things: the sum of my mistakes, my hurtful deeds and careless speech, my aid to others, as well as the love and assistance I extend to others. During quiet moments of reflection when I ponder the sum of my deeds and actions, I ask myself whether my life is one I would be proud to acknowledge. After all, it is the sum of all these things that ultimately determines my feelings of fulfilment and worth. I know I inherit my present from my past. But I cannot change my past. I can only influence the future. So my remaining span of life is the only time I have to change my life. These are no new thoughts. Such thoughts form part of the teachings of even ancient religions. Indeed, the prophet Zoroaster[12] taught these same things more than two thousand years ago, saying:

> 'But without any reason men adhere to that evil guide, passion, created by the demons; so that they do not think of fate,
> And by the bent of their nature they forget death.
> They do not keep in mind the working of time and the transientness of the body,
> They ever go wandering about on the way of desire,
> They are tossed in doubt by evil passion,
> They clothe themselves with spite, in the course of strife, for the sake of vanishing goods;
> They are intoxicated with pride in their youth,
> And shall be full of regrets at the end of their time.
> For if one say: "On this earth of the seven Karshvares[13] there is somebody going to die", everybody ought to think: "Perhaps it is I",
> Had he sense enough to know that every creature that has been created and has had existence shall die, and that the unseen, deceiving Astivihad[14] comes for every one.[15]

Knowing these things, I understand that the most terrible realisation I can have, is to realise shortly before I die that I wished my life were different. I do not want to realise shortly before I die, or at a time when I can do nothing to change my life, that my life was evil, despicable, loathsome, shameful, or even wasted. Such a realisation is truly terrible. For then death will no longer be an ending to a worthy life, but the most becoming deed in my life. I will be remembered as a vile person. I will be remembered as a person who wasted his most precious possession: his life.[16] My children, my family, my friends, and all other people will be glad when I am dead. They will say the best thing I did in life was to die. Even if others do not know of my nature or my deeds, I will know the truth about myself, and such a realisation can only make me bitter and sad.

So I must strive to live a life that I, my children, family, friends, and others are proud to acknowledge. I must strive to live a life that is worthy and fulfilled. Fulfilment in life comes in many forms. It may be a life filled with quiet performance of duty. It may be a life dedicated to raising children to become fine adults. It may be a life filled with pleasure and feasting. It may be a life filled with hard work. It may be a life filled with selfless service to others. It may be a life filled with adventure. Or it may be a life filled with struggle against injustice and evil. But regardless of whether I am rich or poor, beggar or emperor; fulfilment in my life is what I regard as fulfilment. At the end of such a life, I will know what my life has meant to me and to others. Such thoughts lead me inexorably to three precepts underpinning my being.

1. There is no life before birth, and there is no life after death. Life and consciousness exist only between birth and death.
2. Life and mind have a biological basis, because each person is a biological mechanism formed and sustained by food, water, and air. Accordingly, all thoughts, emotions, sensations, perceptions, speech, actions, and experiences are rooted in the biological nature of the body.
3. Each person is immortal, because of the fact of his existence, the effects of his existence, and the memories he leaves behind him.

To understand these three precepts is to know the basis of my individual being. So I celebrate and honour my body, thoughts, senses, emotions, and desires. All these things make me a unique individual, because I am the sum of all these things. This understanding gives me freedom. Indeed, true freedom comes from an understanding of the knowledge revealed in this book. This knowledge frees me from the tyranny of repeated reincarnations in a succession of bodies: I have no soul, so I cannot be reincarnated in a succession of mortal bodies. This knowledge frees me from all fear of the drear horror of an eternal life after death: I have no soul, so there is no life after death. This knowledge frees me from the necessity to conduct my life in the expectation of eternal punishment or reward in a life after death: I have no soul, so I will undergo no punishment or reward in a life after death. This knowledge frees me from the toils of religions, religious dogmas, and religious fanaticism: I have no soul, so I am free of any enslavement to expectations of reward or punishment in a life after death as determined by religion, religious dogma, or religious fanatics. This knowledge frees me from mental enslavement to my fellows: I know they are as mortal as I am, and are driven by the same emotions, lusts, and desires. This knowledge frees me from uncertainty as to my place in this universe: by explaining the nature and meaning of my life and death, this knowledge clarifies my relationship to the universe. This knowledge frees my thoughts, because I now have a more complete understanding of my own nature and my being.

Yet this does not mean Friedrich Nietzsche was correct when he wrote, 'All gods are dead!'[17] The gods are far from dead. I cannot prove the reality, or the non-existence of a God, or of many gods. Who knows, there may be a God, there may even be many gods. The idea of a God, or of many gods, may be no more than a phantasm born of a desire for parental protection and comfort in a harsh, and otherwise seemingly empty universe. But I cannot prove this. I can only believe or not believe. Either I live in a universe together with a God, or many gods, or I live in a universe in which there is only a belief in a God, or many gods. Nonetheless, these possible realities are irrelevant to me, because I have no soul, and this single fact frees me from the fetters of the gods. So the gods are not dead, instead, the gods are irrelevant! No gods determine my destiny. I am the master of my own destiny.

I know I am a product of my upbringing, the functioning of my body, and my interactions with the world. I know I will eventually die. I know that upon my death I will pass from a state of conscious awareness into a state of nothingness and bodily dissolution. I hope that those who survive me will treat my remains with respect, that they will remember me, and honour my achievements. Yet, even though my consciousness will cease upon my death, and even though my body will decay into its component elements, I am alive now, and my existence is forever imprinted upon the fabric of the universe. This means I am alive now and forever. I am immortal!

The workings of my body and the universe teach me these things. I accept this knowledge and am content.

Appendices

Appendix 1

Mortality in different centuries

Survival at different ages per 1000 live births in different centuries

Age (years)	0-300 CE [1]	1700 CE [2]	1900 CE [3]	1991 CE [3]
0	1000	1000	1000	1000
10	752	531	734	988
20	542	481	712	983
30	372	426	673	972
40	222	356	616	956
50	112	275	531	928
60	42	191	410	865
70	12	110	247	732
80	1	0	82	489

This table shows the life tables for people living in the ancient Roman Empire during the period of about 0-300 CE, for people living in England during the periods around 1700 CE and 1900 CE, as well as for people living in the United States of America in 1991 CE. These figures are expressed in terms of numbers surviving per 1000 live births. For example, if an English person was thirty years old in 1700 CE, more than half the people born in the same year as they were born would already have died. Furthermore, this table shows that very few of our ancestors ever became old, because before 1700 CE most of our ancestors died before they reached thirty years of age.

Appendix 2

Numbers of people in the world with hearing and visual disabilities

		% with disability in USA during 1992 CE[5]	USA during 1998 CE [4] Population 270,000,000 Number with disability in USA during 1998 CE	World during 1998 CE [4] 5,926,000,000 Number with disability in world during 1998 CE
Visual disability	Totally blind in both eyes	0.13	351,000	7,703,000
	Visually disabled	0.52	1,404,000	30,815,000
Hearing disability	Totally deaf in both ears	0.07	189,000	4,148,000
	Hearing disabled	0.48	1,296,000	28,444,000
Visual & hearing disability	Totally blind & deaf	0.0091	24,600	539,000
	Visual & hearing disability	0.25	675,000	14,815,000

This table shows the approximate numbers of people in the USA and the world disabled with blindness, and or deafness such that they were unable to perform work or normal daily activities because of these disabilities. These numbers are extrapolated from data in the USA for the year 1992 CE, and make the assumption that the percentages afflicted with these disabilities in both the USA and world-wide are the same.

Appendix 3

Degrees of arterial oxygen saturation (SaPO2) defining different levels of oxygen starvation

Severity of oxygen starvation	% Saturation of hemoglobin with oxygen (S_aPO_2)	Manifestations
Mild	100-80	No effects
Moderate	85-40	Cyanosis[6] + altered mental function, but no loss of consciousness
Severe	60-30	Cyanosis + apparent unconsciousness
Extreme	40-0	Cyanosis + unconsciousness

The percentage arterial hemoglobin oxygen saturations (S_aPO_2) at which the various degrees of oxygen starvation occur are listed in the table above, together with a general description of the manifestations of those degrees of oxygen starvation. Readers should note that these various degrees of oxygen starvation are defined for people with a normal blood hemoglobin concentration between 7.5-9.0 mmol/l, normal heart function, normal blood composition, and not under the influence of drugs or substances affecting the functioning of the lungs, heart or blood.

The reader should read chapter nine for a detailed description of the manifestations of these different degrees of oxygen starvation.

Appendix 4

World-wide causes of death by oxygen starvation

Main causes of death in 1990 CE	Deaths
Heart & blood vessel diseases	14,327,000
Infectious & parasitic diseases	9,329,000
Cancers of all types	6,130,000
Lung infections	4,380,000
Unintentional injuries	3,233,000
Lung diseases	2,935,000
Infant disorders	2,443,000
Digestive disorders	1,851,000
Intentional injuries (fighting, murder, suicide, wars)	1,851,000
Total number of deaths due to oxygen starvation	**46,479,000**
Total number of deaths in 1990 CE	50,467,000
% deaths due to oxygen starvation	92%

This table shows the numbers of people dying world-wide during the year 1990 CE of causes of death where terminal brainstem failure resulted from oxygen starvation.[7] During that year, world population was about 5,500,000,000 people, with a world-wide death rate of about 0.9 people dying per year per 100 head of population.

Appendix 5

Atmospheric composition

Gas	Percentage composition (volumes%)	Pressure (millibars at sea-level)
Nitrogen	78.09	791
Oxygen	20.95	212
Argon	0.93	94
Carbon dioxide	0.03	3
Neon	0.0018	1.8
Helium	0.0005	0.51
Methane	0.0002	0.2
Krypton	0.0001	0.1
Xenon	0.00001	0.01

Air is a mixture of many gases whose total combined pressure at sea-level is 1013.25 millibars, (equal to a pressure of 760 millimetres of mercury). This pressure is referred to as a pressure of 'one standard atmosphere'. The table presented here shows the percentage composition of atmospheric air, and the pressures of each of the gases forming the air in millibars at sea-level.[8]

The reader should note that even though air pressure decreases with altitude, the percentage volume composition of air does not change. For example, air pressure is one half that at sea-level at an altitude of about 5000 metres, but the percentage volume of oxygen at this altitude is still 20.95%, the same as at sea-level.

Appendix 6

Effects of different oxygen pressures on mental function

	Oxygen Pressure (% of one atmosphere)	Oxygen pressure (millibars)
Normal mental function	21%	210
Altered mental function	< 11%	< 110[9]
Unconsciousness	< 6.5%	< 66[10]

The symbol < before a figure is a standard notation meaning 'less than'

Appendix 7

Altitude, oxygen pressure, and mental function

Altitude (metres)	Air pressure (% of one atmosphere)	% oxygen in air	Oxygen pressure (millibars)	Mental function
0	100	21	210	Normal
> 5,000[11]	53	21	110	Abnormal
8,848[12] (Mt. Everest)	31	21	66	Limit of consciousness and activity for trained people
> 9000	< 31	21	< 66	Unconsciousness, brain damage, and death

Acclimatised adults can tolerate oxygen starvation at altitudes at which an non-acclimatised person will lose consciousness. For example:
- a trained and acclimatised person can be conscious and physically active for several days at an altitude of 7,620 metres (25,000 feet), while a non-acclimatised person who normally lives at sea level will lose consciousness within 10 minutes at this altitude[13];
- a trained and acclimatised person can be conscious and physically active for several days at an altitude of 8,534 metres (28,000 feet), while a non-acclimatised person who normally lives at sea level will lose consciousness within 5 minutes at this altitude.[14]

Appendix 8

Heart function and mental function

The heart is no more than a pump, pumping blood to all parts of the body. Brain oxygen starvation occurs when the flow of blood pumped by the heart through the brain is reduced below what is required for normal brain function. The approximate thresholds listed below apply to normal people with a normal concentration of haemoglobin in their blood, and whose blood contains the maximum possible amount of oxygen.

- Altered mental function caused by brain oxygen starvation may occur when the flow of blood through the brain is less than 80% of normal.[15]
- Altered mental function caused by brain oxygen starvation always occurs when the flow of blood through the brain is less than 40% of normal.[16]
- Loss of consciousness caused by brain oxygen starvation always occurs when the flow of blood through the brain is less than 30% of normal.[17]

Appendix 9

Definitions

Different people interpret the terms such as soul, mind, death, and dying very differently. Any discussion of these subjects requires very careful definitions of what is precisely meant by these terms within the context of the discussion. So, even though these terms are carefully defined within the text of this book, I have made a list of their definitions to aid the reader who skips from one chapter to another.

- 'Mind' is the sum total of all conscious will, intellect, personality, emotions, memory, and behaviour patterns.
- An 'illusion' is a false interpretation of a sense perception.
- A 'delusion' is a fixed false idea relating to the interpretation of a sense perception, or a fixed and incorrect way of thinking about something.
- A 'hallucination' is a perception or experience generated within the mind that has no relation with external sensations.
- 'Life' is the period between conception and death.
- 'Dying' is a condition where a series of changes in body functions begins that ultimately ends in death.
- 'Death' is a condition when the body is no longer conscious and able to sustain the integrity and function of the organ systems of the body.
- The 'soul' is an invisible, immaterial, and immortal part of the living body. All religions say that the soul is the vehicle of the mind, interacting with the body to animate the body, and to control all conscious thoughts and actions. This definition is derived in Chapter 4 'The Soul'.

References

Chapter 1 – Questions

1   This verse is translated from the Dutch song 'Credo – Mien Bestoan' written and sung by Ede Staal. Ede Staal was a singer and songwriter who lived in the province of Groningen in the Netherlands. He wrote and sang in the local dialect of Groningen. In the local Groningen dialect the verse reads: *Ik wait, der is n tied van komen / En ook n tied van goan / En alles wat doar tussen ligt / Ja, dat is mien bestoan.*

2   Died.

3   The universe inhabited by the dead.

4   Owen, G Vale. The Life Beyond the Veil. Book 1; The Lowlands of Heaven. England: Thornton Butterworth Ltd.; 1920. Preface, p. xiii-xiv.

5   'Buddha' was the name bestowed upon this man after he became a religious leader. His actual name was Siddhartha Gautama, and he was born a prince in a Northern Indian state. The period that he lived is rather uncertain, but is thought to be about 624-544 BCE by some, or about 448-368 BCE, or about 566-486 BCE by others.

6   Warren, Henry Clarke. Buddhism in Translations. Passages Selected from the Buddhist Sacred Books and Translated from the Original Pali into English. Cambridge (MA): The Harvard University Press; 1915. Chapter 13, p. 117-22.

Chapter 2 – Death of the Body

1   Her heart stopped beating.

2   Moody, RA. Life after Life. USA. Bantam Books; 1988. Chapter 2, p. 27 (ISBN 0-553-27484-8).

3   Edgar Allen Poe was an American short story writer who lived from 1809-1849 CE.

4   'The Premature Burial' was written in 1844 CE.

5   God.

6   The Holy Bible, King James Version, Leviticus, chapter 17, verse 11.
The 'Holy Bible' is a collection of Jewish and Christian religious texts. It consists of two parts. The 'Old Testament' contains 39 books. The content of the Old Testament was finalised about 100 CE. Then there are several other Apocryphal texts, whose divine origin is disputed and which are added to the Old Testament in some versions of the Holy Bible. The 'New Testament' contains 27 books. The definitive content of the New Testament was first listed in the 'Easter Letter' written by Bishop Athanasius dated in 376 CE. The version quoted in this book is the King James version, a translation of the Holy Bible made between 1604 and 1611 CE.

7   Rossen R, et al. Acute arrest of cerebral circulation in man. Archives of Neurology & Psychiatry 1943; 50: 510-528.
Aminoff MJ, et al. Electro-cerebral accompaniments of syncope associated with malignant ventricular arrhythmia's. Annals of Internal Medicine 1988; 108: 791-6.
Gastaut H, Fischer-Williams M. Electro-encephalographic study of syncope. Its differentiation from epilepsy. Lancet 1957; (II): 1018-25.

8   The minimum cerebral blood flow required to sustain consciousness is about 15-18 millilitres per 100 grams brain tissue per minute. (See data from Trojaborg W, Boyson G. Relation between EEG, cerebral blood flow and internal carotid artery pressure during carotid endarterectomy. Electroencephalography and Clinical Neurophysiology 1973; 34: 61-9. Sundt T.M., et al. Correlation of cerebral blood flow and electroencephalographic changes during carotid endarterectomy. Mayo Clinic Proceedings 1981; 56: 533-43.)
The weight of the average adult human brain is up to about 1500 grams. About 15% of the blood pumped out of the heart goes to the brain. So closed-chest heart massage must generate a cardiac output greater than 1.5 to 1.8 litres per minute in order to sustain consciousness in persons undergoing closed chest heart massage. Careful medical studies show that the cardiac output generated by closed-chest heart massage is sufficient to sustain such a level of cerebral blood flow in about 20% of persons (one in five). (See data from Guercio del LRM, et al. Comparison of blood flow during external and internal cardiac massage. Circulation 1965; 31(suppl. 1): 171-80. Guercio de LRM, et al. Cardiac output and other haemodynamic variables during external cardiac compression in man. New England Journal of Medicine 1963; 269: 1398-1404. Haemodynamic effects of external cardiac compression. Lancet 1964; (1): 1342-5.)

9   News releases from the LDS Hospital in Salt Lake City, Utah, in the United States of America. These are to be found on the internet at the address: www.ihc.com/ldsh/

10   His Divine Grace A.C. Bhaktivedanta Swami Prabhupada, translator. Bhagavad-Gita As It Is. Complete edition. The Bhactivedanta Book Trust. Chapter 15, text 14, p. 729 (ISBN 0-89213-268-X).

11   Ferrara BE: Hemicorporectomy: a collective review. Journal of Surgical Oncology 1990; 45: 270-278.
Stelly TC, et al. Hemicorporectomy. Clinical Anatomy 1995; 8: 116-23.
Mackenzie AR: Translumbar amputation: the longest survivor – a case update. Mount Sinai Journal of Medicine 1995; 62: 305-7.

12   Mackenzie AR: Translumbar amputation: the longest survivor – a case update. Mount Sinai Journal of Medicine 1995; 62: 305-7.

13   The nerves controlling breathing are called the 'phrenic nerves'. There are two phrenic nerves, one on the right side of the body that causes the muscles of the right diaphragm to contract and breathe, and one on the left side of the body which causes the muscles of the left diaphragm to contract and breathe. The phrenic

nerves are formed from the fusion of three nerves arising from the spinal cord at the level of the 3rd, 4th and 5th neck vertebrae.

14 Gardner WJ, et al. Residual function following hemispherectomy for tumour and for infantile hemiplegia. Brain 1955; 78: 487-502.
Gott P: Language after dominant hemispherectomy. Journal of Neurology, Neurosurgery, and Psychiatry 1973; 36: 1082-8.

15 Serafetinides EA, et al. Intracarotid sodium amylobarbitone and cerebral dominance for speech and consciousness. Brain 1965; 88: 107-30.
Perria L, et al. Determination of side of cerebral dominance with amybarbital. Archives of Neurology 1961; 4: 173-181.

16 Canfield MA, et al. Hispanic origin and neural tube defects in Houston/Harris County, Texas. I, translator. Descriptive epidemiology. American Journal of Epidemiology 1996; 143: 1-11.

17 Nielson JM, Sedgwick RP: Instincts and emotions in an anencephalic monster. Journal of Nervous and Mental Disease 1949; 110: 387-94.

18 The anencephalic baby.

19 Kramer W: From reanimation to deanimation. Acta Neurologica Scandinavica 1963; 39: 139-53.
Statement issued by the honorary secretary of the Conference of Medical Royal Colleges and their Faculties in the United Kingdom on 11 October 1976: Diagnosis of brain death. British Medical Journal 1976; 2: 1187-8.
Guyton AC. 'Activation of the Brain – The Reticular Activating System; The Generalised Thalamocortical System; Brain Waves; Epilepsy; Wakefulness and Sleep'. In: Textbook of Medical Physiology. 6th edition. USA. W.B. Saunders Co.; 1981. Chapter 54, p. 671-83 (ISBN 0-7216-4394-9).

20 Ganong WF. Chapter 11. In: Review of Medical Physiology. Lange Medical Publications; 1977. (ISBN 0-87041-134-9.)

21 Ganong WF. Chapter 36. In: Review of Medical Physiology. Lange Medical Publications; 1977. (ISBN 0-87041-134-9.)

22 Ganong WF. Chapter 31. In: Review of Medical Physiology. Lange Medical Publications; 1977. (ISBN 0-87041-134-9.)

23 Ganong WF. Chapter 14. In: Review of Medical Physiology. Lange Medical Publications; 1977. (ISBN 0-87041-134-9.)

Chapter 3 – Separate Body, Mind & Soul

1 This was a true story told to me by a patient during the course of a visit to the anaesthetic outpatient clinic in the year 1995 CE. He dreamt he was flying above the

lawn at the back of the Elisabeth Hospital in Leiderdorp in the Netherlands. He was not alarmed during his dream. Instead he found it very interesting.

2   This was an experience told to me by a woman in September 1997 CE, during the course of a conversation with her just before I induced general anaesthesia for another operation. The operation she had undergone was a small gynaecological operation performed under general anaesthesia at the end of 1996 CE.

3   The soul of the dead person.

4   Wallis Budge EA, translator. The Egyptian Book of the Dead. USA. Dover Publications; 1967. Introduction 'The Doctrine of Eternal Life', p. lxxv-lxxvi (ISBN 0-486-21866-X).

5   Saint Augustine was a prominent early Christian holy man. He was a Bishop, a functionary of the Christian religion in the city of Hippo in the region called Numidia in ancient times, which is now a country called Algeria. He lived from 354 to 430 CE.

6   The City of God. Book 13, chapter 6 – Of the Evil of Death in General, Considered as the Separation of Soul and Body, by Saint Aurelius Augustine (354-430 CE).

7   A Treatise on the Soul. Chapter XLIII. Sleep a Natural Function as Shown by Other Considerations, and by the Testimony of Scripture, by Tertullian. Tertullian was one of the founding fathers of early Christian philosophy. He lived from about 160 to 220 CE.

8   Marcus Tullius Cicero. De Senectute, xxiii:81, p. 93. [Translated by WA Falconer in Loeb Classical Library, Harvard University Press, 1996, ISBN 0-674-99170-2.] Marcus Tullius Cicero lived from 106 to 43 BCE.

9   The Holy Bible, King James Version, Hebrews, chapter 11, verse 1.

10   Marcus Tullius Cicero. De Senectute, xxiii:85, p. 97. [Translated by WA Falconer in Loeb Classical Library, Harvard University Press, 1996, ISBN 0-674-99170-2.]

Chapter 4 – Properties of the Soul

1   See various books such as: A Treatise on the Soul (Tertullian, 155-220 CE); A Treatise on the Soul (Augustine, 354-430 CE); City of God (Augustine, 354-430 CE); On the Soul (Aristotle, 384-322 BCE); The Greatness of the Soul (John Bunyan, 1628-1688 CE).

2   See note 6, Chapter 2.

3   The mortal, or physical human body.

4   The Holy Bible, King James Version, 1-Corinthians, chapter 15, verse 44.

5   Humankind.

6   The Holy Bible, King James Version, Genesis, chapter 2, verse 7.

7   People once thought that the nerves animated the body. This writer presumably means the nervous activity of the brain.

8   The soul.

9   Muldoon SJ, Carrington H. The Projection of the Astral Body. USA. Samuel Weiser; 1973. Chapter 1, p. 48 (ISBN 0-87728-069-X).

10   Muldoon SJ, Carrington H. The Projection of the Astral Body. USA. Samuel Weiser; 1973. Chapter 3, p. 79 (ISBN 0-87728-069-X).

11   The 'Upanishads' are a collection of about 108 texts forming a major body of sacred writings of the Hindu religion. The earliest Upanishads date from about 1000-600 BCE.

12   'Atman' is another name for the soul.

13   Breathing.

14   I have improved the grammar slightly in this translation which is derived from the Bhadaranyaka Upanishad, on p. 494, in the book Sixty Upanishads of the Veda, translated into German by P. Deussen, and into English from German by V.M. Bedekar and G.B. Palsule (Motilal Banarsidass Publishers Pty Ltd, India, 1990, ISBN 81-208-0431-7).

15   Muldoon SJ, Carrington H. The Projection of the Astral Body. USA. Samuel Weiser; 1973. Chapter 3 (ISBN 0-87728-069-X).

16   The 'Holy Koran' is a collection of the revelations of God to Mohammed, and is the holy book of the Moslem religion. It achieved its final form in the period 644-656 CE.

17   Dawood NJ, translator. , The Koran. England: Penguin Books; 1990. Sura 39, verse 42.

18   The 'Egyptian Book of the Dead' is a collection of ancient Egyptian funerary texts found in the tombs of wealthier ancient Egyptians. Early versions of some of the texts date to about 3500 BCE, and the final version of the text became standardised sometime between 2000-1000 BCE.

19 Hart G. A Dictionary of Egyptian Gods and Goddesses. England: Routledge; 2001. p. 214-8 (ISBN 0-415-05909-7). 'Thoth' is the scribe of the gods of ancient Egypt.

20 Hart G. A Dictionary of Egyptian Gods and Goddesses. England: Routledge; 2001. p. 151-67 (ISBN 0-415-05909-7). 'Osiris' was the ancient Egyptian king, and judge of the souls of the dead.

21 'Osiris' is not only the name of an Egyptian god, but was also used as a general name for the soul of a deceased person.

22 The good and evil committed during a person's lifetime were weighed up against each other to judge whether the soul of the deceased was worthy enough to enter the paradise inhabited by the immortal souls of the deceased persons.

23 The soul of the deceased.

24 Hart G. A Dictionary of Egyptian Gods and Goddesses. England: Routledge; 2001. p. 3-4 (ISBN 0-415-05909-7). 'Amemet' was the god in the Egyptian pantheon whose task was to destroy the souls of the evil after judgement had been passed. Amemet is usually depicted with the head of a crocodile, the upper body of a lion, and the legs of a hippopotamus.

25 Wallis Budge EA, translator. The Egyptian Book of the Dead. USA. Dover Publications; 1967. p. 258-9 (ISBN 0-486-21866-X).

26 The Jewish people lived in Egypt during the period from 1700-1250 BCE.

27 The text of the Jewish holy book of Ecclesiastes evolved to its present form during 1000-400 BCE.

28 The Holy Bible, King James Version, Ecclesiastes, chapter 12: verse 14.

29 Mohammed, the founding prophet of the Mohammedan, or Islamic religion, 'Islam' was born in the Arabian city of Mecca about 570 CE and died in the year 632 CE. He received his first revelations from God when he was about 40 years of age, after which he preached what was revealed to him.

30 God.

31 Ahmed Ali , translator. *Al-Qur'an. A Contemporary translation*. USA. Princeton University Press; 1990. Sura 39, verses 69-70 (ISBN 0-691-02046-9).

32 The womb of a woman of high social and religious caste.

33 The womb of a woman of low social and religious caste.

34 Chandogya Upanisad, tenth part, verse 7, on p. 145-146. In the book Sixty Upanishads of the Veda, translated into German by P. Deussen, and into English from German by V.M. Bedekar and G.B. Palsule (Motilal Banarsidass Publishers Pty Ltd, India, 1990, ISBN 81-208-0431-7).

35   An intelligence greater than that of the physical body.

36 Muldoon SJ, Carrington H. The Projection of the Astral Body. USA. Samuel Weiser; 1973. Chapter 1, p. 48-49 (ISBN 0-87728-069-X).

37   The 'Bhagavad Gita' is one of many Hindu religious texts. It achieved its current form sometime about 200 BCE to 200 CE.

38   The soul.

39   The soul.

40 His Divine Grace A.C. Bhactivedanta Swami Prabhupada, translator. Bhagavad-Gita As It Is. Complete edition. The Bhactivedanta Book Trust. Chapter 13, Text 34, p. 729 (ISBN 0-89213-268-X).

41   The body.

42   The mind.

43   The soul.

44 Kausitaki Upanishad, third Adhyaya, verse 4, on p. 47, in the book Sixty Upanishads of the Veda, translated into German by P. Deussen, and into English from German by V.M. Bedekar and G.B. Palsule (Motilal Banarsidass Publishers Pty Ltd, India, 1990, ISBN 81-208-0431-7).

Chapter 5 – Animation by the Soul

1   A pacemaker is a device that electrically stimulates a heart to beat that no longer beats normally.

2   Kramer W. From reanimation to deanimation. Acta Neurologica Scandinavica 1963; 39: 139-53.

3   The colour of the brain.

4   Kramer W. From reanimation to deanimation. Acta Neurologica Scandinavica 1963; 39: 139-53.

5   The 'Portable Organ Preservation System' is a device developed by the 'TransMedics' company based in Woburn, Massachusetts in the USA. It first underwent trials with human organs excised from deceased persons in 2001 CE.

This machine simulates the conditions of these organs within the human body by maintaining these excised organs at normal body temperature, pumping blood containing oxygen and nutrients through these organs, and removing waste products and carbon dioxide, so keeping these organs alive for many hours. Information about this development was found on the internet at various sites on 31 January 2002 CE, among which the following address: www.popularmechanics.com/science/medicine/2001/11/changing_hearts/print.phtml

6   Safar P: Resuscitation from clinical death: Pathophysiologic limits and therapeutic potentials. Critical Care Medicine 1988; 16: 923-41.

7   Magovern JA, et al. The mature and immature heart: Response to normothermic ischemia. Journal of Surgical Research 1989; 46: 366-369.
Clowes GHA, Neville WE: Experimental exposure of the aortic valve. Laboratory studies and a clinical trial. Surgical Forum 1955; 5: 39-45.
Carmeliet E: Myocardial ischemia: Reversible and irreversible changes. Circulation 1984; 70: 149-151.

8   Dittmer DS, Grebe RM, editors. Handbook of Circulation. USA. W.B. Saunders Co.; 1959. p. 135.
Weinberger LM, et al. Temporary arrest of the circulation to the central nervous system. Archives of Neurology & Psychiatry 1940) 43: 961-86.

9   Moussa ME, et al. Effect of total hepatic vascular exclusion during liver resection on hepatic ultrastructure. Liver Transpl. Surg. 1996; 6: 461-7.

10   Harley LCJ, et al. Kidney preservation for transportation. Function of 29 human cadaver kidneys preserved with an intracellular perfusate. New England Journal of Medicine 1971; 285: 1049-52.

11   Fletcher IR, Healy TEJ: The arterial tourniquet. Annals of the Royal College of Surgeons of England 1983; 65: 409-17.

Chapter 6 – Control by the Soul

1   Prescott F, et al. Tubocurarine chloride as an adjunct to anaesthesia. Report on 180 cases. Lancet 1946; 2: 80-4.

2   Stuss DT, Benson DF. The Frontal Lobes.New York: Raven Press; 1986. Chapter 5, p. 87-8 (ISBN 0-88167-153-3).
Roland PE. Cortical organization of voluntary behaviour in man. Human Neurobiology 1985; 4: 155-67.
Roland PE, et al. Different cortical areas in man in organization of voluntary movements in extrapersonal space. Journal of Neurophysiology 1980; 43: 137-50.
Roland PE: Metabolic measurements of the working frontal cortex in man. Trends in Neuroscience 1984; 7: 430-5.

3   Kolb B, Whishaw IQ. Fundamentals of Human Neuropsychology. USA. W.H. Freeman; 1990. Chapter 17, p. 424-7 (ISBN 0-7167-1973-8).

4   Elithorn A, et al. Leukotomy for pain. Journal of Neurology, Neurosurgery and Psychiatry 1958; 21: 249-61.
Lewin W. Observations on selective leukotomy. Journal of Neurology, Neurosurgery and Psychiatry 1961; 24: 37-44.
Gardner WJ, et al. Residual function following hemispherectomy for tumour and for infantile hemiplegia. Brain 1955; 78: 487-502.
Perria L, et al. Determination of side of cerebral dominance with amybarbital. Archives of Neurology 1961; 4: 172-81.

5   Paraphrased from a variety of sources.

6   His Divine Grace A.C. Bhactivedanta Swami Prabhupada, translator. Bhagavad-Gita As It Is. Complete edition. The Bhactivedanta Book Trust. Chapter 2, text 24 (ISBN 0-89213-268-X).

7   His Divine Grace A.C. Bhactivedanta Swami Prabhupada, translator. Bhagavad-Gita As It Is. Complete edition. The Bhactivedanta Book Trust. Chapter 2, text 17 (ISBN 0-89213-268-X).

8   Her husband.

9   The diagnosis is based upon the criteria set in the DSM-III-R (APA, 1987). This citation was found in 1998 at: www.science.wayne.edu/~bio340/studentPages/PMS.html

Chapter 7 – Paranormal Senses

1   The Holy Bible, King James Version, Leviticus, chapter 20, verse 27.

2   Blackmore S: Psychic Experiences: Psychic Illusions. Skeptical Enquirer 1992; 16: 367-376.
Zangari W, Machado FR. Incidencia e importancia social de las experiencias psiquicas de los estudiantes universitarios brasileros. Informe presentado originalmente en la Trigesimo Séptima Convención Anual de la Parapsychological Association (PA), realizada en Amsterdam (Holanda) en Agosto de 1994.
Goeritz A, Schumacher J: The www as a research medium: An illustrative survey on paranormal belief. Published in 2002 CE on the internet address: www.wiso-psychologie.uni-erlangen.de/Download/www_research.pdf
Surveys of Psi Experiences, published during 2002 CE on the internet address: www.psiexplorer.com/survey2.htm.

3   Ebon M, editor. The Signet Handbook of Parapsychology. USA. Signet books; 1978. p. 404-5.

4 World War II started in 1939 CE and ended in 1945 CE. The Russian campaign, or Eastern Front lasted from 1941 to 1944 CE. According to reasonably accurate statistics, the mid year troop strengths in Russia were: 1941 – 3.3 million soldiers, 1942 – 3.1 million soldiers, 1943 – 2.9 million soldiers, and 1944 – 3.1 million soldiers. The Russian campaign was exceptionally bitter and bloody, and the numbers killed and wounded were: 1,419,728 killed in action, 997,056 missing in action (most likely dead, but never found and identified), 3,498,060 wounded in action. This is a total of 5,914,844 casualties. So about one half of all soldiers sent to the Russian front were wounded or killed. (See Jason Pipes, 2002 CE, at the site www.feldgrau.com , and Brandon Leniart, 2002 CE, at the site www.angelfire.com/ct/ww2europe/stats.html).

5 Duane TD, Behrendt T: Extrasensory electronencephalographic induction between identical twins. Science 1965) 150: 367.

6 Ebon M, editor. The Signet Handbook of Parapsychology. USA. Signet books; 1978. p. 66-78

7 Grey M. Return from Death. An Exploration of the Near-Death Experience.England: Arkana; 1986. Chapter 4, p. 31 (ISBN 1-85063-019-4).
Sabom MB. Recollections of Death. USA. Harper & Row; 1982. Appendix, table IX.
Greyson B, Stevenson I. The phenomenology of near-death experiences. American Journal of Psychiatry 1980; 137: 1193-6.
Greyson B. The near-death experience scale. Construction, reliability, and validity. Journal of Nervous and Mental Disease 1983; 171: 369-75.

8 Rawlings M. Beyond Death's Door. USA. Bantam Books; 1978. Chapter 6, p. 74-5 (ISBN 0-553-22970-2).

9 Moody RA. The Light Beyond. USA. Bantam Books; 1988. Chapter 7, p. 173 (ISBN 0-553-27813-4).

10 'Coma' is a state of unconsciousness during which a person is unresponsive to pain and manifests no reflex activity whatsoever. A comatose person is unconscious, sometimes they are able to breathe normally, and sometimes they do not breathe. The efficiency of the breathing of a comatose person depends upon how severely their brainstem is affected by the disorder causing them to lose consciousness. People with severely unregulated diabetes mellitus can lose consciousness and become comatose. Such a 'diabetic coma' is a life-threatening condition with a high mortality rate, because diabetic coma affects all vital functions controlled by the brainstem, (consciousness, breathing, heartbeat, and swallowing).

11 Hamblin PS, et al. Deaths associated with diabetic ketoacidosis and hyperosmolar coma: 1973-1988. Medical Journal of Australia 1989; 439: 441-2.
Khardori R, et al. Hyperosmolar hyperglykemic nonketotic syndrome. Report of 22 cases and brief review. American Journal of Medicine 1984; 77: 899-904.
Pinies JA, et al. Course and prognosis of 132 patients with diabetic nonketotic hyperosmolar state. Diabetes and Metabolism 1994; 20: 43-8.

Rimailho A, et al. Prognostic factors in hyperglycaemic hyperosmolar syndrome. Critical Care Medicine 1986; 14: 552-4.

12 Maria.

13 Wilson I. The After Death Experience.New York: Quill; 1987. Chapter 10, p. 132-3 (ISBN 0-688-09419-8).

14 Wilson I. The After Death Experience.New York: Quill; 1987. Chapter 10, p. 132-3 (ISBN 0-688-09419-8).

15 The Case of Kimberly Clark & 'Maria', Critically Examined, Shown to Not Support NDE Claims. This article was found on the internet during 2002 CE at the internet address: www.cincinnatiskeptics.org/blurbs/nde-case.html.

16 Honorton C. Psi and Internal Attention States. In: Wolman BB, editor, Handbook of Parapsychology. USA. Van Nostrand Reinhold; 1977. p. 435-72 (ISBN 0-442-29576-6).

17 Schmeidler GR. Personality Differences in the Effective use of ESP. In: Ebon M, editor, The Signet Handbook of Parapsychology. Signet; 1978. Part VI, p. 354-64 (ISBN 0-451-15478-9).
Rao KR. Psi en Persoonlijkheid. In: Beloff J, editor, Parapsychologie Vandaag – Nieuwe Vormen van Onderzoek, Rotterdam: Lemniscaat; 1975. Chapter 3, p. 95-112 (ISBN 90-6069-209-8). [Translated from 'New Directions in Parapsychology' published by Elek Books Ltd, in 1974].

18 Hansel CEM. ESP and Parapsychology. A Critical Re-evaluation. USA. Prometheus Books; 1980.
Blackmore SJ: Unrepeatability: Parapsychology's only finding. Science Tribune, 1999 (Spetember), published on the internet during 2002 CE on the internet address: www.tribunes.com/tribune/art99/blackmor.htm
Austin Society to Oppose Pseudoscience: Pseudoscience Fact Sheets: Extrasensory Perception and Telepathy 2002
Thomas JA. Extra-Sensory Perception Fact Sheet. Prepared by the North Texas Skeptics 1997
Utts J. Replication and meta-analysis in parapsychology. Statistical Science 1991; 6: 363-403.
Carroll RT. Skeptic's Dictionary: Parapsychology. Published during 2001 CE on the internet address: www.skepdic.com

19 Tenhaeff WHC, Spontane paragnosie. II. Spontane telepathie en telaesthesie. Tijdschrift voor Parapsychologie 1954; 22: 45-78. See p. 59.

Chapter 8 – Dreams & Visions

1 Rattet SL, Bursik K: Investigating the personality correlates of precognitive belief and paranormal experience. Personality and Individual Differences 2001; 31: 433-444.

2 Gordon Fisher wrote a very good essay on these aspects of divination titled, 'Marriage and Divorce of Astronomy and Astrology, A History of Astral Prediction from Antiquity to Newton', which he published on the internet in 2002 CE at the address: http://gfisher.org/index.htm

3 Hansel CEM. ESP and Parapsychology. A Critical Re-evaluation. USA. Prometheus Books; 1980.

4 McCrone J. Psychic ability? The micro-PK experiments. New Scientist 1994 (26 November).
Radin DI, Rebman JM. Seeking psi in the casino. Journal of the Society for Psychical Research 1998; 62: 193-219.

5 Honorton C. Buitenzintuigelijke waarneming en veranderd bewustzijn. In: Beloff, editor, Parapsychologie Vandaag – Nieuwe Vormen van Onderzoek. Rotterdam: Lemniscaat; 1975. p 75-7 (ISBN 90-6069-209-8). [Translated from 'New Directions in Parapsychology' published by Elek Books Ltd, in 1974].
Tenhaeff WHC. Para-psychologische verschijnselen in het dagelijkse leven. Zeist: W. de Haan/Standaard Boekhandel; 1964. p. 127-33.

6 Ganong WF. Review of Medical Physiology. Lange Medical Publications; 1977. 'The Reticular Activating System, Sleep, & the Electrical Activity of the Brain', Chapter 11, p. 128 (ISBN 0-87041-134-9).

7 Bunyan J. The greatness of the soul, and unspeakableness of the loss thereof; with causes of the losing it. 1682 CE. [*Powers and Properties of the Soul*]

8 Hansel CEM. ESP and Parapsychology. A Critical Re-evaluation. USA. Prometheus Books; 1980.
Lange R, et al. What Precognitive Dreams are Made of: The Nonlinear Dynamics of Tolerance of Ambiguity, Dream Recall, and Paranormal Belief. Published on the internet during the year 1999 CE, at the address: http://goertzel.org/dynapsyc/2000/Precog%20Dreams.htm
Blackmore SJ. Unrepeatability: Parapsychology's only finding. Science Tribune 1999 (September). Published on the internet during 2002 CE at the internet address: www.tribunes.com/tribune/art99/blackmor.htm

9 Mark Twain's Autobiography. Volume 1. USA. 1924. Chapter 16, 'New York, January 13, 1906'.

10 Ganong WF. Review of Medical Physiology. Lange Medical Publications; 1977. Chapter 11, p. 128, 'The Reticular Activating System, Sleep, & the Electrical Activity of the Brain' (ISBN 0-87041-134-9).

11 Geller Uri. Uri Geller's fortune secrets. Sphere Books; 1987. Chapter 13, 'Psi and the cosmic forces' (ISBN 0-72213-812-1).

12 Hess EH: Attitudes and pupil size. Scientific American 1965; (April): 46-54. Hess EH: The role of pupil size in communication. Scientific American 1975; (November). p. 110-9.

13 Seeing, Hearing, and Smelling the World. New Findings help Scientists make Sense of our Senses. USA. Howard Hughes Medical Institute; 1995.
Kohl JV, et al. Human Pheromones: Integrating Neuroendocrinology and Ethology. Neuroendocrinology Letters 2001; 22: 309-21.
Porter RH, Olfaction and Human Kin Recognition. Paper from the Laboratoire de Comportement Animal, CNRS URA 1291 – PRMD (France), read during the International Symposium 'MHC and Behaviour', held at the University of Kiel on July 13, 1996.
Chen D, Haviland-Jones J. Human olfactory communication of emotion. Perceptual and Motor Skills 2000; 91: 771-81.

14 The Holy Bible, King James Version, Isaiah, chapter 6, verses 1-12.

15 The Holy Bible, King James Version, Kings II, chapter 20, verses 12-18.

16 An excerpt from a website called 'An Angel in Your Pocket?', published by Jacky Newcomb during 2002 CE at the address: www.holisticshop.co.uk/library/angels.html

17 Gloor P, et al. The role of the limbic system in experiential phenomena of temporal lobe epilepsy. Annals of Neurology 1982; 12: 129-44.
Gloor P, et al. Experiential phenomena of temporal lobe epilepsy. Brain 1990; 113: 1673-94.
Weingarten SM, et al. Relationship of hallucinations to the depth structures of the temporal lobe. In: Sweet WH, et al, editors. Neurosurgical Treatment in Psychiatry, Pain and Epilepsy. USA. University Park Press; 1975. p. 553-68 (ISBN 0-8391-0881-8).
Dewhurst K. Sudden religious conversions in temporal lobe epilepsy. British Journal of Psychiatry 1970; 117: 497-507.

18 Louis S: 'Normal EEG variants', published during 2001 CE in eMedicine, on the internet at the address: www.emedicine.com

19 Makarec K, Persinger MA. Temporal lobe signs: electroencephalographic validity and enhanced scores in special populations. Perceptual and Motor Skills 1985; 3: 831-42.
Wright PA. The interconnectivity of mind, brain, and behavior in altered states of

consciousness: focus on shamanism. Alternative Therapies in Health and Medicine 1995; 1: 50-6.

20 Richards MA, et al. Circumcerebral application of weak magnetic fields with derivatives and changes in electroencephalographic power spectra within the theta range: implications for states of consciousness. Perceptual and Motor Skills 2002; 95: 671-86.

21 Cook CM, Persinger MA. Experimental induction of the 'sensed presence' in normal subjects and an exceptional subject. Perceptual and Motor Skills 1997; 85: 683-93.
Cook CM, Persinger MA. Geophysical variables and behavior: XCII. Experimental elicitation of the presence of a sentient being by right hemispheric, weak magnetic fields: interaction with temporal lobe sensitivity. Perceptual and Motor Skills 2001; 92: 447-8.
Persinger MA, Healey F. Experimental facilitation of the sensed presence: possible intercalation between the hemispheres induced by complex magnetic fields. Journal of Nervous and Mental Disease 2002; 190: 533-41.
Tiller SG, Persinger MA. Geophysical variables and behavior: XCVII. Increased proportions of the left-sided sense of presence induced by induced experimentally by right hemispheric specific (frequency modulated) magnetic fields. Perceptual and Motor Skills 2002; 94: 26-8.

22 Cook CM, Persinger MA. Geophysical variables and behavior: XCII. Experimental elicitation of the presence of a sentient being by right hemispheric, weak magnetic fields: interaction with temporal lobe sensitivity. Perceptual and Motor Skills 2001; 92: 447-8.

23 Persinger MA, et al. Experimental stimulation of a haunt experience and elicitation of paroxysmal electroencephalographic activity by transcerebral complex magnetic fields: induction of a synthetic 'ghost'? Perceptual and Motor Skills 2000; 90: 659-74
Persinger MA, et al. Geophysical variables and behavior: CIV. Power-frequency magnetic field transients (5 microtesla) and reports of haunt experiences within an electronically dense house. Perceptual and Motor Skills 2001; 92: 673-4
Persinger MA, Koren SA. Experiences of spiritual visitation and impregnation: potential induction by frequency-modulated transients from an adjacent clock. Perceptual and Motor Skills 2001; 92: 35-6
Persinger MA. Geophysical variables and behaviour: XCVIII. Ambient geomagnetic activity and experiences of 'memories': interactions with sex and implications for receptive psi experiences. Perceptual and Motor Skills 2002; 94: 1271-82
Suess LA, Persinger MA. Geophysical variables and behaviour: XCVI. 'Experiences' attributed to Christ and Mary at Marmora, Ontario, Canada, may have been consequences of environmental electromagnetic stimulation: implications for religious movements. Perceptual and Motor Skills 2001) 93: 435-450.

24 Wright PA. The interconnectivity of mind, brain, and behaviour in altered states of consciousness: focus on shamanism. Alternative Therapies in Health and

Medicine 1995; 1: 50-6.
Noelle DSC. 'Searching for God in the machine.' An article published on the internet in 2002 CE at the address: http://secularhumanism.org

Chapter 9 – The Aura

1 This is quoted from an article about the aura, 'Auras', by R. Bruce, published on the internet during 2001 CE on the address: www.spiritweb.org./Spirit.aura.html

2 'Bagnall' is the name of a man who conducted research into the human aura at about the beginning of the 20th century.

3 Watson L. Supernature. Sceptre; 1989. Chapter 4, p. 141 (ISBN 0-340-40419-1).

4 Redfield J. The Celestine Prophecy. USA. Warner Books; 1993. Chapter 3, p. 51 (ISBN 0-446-67100-2).
Watson L. Supernature. Sceptre; 1989. Chapter 4, p. 139-46 (ISBN 0-340-40419-1).

5 The seven different colours of light visible to the human eye and their wavelengths are: red 740-620 nanometers: orange 620-585 nanometers: yellow 585-575 nanometers: green 575-500 nanometers: blue 500-445 nanometers: indigo 445-425 nanometers: violet 425-390 nanometers
Hsia Y, Graham CH: Spectral luminosity curves for protanopic, deuteranopic, and normal subjects. Proceedings of the National Academy of Science USA 1957; 43: 1011-9.

6 Guyton AC. Textbook of Medical Physiology. 6th edition. USA. W.B. Saunders; 1981. Chapter 59, p. 742-3 (ISBN 0-7216-4394-9).

7 Photography was actually discovered by a Frenchman called Joseph Nicephore Niepce in 1816 CE. However, the first techniques and methods were extremely impractical, and used highly toxic chemicals. But the developments introduced by William Talbot in 1839 CE were what transformed photography into a practical technique.

8 LaPlante MP, Carlson D. Disability in the United States: Prevalence and Causes, 1992. From the National Health Interview Survey. Disability Statistics Report (7). Washington DSC. National Institute of Disability and Rehabilitation Research; 1992. See table in Appendix 2.

9 Bruce R. Auras. Published on the internet during 2001 CE on the internet address: www.spiritweb.org./Spirit.aura.html
Redfield J. The Celestine Prophecy. USA. Warner Books; 1993. Chapter 3, 'A Matter of Energy' (ISBN 0-446-67100-2)
Watson L. Supernature. Sceptre; 1989. Chapter 4, p. 139-46 (ISBN 0-340-40419-1).

10 Jenkins FA, White HE. Fundamentals of Optics. 4th edition. USA. McGraw-Hill; 1976. Chapter 9, 'Lens Aberrations', p. 149-87 (ISBN 0-07-032330-5).

11 Guyton AC. Textbook of Medical Physiology. 6th edition. USA. W.B. Saunders; 1981. Chapter 58, p. 729-30 (ISBN 0-7216-4394-9).

12 A distance of about 30-60 centimeters.

13 This is quoted from Bruce R. Auras. Published on the internet during 2001 CE on the address: www.spiritweb.org./Spirit.aura.html

14 Bruce R. Auras. Published on the internet during 2001 CE on the internet address: www.spiritweb.org./Spirit.aura.html
Redfield J. The Celestine Prophecy. USA. Warner Books; 1993. Chapter 3, 'A Matter of Energy' (ISBN 0-446-67100-2)
Watson L. Supernature. Sceptre; 1989. Chapter 4, p. 40 (ISBN 0-340-40419-1).

15 Bruce R. Auras. Published on the internet during 2001 CE on the internet address: www.spiritweb.org./Spirit.aura.html
Redfield J. The Celestine Prophecy. USA. Warner Books; 1993. Chapter 3, 'A Matter of Energy' (ISBN 0-446-67100-2)
Watson L. Supernature. Sceptre; 1989. Chapter 4, p. 40 (ISBN 0-340-40419-1).

16 Ravioloa E, Torsten NW: The neural basis for myopia. On The Brain: The Harvard Mahoney Neuroscience Institute Letter 1995; 4(3): 2. Published on the internet at: www.med.harvard.edu/publications/On_The_Brain/Volume4/Number3/Myopia.html

17 In Australia, about 21% of people have low myopia (less than -5 diopters), 3.2% have high myopia (-5 to -10 diopters), and 0.3% have high myopia (more than -10 diopters). See: McCarty CA, et al. Prevalence of Myopia in adults: Implications for refractive surgeons. Journal of Refractive Surgery 1997; 13: 229-34.

18 Papastergiou GI, et al. Induction of axial eye elongation and myopic refractive shift in one-year-old chickens. Vision Research 1998; 12: 1883-8.
Yoshino Y, et al. Visual deprivation myopia with translucent and black goggles. Ophthalmologica 1997; 211: 4-7.
Wong L, et al. Education, reading, and familial tendency as risk factors for myopia in Hong Kong fishermen. J. Epidemiol Community Health 1993; 47: 50-3.
Parssinen O, et al. Myopia, use of eyes, and living habits among men aged 33-37 years. Acta Ophthalmol (Copenh) 1985; 63: 395-400.
Paritsis N, et al. Epidemiologic research on the role of studying and urban environment in the development of myopia during school-age years. Ann. Ophthalmol. 1983; 11: 1061-5.

19 McCollin RJ: On the nature of myopia and the mechanism of accommodation. Medical Hypotheses 1989; 3: 197-211.
Drexler W, et al. Eye elongation during accomodation in humans: differences between emmetropes and myopes. Invest. Ophthalmol. Vis. Sci. 1998; 39: 2140-7.
Ciuffreda KJ, Ordonez X: Vision therapy to reduce abnormal nearwork-induced transient myopia. Optom. Vis. Sci. 1998; 75: 311-5.

20 Gelder Kunz D van. The Personal Aura. USA. Quest Books; 1991. (ISBN 0-8356-0671-6.)

Chapter 10 – Disembodiment Defined

1 Steiger Brad. Astral Projection. USA. Para Research; 1982. Chapter 6, p. 45. (ISBN 0-914918-36-2, Distributed by Schiffer Publishing Ltd, USA.)

2 Twemlow SW, et al. The out-of-body experience: A phenomenological typology based on questionnaire responses. American Journal of Psychiatry 1982; 139: 450-5.

3 This report of an out-of-body experience occurring during sleep was published by Jim Lagerkvist on the internet on 16 Jan 1995 at the address: www.spiritweb.org

4 Grey M. Return from Death. An Exploration of the Near-Death Experience. London: Arkana; 1985. Chapter 4, p. 35 (ISBN 1-85063-019-4).

5 Twemlow SW, et al. The out-of-body experience: A phenomenological typology based on questionnaire responses. American Journal of Psychiatry 1982; 139: 450-5.

6 A technique where a blood vessel is cut open in order to insert a tube through which a blood transfusion can be administered.

7 After undergoing an operation.

8 Scott Rogo D. The Return from Silence. A Study of Near-Death Experiences. The Aquarian Press; 1989. Chapter 11, p. 222 (ISBN 0-85030-736-8).

9 Penfield W. The role of the temporal cortex in certain psychical phenomena. Journal of Mental Science 1955; 101: 451-65. Case V.F. p. 458.
Blanke O, et al. Stimulating own-body perceptions. Nature 2002; 419: 269-70.

Chapter 11 – Sensation, Body, & Mind

1 Beardsley T. The machinery of thought. Scientific American 1997; 277: 58-63.

2 Silbersweig DA, et al. A functional neuroanatomy of hallucinations in schizophrenia. Nature 1995; 378: 176-9.

Chapter 12 – Disembodied Feelings

1 Kolb B, Whishaw IQ. Fundamentals of Human Neuropsychology. USA. W.H. Freeman; 1990. Chapter 24, p. 643-76 (ISBN 0-7167-1973-8).

2 Lukianowicz N. Autoscopic phenomena. Archives of Neurology & Psychiatry 1958; 80: 199-220.
Noyes R, et al. Depersonalisation in accident victims and psychiatric patients. Journal of Nervous and Mental Disease 1977; 164: 401-7.

3   Lukianowicz N. Autoscopic phenomena. Archives of Neurology & Psychiatry 1958; 80: 199-220.

4   Penfield W: The role of the temporal cortex in certain psychical phenomena. Journal of Mental Science 1955; 101: 451-65.
Blanke O, et al. Stimulating illusory own-body perceptions. Nature 2002; 419: 269-70.

5   Lukianowicz N. Autoscopic phenomena. Archives of Neurology & Psychiatry 1958; 80: 199-220.
Penfield W, Boldrey E. Somatic motor and sensory representation in the cerebral cortex of man as studied by electrical stimulation. Brain 1937; 60: 389-443.
Arias M, et al. Autoscopy and multiple sclerosis. Neurologia 1996; 11: 230-2. [Translated from the original Spanish article.]
Blanke O, et al. Stimulating illusory own-body perceptions. Nature 2002; 419: 269-70.
Blanke O, et al. Simple and complex vestibular responses induced by electrical stimulation of the parietal cortex in humans. Journal of Neurology, Neurosurgery & Psychiatry 2000; 69: 553-6.

6   Woolsey CN, et al. Localisation in somatic sensory and motor areas of human cerebral cortex as determined by direct recording of evoked potentials and electrical stimulation. Journal of Neurosurgery 1979; 51: 476-506.
Penfield W, Boldrey E: Somatic motor and sensory representation in the cerebral cortex of man as studied by electrical stimulation. Brain 1937; 60: 389-443.
Blanke O, et al. Stimulating illusory own-body perceptions. Nature 2002; 419: 269-70.

7   Penfield W: The role of the temporal cortex in certain psychical phenomena. Journal of Mental Science 1955; 101: 451-65.
Blanke O, et al. Stimulating illusory own-body perceptions. Nature 2002; 419: 269-70.

8   Penfield W. The role of the temporal cortex in certain psychical phenomena. Journal of Mental Science 1955; 101: 451-65. Case V.F. p. 458.

9   Arias M, et al. Autoscopy and multiple sclerosis. Neurologia 1996; 11: 230-2 [Translated from the original Spanish article.]

10 Kandel EH, et al, editors. Principles of Neural Science. 3rd edition. USA. Prentice Hall; 1991. Chapters 24 and 37 (ISBN 0-8385-8068-8).

11 Clamann HP. All you ever needed to know about each muscle. Article posted on the internet in 1995 at: www.pylvs3.unibe.ch/www/groups/luescher/muscdata.html

12 McCloskey DI. Kinesthetic sensibility, Physiological Reviews 1978; 58: 763-820.
Gandevia SC, McCloskey DI. Sensations of heaviness. Brain 1977; 100: 345-54.
Gandevia SC, McCloskey DI. Changes in motor commands, as shown by changes in

perceived heaviness during partial curarizasation and peripheral anaesthesia in man. Journal of Physiology 1977; 272: 673-89.
Wei JY, et al. Joint angle signalling by muscle spindle receptors. Brain Research 1986; 370: 108-18.
Ribot-Ciscar E, Roll JP. Ago-antagonist muscle spindle inputs contribute together to joint movement coding in man. Brain Research 1998; 791: 167-76.

13   Kandel EH, et al, editors. Principles of Neural Science. 3rd edition. USA. Prentice Hall; 1991. Chapter 37, p. 571-3 (ISBN 0-8385-8068-8).

14   Kandel EH, et al, editors. Principles of Neural Science. 3rd edition. USA. Prentice Hall; 1991. Chapter 37, p. 573-4 (ISBN 0-8385-8068-8).

15   McCloskey DI. Kinesthetic sensibility, Physiological Reviews 1978; 58: 763-820.
Pederson J, et al. Alterations in information transmission in ensembles of primary muscle spindle afferents after muscle fatigue in heteronymous muscle.
Neuroscience 1998; 84: 953-9.

16   Edin BB, Valbo AB. Muscle afferent responses to isometric contractions and relaxations in humans. Journal of Neurophysiology 1990; 63: 1307-13.
Wilson LR, et al. Increased resting discharge of human spindle afferents following voluntary contractions. Journal of Physiology 1995; 488: 833-40.

17   At frequencies of less than 100 Hertz.

18   McCloskey DI. Kinesthetic sensibility, Physiological Reviews 1978; 58: 763-820. See p. 785-8.
Goodwin GM, et al. The contribution of muscle afferents to kinaesthesia shown by vibration induced illusions of movement and by the effects of paralysing joint afferents. Brain 1972; 95: 705-48.
Inglis JT, Frank JS. The effect of agonist/antagonist muscle vibration on human position sense. Experimental Brain Research 1990; 81: 573-80.
Inglis JT, et al. The effect of muscle vibration on human position sense during movements controlled by lengthening muscle contraction. Experimental Brain Research 1991; 84: 631-4.
Cordo P, et al. Proprioceptive consequences of tendon vibration during movement. Journal of Neurophysiology 1995; 74: 1675-88.

19   Muller N, et al. Diaphragmatic muscle tone. Journal of Applied Physiology 1979; 47: 279-84.
Pivik RT, Mercier L. Motoneuronal activity during wakefulness and non-REM sleep: H-reflex recovery in man. Sleep 1979; 1: 357-67.
Mercier L, Pivik RT. Spinal motoneuronal activity during wakefulness and non-REM sleep in hyperkinesis. Journal of Clinical Neuropsychology 1983; 5: 321-36.
Brylowski A, et al. H-reflex suppression and autonomic activation during lucid REM sleep: a case study. Sleep 1989; 12: 374-8.

20 Grundy BL. Intraoperative monitoring of sensory-evoked potentials. Anesthesiology 1983; 58: 72-87.
Blok RI, et al. Human learning during general anaesthesia and surgery. British Journal of Anaesthesia 1991; 66: 170-8.

21 Russell IF, Wang M. Absence of memory for intraoperative information during surgery under adequate general anaesthesia. British Journal of Anaesthesia 1997; 78: 3-9.

22 Mainzer J. Awareness, muscle relaxants and balanced anaesthesia. Canadian Anaesthetist's Journal 1979; 26: 386-93.&#6;Breckenridge JL, Aitkenhead AR: Awareness during general anaesthesia: a review. Annals of the Royal College of Surgeons 1983; 65: 93-6.
Schwender D, et al. Conscious awareness during general anaesthesia: patients' perceptions, emotions, cognition and reactions. British Journal of Anaesthesia 1998; 80: 133-9.

23 Yamamoto T, et al. Blokade of intrafusal neuromuscular junctions of cat muscle spindles with gallamine. Experimental Physiology 1994; 79: 365-76.

24 Dutia MB: Activation of cat muscle spindle primary, secondary and intermediate sensory endings by suxamethonium. Journal of Physiology (London) 1980; 304: 315-30.
O'Sullivan EP, et al. Perioperative dreaming in paediatric patients who receive suxamethonium. Anaesthesia 1988; 43: 104-6.
Hobbs AJ, et al. Perioperative dreaming and awareness in children. Anaesthesia 1988; 43: 560-2.

25 Lanier WL, et al. The cerebral and systemic effects of movement in response to a noxious stimulus in lightly anesthetized dogs. Possible modulation of cerebral function by muscle afferents. Anesthesiology 1994; 80: 392-401.

26 O'Sullivan EP, et al. Perioperative dreaming in paediatric patients who receive suxamethonium. Anaesthesia 1988; 43: 104-6
Hobbs AJ, et al. Perioperative dreaming and awareness in children. Anaesthesia 1988; 43: 560-2.
Mainzer J. Awareness, muscle relaxants and balanced anaesthesia. Canadian Anaesthetists' Society Journal 1979; 26: 386-93.

27 The author is a physician specialised in anaesthesia. This was a real incident that occurred in 1994 during the course of his normal work as an anaesthetist. The woman concerned underwent an operation under general anaesthesia to correct a deviated nasal septum. This is a common operation, and both operation and anaesthetic technique were in no way unusual. The general anaesthetic was personally administered by the author, which is why all the medical and other circumstances surrounding this report are well known to the author.

28 Parkes JD. Sleep and its Disorders. USA. W.B. Saunders; 1985. Chapter 4, p. 191-2 (ISBN 0-7216-1858-8).

29 Muller N, et al. Diaphragmatic muscle tone. Journal of Applied Physiology 1979; 47: 279-84.
Pivik RT, Mercier L. Motoneuronal activity during wakefulness and non-REM sleep: H-reflex recovery in man. Sleep 1979; 1: 357-67.
Mercier L, Pivik RT. Spinal motoneuronal activity during wakefulness and non-REM sleep in hyperkinesis. Journal of Clinical Neuropsychology 1983; 5: 321-36.
Brylowski A, et al. H-reflex suppression and autonomic activation during lucid REM sleep: a case study. Sleep 1989; 12: 374-8.

30 Oswald I. Sudden bodily jerks on falling asleep. Brain 1959; 82: 92-103.

31 Liddon SC. Sleep paralysis and hypnagogic hallucinations. Archives of General Psychiatry 1967; 17: 88-96.
Armor Ardis J, McKellar P: hypnagogic imagery and mescaline, Journal of Mental Science 1956; 102: 22-9.

32 Parker A. States of Mind: ESP and Altered States of Consciousness. London: Malaby Press; 1975. Chapter 5, p. 102-7 (ISBN 0-460-14009-7).

Chapter 13 – Diabolical Dreams

1 Blackmore S. Abduction by aliens or sleep paralysis. Skeptical Enquirer 1998; (May/June).
Hopkins B, et al. 'The Roper Poll – A report on unusual experiences associated with UFO abductions, based upon the Roper organization's survey of 5947 Americans, 1994'. Published on the internet during 2002 CE at the address: www.spiritweb.org/Spirit/abduction-roperpoll.html

2 Robinson JM, editor. The Nag Hammadi Library: The definitive new translation of the Gnostic Scriptures. The Gospel of Truth, verse 29. The ancient Roman preacher, Valentinus, who lived at some time between 100-160 CE, was the author of this Christian Gnostic text.

3 Gandevia SC, McCloskey DI. Sensations of heaviness. Brain 1977; 100: 345-54.
Gandevia SC, McCloskey DI. Changes in motor commands, as shown by changes in perceived heaviness, during partial curarization and peripheral anaesthesia in man. Journal of Physiology 1977; 272: 673-89.
McCloskey DI. Kinesthetic sensibility. Physiological Reviews 1978; 58: 763-820.

4 Gandevia SC. The perception of motor commands or effort during muscular paralysis. Brain 1982; 105: 151-9.

5 Smith, SM, et al. The lack of cerebral effects of d-Tubocurarine. Anesthesiology 1947; 8: 1-14.

Prescott F, et al. Tubocurarine chloride as an adjunct to anaesthesia. Lancet 1946; 2: 80-4.
Dery R. The effects of precurarization with a protective dose of d-Tubocurarine in the conscious patient. Canadian Anaesthetist's Society Journal 1974; 21: 68-78.

6   Cave, HA. Narcolepsy. Archives of Neurology & Psychiatry 1931; 26: 50-101.

7   Cave, HA. Narcolepsy. Archives of Neurology & Psychiatry 1931; 26: 50-101. Case number 11.

8   Penn NE, et al. Sleep paralysis among medical students. The Journal of Psychology 1981; 107: 247-52.
Browne-Goode G. Sleep Paralysis, Archives of Neurology 1962; 6: 228-34.

9   Mahowald MW, Ettinger MG. Things that go bump in the night: The parasomnias revisited. Journal of Clinical Neurophysiology 1990) 7: 119-43.
Browne-Goode G. Sleep Paralysis, Archives of Neurology 1962; 6: 228-34.
Nan'no H, et al. A neurophysiological study of sleep paralysis in narcoleptic patients. Electroencephalography and Clinical Neurophysiology 1970; 28: 382-90.

10   Browne-Goode G. Sleep Paralysis, Archives of Neurology 1962; 6: 228-34.

11   Cave, HA. Narcolepsy. Archives of Neurology & Psychiatry 1931; 26: 50-101.

12   Liddon SC. Sleep paralysis and hypnagogic hallucinations. Archives of General Psychiatry 1967; 17: 88-96.
Mahowald MW, Ettinger MG. Things that go bump in the night: The parasomnias revisited. Journal of Clinical Neurophysiology 1990; 7: 119-43.

13   Macnish R. The Philosophy of Sleep. New York: Appleton & Co; 1834. [Quoted in Liddon SC. Sleep paralysis and hypnagogic hallucinations. Archives of General Psychiatry 1967; 17: 88-96.]

14   Message, posted on a public computer bulletin board devoted to people suffering from sleep paralysis related problems, by a 27 year old woman called Chrystal Westwood 25 February 1997.

15   Message posted by an Englishman Nick Jewell during 1997 in a discussion forum on 'Sleep Paralysis' held on the internet.

16   Mahowald MW, Ettinger MG. Things that go bump in the night: The parasomnias revisited. Journal of Clinical Neurophysiology 1990; 7: 119-143.

17   The Shorter Oxford English Dictionary. 3rd edition. Oxford (UK); 1956.

18   The Shorter Oxford English Dictionary. 3rd edition. Oxford (UK); 1956.

19   The Shorter Oxford English Dictionary. 3rd edition. Oxford (UK); 1956.

20 The Shorter Oxford English Dictionary. 3rd edition. Oxford (UK); 1956.

21 The Shorter Oxford English Dictionary. 3rd edition. Oxford (UK); 1956.

22 The Shorter Oxford English Dictionary. 3rd edition. Oxford (UK); 1956.

23 The Shorter Oxford English Dictionary. 3rd edition. Oxford (UK); 1956.

24 Malleus Maleficarum by Kremer and Sprenger, first published 1484 CE, translation by Montague Summers, 1928.

25 This was a mythical race of giants called the 'Nephilim', descendants of the children born to women who had sexual union with these 'sons of God'.

26 The Holy Bible, King James Version, Genesis, chapter 6, verse 4.

27 Parkes, JD. Sleep and its Disorders. USA. W.B. Saunders; 1985. Chapter 4, p. 191-2 (ISBN 0-7216-1858-8).

28 See Chapter 11 – 'Disembodied Feelings' for a more extensive explanation.

29 The Shorter Oxford English Dictionary. 3rd edition. Oxford (UK); 1956.

30 Summers M. The History of Witchcraft. England: Senate; 1994 [first published 1925]. Introduction (ISBN 1-85958-026-2).

31 Time-Line of witch-hunts in Western Europe. Published on the internet during 2002.

32 Parson R. 'Deaths from the European Witch Craze.' An e-mail posted on the internet during 2002.
Gibbons J. The great European witch hunt. PanGaia 1999; (21, Autumn): 25-34.

33 The Shorter Oxford English Dictionary. 3rd edition. Oxford (UK); 1956.

34 Summers M. The History of Witchcraft. England: Senate; 1994 [first published 1925]. Chapter 4 (ISBN 1-85958-026-2).

35 The term 'UFO' means an 'Unidentified Flying Object', a name many people call the unidentified flying objects they believe to be the spacecraft of extraterrestrial beings.

36 The hypnotherapist.

37 Harpur P. Daimonic Reality. Understanding Otherworld Encounters. Penguin Arkana; 1994. Chapter 16, p. 215-6.

38 Mack JE. Abduction. Human Encounters with Aliens. Simon & Schuster; 1994. Chapter 2, p. 33-43 (ISBN 0-671-85194-2).
Jacobs DM. Secret Life. Firsthand Documented Accounts of UFO Abductions. Simon & Schuster; 1993. Chapters 3, 4, and 6 (ISBN 0-671-79720-4).

39 Hirschkowitz M, Moore CA. Sleep-related erectile activity. Neurological Clinics 1996; 14: 721-37.
Karacan I, et al. Penile blood flow and microvascular events during sleep-related erections of middle-aged men. Journal of Urology 1987; 138: 177-81.

40 Scharf MB, et al. Penile tumescence in temporally abnormal and pathologic rapid eye movement sleep. Journal of Urology 1983; 130: 909-1011.

41 Abel GG, et al. Women's vaginal responses during REM sleep. Journal of Sexual and Marital Therapy 1979; 5:5-14.
Rogers GS, et al. Vaginal pulse amplitude response patterns during erotic conditions and sleep. Archives of Sexual Behavior 1985; 14: 327-42.

42 Laura Knight-Jadczyk, 'Alien abduction, demonic possession, and the legend of the vampire', an essay published during 2001 on the internet at the address: www.cassiopaea.org

Chapter 14 – Body, Mind & Soul

1   Saint Augustine, Sermons, sermon 43.

Chapter 15 – Dying

1   Murray CJL, Lopez AD. Mortality by cause for eight regions of the world: Global burden of disease study. Lancet 1997; 349: 1269-76. This is one of several articles reporting a study financed by the World Bank to make an inventory of the health problems in different regions of our world. This article reports causes of death, and numbers of people dying world-wide during the year 1990 CE. And in this article I read that about 50,467,000 people died world-wide during 1990 CE. The world population at this time was about 5,500,000,000 people. This means that about one person in one hundred dies each year.

2   Murray CJL, Lopez AD. Mortality by cause for eight regions of the world: Global burden of disease study. Lancet 1997; 349: 1269-76. See table in appendix 4.

3   Rossen R, et al. Acute arrest of cerebral circulation in man. Archives of Neurology & Psychiatry 1943; 50: 510-28.

4   Aminoff MJ et al. Electrocerebral accompaniments of syncope associated with malignant ventricular arrhythmias. Annals of Internal Medicine 1988; 108: 791-6.
Gastaut H, Fischer-Williams M: Electroencephalographic study of syncope. Lancet 1957; (II): 1018-25.

5   Rossen R, et al. Acute arrest of cerebral circulation in man. Archives of Neurology & Psychiatry 1943; 50: 510-28.
Aminoff MJ et al. Electrocerebral accompaniments of syncope associated with malignant ventricular arrhythmias. Annals of Internal Medicine 1988; 108: 791-6.
Gastaut H, Fischer-Williams M: Electroencephalographic study of syncope. Lancet 1957; (II): 1018-25.

6   Murray CJL, Lopez AD. Mortality by cause for eight regions of the world: Global burden of disease study. Lancet 1997; 349: 1269-76. See table in appendix 4.

7   Woerlee GM. Common Perioperative Problems and the Anaesthetist. Kluwer Academic Publishers; 1988. Chapter 14.4 (ISBN 0-89838-402-8).

8   Woerlee GM. Common Perioperative Problems and the Anaesthetist. Kluwer Academic Publishers; 1988. Chapters 4.1, 4.3, and 5.1 (ISBN 0-89838-402-8).

9   Murray CJL, Lopez AD. Mortality by cause for eight regions of the world: Global burden of disease study. Lancet 1997; 349: 1269-76. Table 3.

10   Mortality statistics for the Netherlands for the year 1996. In: The Statistical Year of the Netherlands 1998. The Hague: Statistics Netherlands; 1998. p. 506-7 (ISBN 903573142-5).

11   Hodges M, Williams RA. Registered infant and under-five deaths in Freetown, Sierra Leone from 1987-1991 and a comparison with 1969-1979. West African Journal of Medicine 1998; 17: 95-8.

Chapter 16 – Oxygen Starvation

1   Conclusions of the international colloquium on anoxia and the EEG. In: Gastaut H, Meyer JS, editors. Cerebral Anoxia and the Electroencephalogram. USA: Charles C. Thomas; 1961. Chapter 57, p. 599-617.

2   Conclusions of the international colloquium on anoxia and the EEG. In: Gastaut H, Meyer JS, editors. Cerebral Anoxia and the Electroencephalogram. USA: Charles C. Thomas; 1961. Chapter 57, p. 599-617.

3   Stuss DT, Benson DF. The Frontal Lobes. New York: Raven Press; 1986. Chapter 5, p. 75 and 80-2, Chapter 7, p 108-9, Chapter 14, p. 204-6 (ISBN 0-88167-153-3).

4   Liere EJ van, Stickney JC. Hypoxia. The University of Chicago Press; 1963. Chapter 18, p. 300 (Library of Congress 63-16722).

5   Insertion of a catheter into his subclavian vein.

6   Translated by the author from: Sabom MB. Herinneringen aan de Dood. Strengholt; 1983. Chapter 7, 'Vijfde geval', p. 100-5 (ISBN 90-6010-546-X). [Original title: Recollections of Death, Harper & Row; 1982.]

7   West JB. Do climbs to extreme altitude cause brain damage? Lancet 1986; 2: 387-8.
Regard M, et al. Persistent cognitive impairment in climbers after repeated exposure to extreme altitude. Neurology 1989; 39: 210-3.
Hornbein TF, et al. The cost to the central nervous system of climbing to extreme altitude. New England Journal of Medicine 1989; 321: 1714-9.

8   Moody, RA. The Light Beyond. USA: Bantam Books; 1988. Chapter 2, p. 51-2 (ISBN 0-553-27813-4).

9   West JB. Do climbs to extreme altitude cause brain damage? Lancet 1986; 2: 387-8.
Regard M, et al. Persistent cognitive impairment in climbers after repeated exposure to extreme altitude. Neurology 1989; 39: 210-3.
Hornbein TF, et al. The cost to the central nervous system of climbing to extreme altitude. New England Journal of Medicine 1989; 321: 1714-9.

10   McCloskey DI. Kinesthetic sensibility, Physiological Reviews 1978; 58: 763-820. See p. 801.

11   Liere EJ van, Stickney JC. Hypoxia. The University of Chicago Press; 1963. Chapter 18, p. 302 (Library of Congress 63-16722).

12   About 600 millimeters of mercury.

13   Rossen R, et al. Acute arrest of cerebral circulation in man. Archives of Neurology & Psychiatry 1943; 50: 510-28.

14   Woolsey CN, et al. Localisation in somatic sensory and motor areas of human cerebral cortex as determined by direct recording of evoked potentials and electrical stimulation. Journal of Neurosurgery 1979; 51: 476-506.
Penfield W, Boldrey E. Somatic motor and sensory representation in the cerebral cortex of man as studied by electrical stimulation. Brain 1937; 60: 389-443.

15   Penfield W. The role of the temporal cortex in certain psychical phenomena. Journal of Mental Science 1955; 101: 451-465.

16   Kolb B, Whishaw IQ. Fundamentals of Human Neuropsychology. USA. W.H. Freeman; 1990. Chapters 11, 17, 24 (ISBN 0-7167-1973-8).

17   Newberg A, et al. The measurement of regional cerebral blood flow during the complex cognitive task of meditation. Psychiatry Research 2001; 106: 113-22.

18 Conclusions of the international colloquium on anoxia and the EEG. In: Gastaut H, Meyer JS, editors. Cerebral Anoxia and the Electroencephalogram. USA: Charles C. Thomas; 1961. Chapter 57, p. 599-617.

19 Schiff SJ, Somjen GG. Hyperexcitability following moderate hypoxia in hippocampal tissue slices. Brain Research 1985; 337: 337-340.
Aitken PG, et al. Ion-channel involvement in hypoxia-induced spreading depression in hippocampal slices. Brain Research 1991; 541: 7-11
Fujiwara N, et al. Effects of hypoxia on rat hippocampal neurones in vitro. Journal of Physiology 1989; 384: 131-51.

20 Gloor P, et al. The role of the limbic system in experiential phenomena of temporal lobe epilepsy. Annals of Neurology 1982; 12: 129-44.
Gloor P, et al. Experiential phenomena of temporal lobe epilepsy. Brain 1990; 113: 1673-94.
Weingarten SM, et al. Relationship of hallucinations to the depth structures of the temporal lobe. In: Sweet WH, editor. Neurosurgical Treatment in Psychiatry, Pain and Epilepsy. USA: University Park Press; 1975. p. 553-68 (ISBN 0-8391-0881-8).

21 Dewhearst K, Beard AW. Sudden religious conversion in temporal lobe epilepsy. British Journal of Psychiatry 1970; 117: 497-507.
Tucker DM, et al. Hyperreligiosity in temporal lobe epilepsy: redefining the relationship. Journal of Nervous and Mental Disease 1987; 175: 181-4.
Cook CM, Persinger MA. Experimental induction of the 'sensed presence' in normal subjects and an exceptional subject. Perceptual and Motor Skills 1997; 85: 683-93.

22 The 'Taj Mahal' is a beautiful domed white marble tomb situated upon the a bank of the Jammu River where it winds through the city of Agra in India. It was built between 1632-1643 CE by the Mogul emperor of India, Shah Jahan, as a mausoleum for his favourite wife Mumtaz Mahal.

23 Hunter RCA. On the experience of nearly dying. American Journal of Psychiatry 1967; 124: 84-8.

24 Greyson B. A typology of near-death experiences. American Journal of Psychiatry 1985; 142: 967-9.

25 The 'death-watch' is an ages-old tradition where family members take turns keeping a dying person company so that the dying person does not die alone. Sometimes the burden of maintaining such a death-watch become too much for the family, so they ask family friends to assist in maintaining the watch.

26 Tuberculosis of the lungs.

27 Barrett W. Death Bed Visions. The Psychical Experiences of the Dying. Aquarian Press; 1986 [first published in 1926]. Chapter 3, p. 55-6 (ISBN 0-85030-520-9).

28 Osis K, Haraldsson E. At the Hour of Death. New York: Hastings House; 1986. Chapter 10, p. 105 (ISBN 0-8038-9279-9).

29 Rawlings M. Beyond Death's Door. USA: Bantam Books; 1979. Chapter 6, p. 79-81 (ISBN 0-553-22970-2).

30 Wilkins WJ. Hindu Mythology, Vedic and Puranic. 2nd edition. India: Rupa & Co; 1980. Chapter 10, p. 78-86. 'Yamraj' is another name for the Hindu god of the world of the dead called 'Yama'.

31 Pasricha S, Stevenson I. Near-death experiences in India: A preliminary report. Journal of Nervous and Mental Diseases 1986; 174: 165-70. Note: In India, the surname is an indicator of caste as well as profession. Thus 'Bania' is a trader and 'Kumhar' a potter. Both men had the same given name, 'Chajju'.

32 Conclusions of the international colloquium on anoxia and the EEG. In: Gastaut H, Meyer JS, editors. Cerebral Anoxia and the Electroencephalogram. USA: Charles C. Thomas; 1961. Chapter 57, p. 599-617.

33 Conclusions of the international colloquium on anoxia and the EEG. In: Gastaut H, Meyer JS, editors. Cerebral Anoxia and the Electroencephalogram. USA: Charles C. Thomas; 1961. Chapter 57, p. 599-617.

34 Liere EJ van, Stickney JC. Hypoxia. The University of Chicago Press; 1963. Chapter 18, p. 317 (Library of Congress 63-16722).

35 Lempert T, et al. Syncope: A videometric analysis of 56 episodes of transient cerebral hypoxia. Annals of Neurology 1994; 36: 233-7.

36 Rossen R, et al. Acute arrest of cerebral circulation in man. Archives of Neurology & Psychiatry 1943; 50: 510-28.

37 Carbon monoxide displaces oxygen from haemoglobin in blood and binds tightly to haemoglobin. So when people breathe high concentrations of carbon monoxide, blood transports carbon monoxide to tissues instead of oxygen. But carbon monoxide has no function in the vital energy generating metabolic processes of the body. Accordingly, the vital energy rich substances generated within cells, are no longer generated because of lack of oxygen. This means that carbon monoxide poisoning causes brain damage and death due to oxygen starvation.

38 Liere EJ van, Stickney JC. Hypoxia. The University of Chicago Press; 1963. Chapter 18, p. 317 (Library of Congress 63-16722).

39 Moody, RA. Life after Life. USA: Bantam Books; 1988. Chapter 2, p. 43-4 (ISBN 0-553-27484-8).

40 Stuss DT, Benson DF. The Frontal Lobes.New York: Raven Press; 1986. Chapter 5, p. 87-8 (ISBN 0-88167-153-3).

Roland PE. Cortical organization of voluntary behaviour in man. Human Neurobiology 1985; 4: 155-67.
Roland PE, et al. Different cortical areas in man in organization of voluntary movements in extrapersonal space. Journal of Neurophysiology 1980; 43: 137-51.
Roland PE. Metabolic measurements of the working frontal cortex in man. Trends in Neuroscience 1984; 7: 430-5.

41   Rawlings M. Beyond Death's Door. USA. Bantam Books; 1978. Chapter 6, p. 67-8 (ISBN 0-553-22970-2).

42   Liere EJ van, Stickney JC. Hypoxia. The University of Chicago Press; 1963. Chapter 18, p. 277-9 (Library of Congress 63-16722).

43   Rossen R, et al. Acute arrest of cerebral circulation in man. Archives of Neurology & Psychiatry 1943; 50: 510-28.
Liere EJ van, Stickney JC. Hypoxia. The University of Chicago Press; 1963. Chapter 18, p. 300-12 (Library of Congress 63-16722).

Chapter 17 – Dying Eyes

1   Steen-Hansen JE, et al. Pupil size and light reactivity during cardiopulmonary resuscitation: A clinical study. Critical Care Medicine 1988; 16: 69-70.
Binnion PF, McFarland RJ. The relationship between cardiac massage and pupil size in cardiac arrest dogs. Cardiovascular Research 1968; 3: 247-51.

2   Pupil diameters can vary considerably. The minimum pupil diameter is about one millimeter, and the maximum pupil diameter is about ten millimeters. The difference between the amount of light entering an eye where the pupil diameter widens from one to ten millimeters is about 100 times. So pupil widening can considerably increase the amount of light entering our eyes.

3   Copenhaver RM, Perry NW. Factors affecting visually evoked cortical potentials such as impaired vision of varying etiology. Investigative Ophthamlmology 1964; 3: 665-75
Halliday AM, et al. Problems in defining the normal limits of the visual evoked potential. Advances in Neurology 1982; 32: 1-9.

4   Guyton AC. Textbook of Medical Physiology. 6th edition. USA. W.B. Saunders; 1981. Chapter 58, p. 729-30 (ISBN 0-7216-4394-9).

5   Hess EH, Attitudes and pupil size. Scientific American 1965; (April): 46-54.
Hess EH, The role of pupil size in communication. Scientific American 1975; (November): 110-9.

6   This is because the oxygen consumption of the retina is greater than that of the brain. Retinal oxygen consumption is about 5 ml oxygen/100 gram retina tissue/minute, while brain oxygen consumption is about 3.5 ml oxygen/100 gram brain tissue/minute. See any textbook of physiology for human brain oxygen

consumption, and for retinal oxygen consumption see:
Zuckerman R, et al. Optical mapping of inner retinal tissue PO2. Current Eye Research 1993; 12: 809-25.
Linsenmeier RA, Braun RD. Oxygen distribution and consumption in the cat retina during normoxia and hypoxemia. Journal of General Physiology 1992; 99: 177-97.

7   Linsenmeier RA. Electrophysiological consequences of retinal hypoxia. Graefe's Archive for Clinical and Experimental Ophthalmology 1990; 228: 143-50.
Rimmer TJ, et al. Effects of hypoxaemia on the electroretinogram in diabetics. Doc. Ophthalmol. 1995-6; 91: 311-21.
Rossen R, et al. Acute arrest of cerebral circulation in man. Archives of Neurology & Psychiatry 1943; 50: 510-28.
Andina F. von: Ueber 'Schwarzsehen' als Ausdruck von Blutdruckschwankungen bei Sturzflugen. Schweizerische Medizinische Wochenschrift 1937; 67: 753-6.

8   Ring HG, Fujina T. Observations on the anatomy and pathology of the choroidal vasculature. Archives of Ophthalmology 1967; 78: 431-44.
Alm A, Bill A. Optic and ocular nerve blood flow at normal and increased ocular pressures in monkeys (Macaca iris): a study with radioactively labelled microspheres including flow determination in brain and other tissues. Experimental Eye Research 1973; 15: 15-29.

9   Liere EJ van, Stickney JC. Hypoxia. The University of Chicago Press; 1963. Chapter 18, p. 336-7 (Library of Congress 63-16722).
Andina F. von. Über 'Schwarzsehen' als Ausdruck von Blutdruckschwankungen bei Sturzflugen. Schweizerische Medizinische Wochenschrift 1937; 67: 753-6.
Duane TD. Experimental blackout and the visual system. Transactions of the American Ophthalmological Society 1966; 64: 488-542.

10   Zorpette G. A pound of flesh. Scientific American 1999; 281(August): 13.

11   Liere EJ van, Stickney JC. Hypoxia. The University of Chicago Press; 1963. Chapter 18, p. 277-9 (Library of Congress 63-16722).

12   Rossen R, et al. Acute arrest of cerebral circulation in man. Archives of Neurology & Psychiatry 1943; 50: 510-28.

13   Eijk P van der. Naar het hiernamaals en terug. The Hague: BZZTôH; 1991. p. 58-9 (ISBN 90-6291-628-7).

14   Grey M. Return from Death. An Exploration of the Near-Death Experience. Arkana; 1985. Chapter 4, p. 46 (ISBN 1-85063-019-4).

15   Barrett W. Death Bed Visions. The Psychical Experiences of the Dying. Aquarian Press; 1986 [first published in 1926]. Chapter 2, p. 10-4 (ISBN 0-85030-520-9).

Chapter 18 – The Experience of Dying

1   Murray CJL, Lopez AD. Mortality by cause for eight regions of the world: Global burden of disease study. Lancet 1997; 349: 1269-76. See also appendix 4.

2   Judson IR, Wiltshaw E. A near Death Experience. Lancet 1983; 2: 516-562.

3   Klug I. Het Katholieke Geloof: Een Apologetisch, Dogmatisch Kerkhistorisch Overzicht. Heemstede: De Toorts; 1939. p. 596.

4   Osis K, Haraldsson E. At the Hour of Death. USA: Hastings House; 1986. Chapter 11, p. 130-1 (ISBN 0-8038-9279-9).

5   His physician.

6   Rawlings M. Beyond Death's Door. USA: Bantam Books; 1979. Chapter 6, p. 68-9 (ISBN 0-553-22970-2).The angel.

7   The City of God. Book 1, chapter 11 – Of the End of This Life, Whether It is Material that It Be Long Delayed, by Saint Aurelius Augustine, 426 CE.

Chapter 19 – A Vision of Eternity

1   Susan Ertz (1894-1985) wrote this in a book called Anger in the Sky (1943 CE).

2   The universe is about fifteen to twenty billion years old, that is, 15,000,000,000 to 20,000,000,000 years . The solar system and the planet upon which we live are about 3,000,000,000 years . Humans have achieved their present form during the last 100,000 years.

3   Friedrich Nietzsche was an influential German philosopher, born in 1844 CE, died 1900 CE. The name of the book, 'Thus Spoke Zarathustra. A Book for Everyone and No-one' is derived from 'Zarathustra' [Greek name – 'Zoroaster'] and was first published in the German language in 1885 CE

4   The tightrope walker.

5   Nietzsche F. Thus Spoke Zarathustra. A Book for Everyone and No-one [English translation by R.J. Hollingdale]. Penguin Classics; 1969. p.48 of Part One, 'Zarathustra's Prologue'.

6   Based upon the biography of Confucius.from many sources.

7   Davies P. That mysterious flow. Scientific American 2002; 287(September): 24-9.

8   Percy Bysshe Shelley was an English poet, born 1792 CE, died 1822 CE.

9   The human body.

10   Determinism, or the force of fate.

11   Carus P. The Gospel of Buddha, Compiled from Ancient Records. Open Court Publishing Company; 1915. Chapter 9, verse 16.

12   The prophet Zoroaster was born in the region of the present Iran somewhere between 1400 to 1200 BCE. He was a Babylonian priest. Sometime between the ages of 35 to 40 years he received revelations, after which he preached a new religion, now called 'Zoroastrianism'. He preached a dualistic religion whose central theme was an eternal struggle between the forces of good and evil. Zoroastrianism had a large following in the ancient world until replaced by Christianity in the west and by Islam in the Middle East. Finally, around 650 CE, conquering Islamic hordes either killed or forcibly converted nearly all the remaining Zoroastrians to Islam, and the few remaining believers fled into exile in India. The descendants of these exiles are called Parsi's, most of who still live in the Indian city of Bombay. Parsi's are the only group of people still practising the religion preached by Zoroaster.

13   The religions of the ancient Indo-Iranians taught that the Supreme God, as well as the worlds over which he ruled, had a sevenfold existence. Ancient Persians called these seven worlds, the seven KARSHVARE of the world and only one of these seven KARSHVARE is known and accessible to man the world in which we mortals live.

14   Apparently a Zoroastrian demon.

15   The Aogemadaeca Avesta is one of the holy books of the Zoroastrian religion. Verses 31-40.

16   'Nothing in his life became him like the leaving it;' See Macbeth Act 1, Scene IV, written by William Shakespeare, the leading playwright of English literature (1564 – 1616 CE). The character Malcolm says this to Duncan regarding the execution of the previous Thane of Cawdor.

17   Nietzsche F. Thus Spoke Zarathustra. A Book for Everyone and No-one [English translation by R.J. Hollingdale]. Penguin Classics; 1969. p. 104 in Part One – 'Of the Bestowing Virtue'.

Appendices

1   Data for people living in the Roman Empire from about 0-300 CE, derived from Parkin TG, 'Friar's Life Table for the Roman Empire'. In: Demography and Roman Society. 1992. p. 144. Obtained from the internet at the address: www.columbia.edu/~rcc20/romans/lifetabl.html

2   Data for 1700 CE and 1900 CE are for Western Europe and are derived from Acheson RM, Hagard S. Health, Society and Medicine. An Introduction to

Community Medicine. 3rd edition. Blackwell Scientific Publications; 1984. (ISBN 0-632-00965-9.)

3   Data for 1991 CE are from 'Table 1: Life Table for the total population: United States, 1989-1991', published in US decennial life tables for 1989-91, vol. 1, no. 1. Hyattsville (MD): National Center for Health Statistics; 1997 (Library of Congress card no. 85-600190).

4   Population figures are those for the middle of the year 1998 CE from the 'Population Reference Bureau' in the USA at the internet adress: http://www.prb.org

5   Data are from LaPlante MP, Carlson D. Disability in the United States: Prevalence and Causes. From the National Health Interview Survey. Disability Statistics Report (7). Washington DSC: National Institute of Disability and Rehabilitation Research; 1992.

6   Cyanosis is a blue to black coloration of the lips and tongue caused by oxygen starvation.

7   Murray CJL, Lopez AD. Mortality by cause for eight regions of the world: Global burden of disease study. *Lancet* 1997) 349: 1269-76.

8   Harrison RD. (editor) Book of Data: Chemistry, Physical Science, Physics. Longman Group Limited, England, 1972, page 63, (ISBN 0-582-82672-1).

9   Otis AB, et al. Performance related to composition of alveolar air. American Journal of Physiology 1946; 146: 207-21.
Liere EJ van, Stickney JC. Hypoxia. The University of Chicago Press; 1963. Chapter 18, p. 305-11 (Library of Congress 63-16722).
Consolazio WV, et al. Effects on man of high concentrations of carbon dioxide in relation to various oxygen pressures during exposures as long as 72 hours. American Journal of Physiology 1947; 151: 479-503.

10 Boothby WM. Respiratory Physiology in Aviation. Air University, USAF School of Aviation Medicine; 1954. Chapter 8, p. 140, and chapter 9, p. 151.

11 Otis AB, et al. Performance related to composition of alveolar air. American Journal of Physiology 1946; 146: 207-21.
West JB. Do climbs to extreme altitude cause brain damage? Lancet 1986; 2: 387-8.
Regard M, et al. Persistent cognitive impairment in climbers after repeated exposure to extreme altitude. Neurology 1989; 39: 210-3.
Hornbein TF, et al. The cost to the central nervous system of climbing to extreme altitude. New England Journal of Medicine 1989; 321: 1714-9.

12 Boothby WM. Respiratory Physiology in Aviation. Air University, USAF School of Aviation Medicine; 1954. Chapter 8, p. 140, and Chapter 9, p. 151.

13   Boothby WM. Respiratory Physiology in Aviation. Air University, USAF School of Aviation Medicine; 1954. Chapter 9, p. 155.

14   Boothby WM. Respiratory Physiology in Aviation. Air University, USAF School of Aviation Medicine; 1954. Chapter 9, p. 155.

15   Finnerty JA, et al. Cerebral hemodynamics during cerebral ischemia produced by acute hypotension. Journal of Clinical Investigation 1954; 33: 1227-32.

16   Finnerty JA, et al. Cerebral hemodynamics during cerebral ischemia produced by acute hypotension. Journal of Clinical Investigation 1954; 33: 1227-32.

17   Trojaborg W, Boysen G. Relation between EEG, cerebral blood flow and internal carotid artery pressure during carotid endarterectomy. Electroencephalography and Clinical Neurophysiology 1973; 34: 61-9.
Sundt T.M., et al. Correlation of cerebral blood flow and electroencephalographic changes during carotid endarterectomy. Mayo Clinic Proceedings 1981; 56: 533-43.